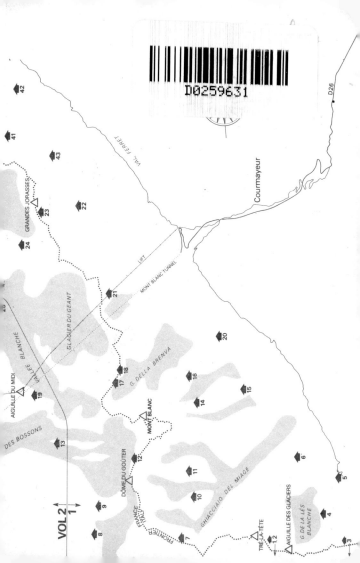

Mont Blanc Massif   Volume II   *Selected Climbs*

# Mont Blanc Massif    Volume II

SELECTED CLIMBS
by Lindsay Griffin

General Editor: Les Swindin

eeer JUL 0 1999
050343

ALPINE CLUB · LON
1991

050343

Mont Blanc Massif, Volume II *Selected Climbs*

Published *(with Addendum)* in Great Britain by the
Alpine Club, 55/56 Charlotte Road, London EC2A 3QT

This edition first published, Copyright © 1991 by the Alpine Club
This edition *(with Addendum)* Copyright © 1996 by the Alpine Club

First Edition *(Collomb, Crew)* 1967 in two volumes
Second Edition *(Collomb, O'Connor, Griffin)* 1978 in three volumes

Produced by the Alpine Club

Topo diagrams drawn by Rod Powis

Mont Blanc Massif in 2 volumes:
    I  Col de la Bérangère to Col de Talèfre.
    II  Col de Talèfre to Swiss Val Ferret, Chamonix Aiguilles
       and Aiguilles Rouges.

Cover photographs
*Front:* On La Nonne, Aig Verte and Cardinal in background *(Roger Payne)*
*Back:* Les Droites, North Face in winter *(Les Swindin)*

Typeset in Plantin from the author's word processor
by Factel Limited, Cheltenham

Produced by The Ernest Press, Glasgow
Printed in Hong Kong by Colorcraft Ltd.

30 JUN 1999

050343

REGIONAL TECHNICAL COLLEGE GALWAY
CASTLEBAR CAMPUS LIBRARY

796.52209
4469

£16.28

British Library cataloguing in Publication Data

    Griffin, Lindsay
    Mont Blanc Massif. – 3rd ed. Vol.II, *Selected Climbs*
    1. Europe. Mont Blanc range. Mountaineering
    I. Title II. Collomb, Robin G.  Mont Blanc range III.
    796.522094449

    ISBN 0-900523-58-1

# Contents

# List of topo diagrams and photographs

Text photographs:
Alpine Club Collection AC, Trevor Braham TB, Gino Buscaini GB,
Maurice Brandt MB, John Cleare JC, David Cuthbertson DC,
Rob Durran RD, Lindsay Griffin LG, Malcolm Campbell MC,
Stephen Hartland SH, Joyce Hodgson JH, Will Hurford WH,
Douglas Milner DM, Bill O'Connor BOC, Stephen Parr SP,
Roger Payne RP, Les Swindin LS, Dave Walsh DW,
Jeremy Whitehead JW

# General Editor's Preface

This edition and its companion volume form the third in the new series of guidebooks to the major European alpine regions being prepared by the Alpine Club. These two volumes replace the three volume edition published in 1978. Although the number of volumes has been reduced the number of routes that are described has been more than doubled. The features introduced in the two guidebooks already published in this new series, Ecrins Massif and Dolomites, have been retained whilst a new feature in these volumes is the inclusion of topo diagrams for the first time in Alpine Club guidebooks.

These two volumes between them provide the reader with a very wide selection of routes in all grades that will suit everyone from the novice to the experienced alpinist and the dedicated rock climber who may have little or no interest in actually reaching summits. The policy adopted has been to maximise choice, so that whilst some routes have been described in considerable detail, others have only brief descriptions. Thus, in the latter case, experienced alpinists will know whether or not a route is suitable for their ability and degree of commitment but will be left on their own to judge the exact details of routes. At the very least this should enable them to select routes that are much less frequented and uncrowded. The former will almost certainly include the sort of route that a novice alpinist or first time visitor to the region might undertake. Those who wish to climb the magnificent rock in the massif either at high or low altitude, should find plenty here to suit them. Most of the rock climbs are described with topo diagrams whilst the selection made in general allows the climb to be used as a means of ascent to a summit.

Lindsay Griffin, the author, is a well known name among mountaineers. He is a member of the Alpine Climbing Group wth a wealth of experience of climbing in the Alps in both summer and winter and was co-author of the previous guidebooks to the Mont Blanc Range. Whilst working with him in the preparation of these volumes I have been greatly impressed by his attention to detail and to the sheer volume of work that he has put into the task. Lindsay has many friends and as you will see from the acknowledgements he has called on many of them to help with the detail. My personal thanks go to them all.

As with all our guidebooks the Alpine Club welcomes helpful comments about the climbs described and any worthwhile ones that we have omitted that might be included in future editions. We also welcome offers of good quality photographs that might be used in the preparation of photo-diagrams. All comments or offers should be addressed to the general editor at the Alpine Club.

My thanks too go to those people who have helped me in the work and are not mentioned elsewhere, particularly Jeremy Whitehead for his proof reading of text.

Les Swindin

# Author's preface

There is no doubt that the Mont Blanc Range provides the alpinist with some of the finest quality routes in Europe, whether it be along the delicate snow crests, on rough red granite or steep ice.

For such a relatively compact range, a staggeringly large number of climbs have been recorded, approximately 4000. This guide covers the whole area in two volumes and although recording only one quarter of that number and therefore in no way definitive, does indicate most of the worth-while projects available to the visitor.

Inevitably, for this is the Mecca to which most alpinists aspire, over-crowding can now be a serious problem during the summer months in certain parts of the range and on high quality classic routes. Lovers of tranquillity may now have to seek the more esoteric corners or climb outside the main season; information is provided to help them on their way.

I hope that this guide will not only allow the reader to make the best use of weather and mountain conditions when visiting the area, but will also stimulate inspiration during the preceding months of planning. Throughout the text you will be treading in the footsteps of the great pioneers – Whymper, Mummery, Ravanel, Charlet and Contamine – and frequently following Bonatti, Desmaison, Rébuffat, Seigneur and in more recent years Gabarrou, Grassi and Piola. Whatever your ambitions, from mountain walking in spectacular scenery through to the most demanding alpine climbs in the world, there is plenty to go at.

Special thanks must go to the series editor Les Swindin for contributing a tremendous amount of work to the project and making allowances for my interim expeditions to other regions over the last two years. Simon Richardson and Jon Silvester provoked argumentative discussion and helped enormously with the text. Sheila Harrison took on the mammoth job of word-processing.

Other people who helped with the text are Gino Buscaini, Chris Dale, Rob Durran, Roger Everett, Andy Perkins, Roger Payne, Godefrey Perroux, Christine Richardson, W.L. Robinson and Mike Woolridge. Monique Faussurier, Pietro Giglio, Jerry Gore, Mark Miller, Martin Moran, Efusio Noussan, Tony Penning and D 'Smiler' Cuthbertson. Credits for photographs are given with the list of photographs elsewhere in the book but my thanks must be extended to Bob Lawford, Frank Solari and Paul Kent for all they did in preparing photographs and to John Bowler for all the art work on them. I must also thank Rod Powis for all his efforts in interpreting and drawing topo diagrams from my originals.

Lindsay Griffin, North Wales 1991                                    11

# General information

## RECENT DEVELOPMENTS

Whereas the seventies saw a concentration in and development of the ice/mixed climbing potential due to the introduction of curved tools, this has been superceded in the eighties by the enormous development of climbing on the granite faces throughout the range.

The style in which these ascents have been made has undergone several changes and it is important to differentiate between 'mountaineering' with its associated level of commitment and what could now be termed a climbing exercise.

These days, climbs are quite often terminated at the natural finish to the route, be this a mountain ridge, the top of a pillar or simply a ledge at the end of the difficulties. Descent is then effected by rappeling the route of ascent or one close at hand. By leaving boots and rucksacks at the foot of the climb, together with any ice gear required on the approach, a fast ascent in rock shoes can be made of a route that traditionally might have necessitated the carrying of bivouac equipment.

Short routes completed in this fashion are very much in vogue as relatively unsettled weather can still allow a good deal of climbing to be achieved in a limited holiday period. Many modern rock routes are now created and climbed in this style, though it must be emphasised that some of these entail long and badly-protected runouts that require a high degree of boldness and commitment. Popular routes now have well-equipped fixed rappel points allowing a rapid retreat at the first sign of inclement weather and give an overall impression of non-seriousness. However a lightweight approach can produce dire consequences at higher altitudes when indecision prevents parties from making this retreat in good time. The popularity of certain rock faces has created its own problems. Serious danger areas for rock fall, attributed to parties above, are now considered to lie beneath the W faces of Dru, Blaitière and the L side of the Grand Capucin. The importance of experience, route-finding skills and sound mountaineering judgment have in no way lessened in recent years!

Advances in ice climbing have taken alpinists into the narrow gullies that often face S or E and are rarely in good condition during the summer. Spring or autumn ascents are preferred, when the nights are longer and colder and the routes well plastered in snow and ice. As yet, few parties appear to indulge in this facet of the sport.

The recent mild winters and general lack of snowfall throughout the Alps have been instrumental in creating exceptionally dry conditions during the summer months. Large expanses of bare rock are now viewed with amazement by those expecting the usual snow and ice covered slopes (see for example the photograph of the N face of the Grand Charmoz used in this volume). Stonefall has now reached serious proportions and danger areas are being established on routes of all grades that were until recently considered 'objectively safe'. This current trend suggests that many ice/mixed routes might become a thing of the past for Alpinist visiting this area during the more traditional holiday periods.

Some popular modern rock routes have been affected in a different manner. The remarkable drop in glacier levels has meant that climbers, especially those working from the Envers hut, have been faced with 'impossible starts' up blank, glacial-polished granite to gain the original line.

A number of climatologists view this as simply a transient state. Only time will tell if the Massif is heading for the sort of conditions now being experienced on the arid peaks of the Ecrins.

## MAPS

The guide is designed to be used in conjunction with the French I G N Series 1:25,000 which covers the entire range in two sheets – the 1986 3531 Est, St Gervais-le-bans Mont Blanc and the 1984 3630 Ouest, Chamonix-Mont Blanc. All heights and nomenclature are taken from these maps. Approaches to huts and various peaks/cols are often well-marked, obviating the need for comprehensive guidebook description.

## USING HUTS

Huts allow a night to be spent high in the range and close to the proposed ascent, without the burden of a heavy rucksack. Fees can be reduced on production of a reciprocal rights card (an Alpine Club or UIAA reciprocal rights card, etc). However with more and more overcrowding in high season, many parties are finding it preferable to camp/bivouac a suitable distance away from the hut. In August a veritable 'village' can appear in the Vallée Blanche.

In all CAF wardened huts it is necessary for all groups to pre-book and is generally advisable for individuals to pre-book in order to reserve bedspace. In the case of the Albert Premier it is necessary for individuals to pre-book.

In CAF huts there is usually provision for self-catering, but not at the Grands Mulets or at the Goûter Huts. If you do self-cater then it is advisable to take stove, cooking and eating implements with you. If you borrow these from the guardian you will be charged. The same applies to Italian huts. Please take all your refuse back to the valley with you. The CAF provide polythene bags for the purpose. In Swiss huts there are no self-catering facilities and stoves are not allowed in the huts. The guardian will cook food you provide but don't make his task difficult. Food which can be quickly cooked in a single pan is best. No charge is made for this service but expect to pay for hot water during the day. It should be free at breakfast and in the evening.

Bivouac huts generally have blankets but do not rely on there being fuel for stoves or cooking and eating implements.

## USING THIS GUIDE

ROUTE DESCRIPTIONS vary from one or two line explanations through to very detailed accounts. A number of modern climbs together with several older ascents have seen few, or in some cases no, repeats and descriptions should thus be treated with a degree of caution. Undoubtedly these routes will appeal to those of a more exploratory nature. Some older climbs described with short sections of aid have almost certainly been climbed free but details have been unforthcoming.

Common British usage in naming routes and features has been maintained despite apparent inconsistencies, e.g. 'Fissure Brown' as opposed to 'Mummery Crack'. Modern route names have not been translated.

The terms L and R or L and R side are always used with reference to the direction of movement of the climber. For mountain features such as glaciers or couloirs etc. the orographical reference to L or R banks is applied when viewed in the direction of flow or looking downwards.

Information on certain routes appears in the form of a topo diagram and the appropriate reference number is given in the margin in an open rectangle.

FIRST ASCENT details have been included to supplement information on the climb. Thus it was felt important to include the date and duration of first winter ascents, where known and thought reevant. The UIAA ruling that the period designated for alpine winter ascents should run from 21 December to 20 March inclusive has been adhered to implicitly. Some ascents in this guide are described under winter conditions only and the first ascent is credited accordingly.

GRADING OF CLIMBS as indicated in the margin is determined not only by the general level of technical difficulty but also by the seriousness of the enterprise as reflected by the associated objective danger, length, altitude and commitment.

Shorter rock climbs that are often termined below the summit of the peak, where a quick and efficient rappel descent can be made back down the route, are given an overall numerical grading in an attempt to distinguish them from longer undertakings in a more committing situation. This grading is generally that of the hardest section encountered and the route description or topo will indicate whether or not the climb is sustained at that level.

Other routes and all mixed or snow/ice climbs are given an adjectival grading which should not be confused with British rock climbing grades.

In order of rising difficulty: F Facile (Easy) PD Peu difficile (not very hard) AD Assez difficile (fairly hard) D Difficile (hard) TD Tres difficile (very hard) ED Extremement difficile (extremely hard)

FURTHER REFINEMENT is possible by adding plus or minus signs to the grades TD and below, but the ED grade has been made open-ended to cater for rising standards, e.g. ED1, ED2 etc. On traditional rock climbs, unless otherwise stated, the overall grading reflects a free ascent even though there may be a wealth of in situ protection (aid?) on various pitches. Certain climbs, graded from AD to TD, although not technically demanding under good conditions, are extremely serious for their grade and this has been noted in the introduction to the route in question.

UIAA NUMERICAL GRADING has been used for all rock sections and will avoid the confusion that sometimes occurs with French gradings below 6a. A table of international grading comparisons has been included but should only be used as a general indication, especially at higher levels. Problems often arise when first ascent parties have given a 'blanket' VI or VI+ grade to all the hard sections.

ARTIFICIAL CLIMBING is graded from A1 to A4. On A2 and above, slings and/or etriers will generally be necessary but short sections of A1 with in situ aid points can be overcome by most strong climbers wearing rock shoes simply by pulling on the gear.

SNOW AND ICE. With climbs involving technical difficulty on snow/ice, grading is less precise due to the variable conditions throughout the season and from year to year. Areas of glacier travel can, at certain times, become almost impracticable. Indeed, routes that involve hanging glaciers and ice slopes with serac formations are undergoing constant change. The difficulty and objective danger on these climbs will vary enormously and it would be wise to seek up-to-date information before making an attempt (eg Triolet and Plan N faces). From time to time the Scottish ice grading of 1 to 6 has been used in the text to indicate the difficulty of certain sections. This grading approximates the technical difficulties that are typically encountered on a reasonably protected Scottish climb of that standard. This is not to suggest that a leader who is competent at that grade is fully qualified to attempt the alpine route in question. The latter, in reality, will almost certainly feel considerably more demanding than the Scottish grade would imply.

THE OFFICE DE LA HAUTE MONTAGNE in the Place de l'Eglise in Chamonix Tel 50 53 00 88 provides an excellent service offering information on routes, mountain conditions and detailed weather forecasts. They encourage climbers to leave details (forms are available) of their proposed itinerary with them before setting out on an excursion so that in the event of non-return, search and rescue facilities will be alerted. Do remember to tell them when you do return if you use this service. The office also keep details of new routes climbed in the region and has reference copies of guidebooks to this and other alpine areas.

PHOTOGRAPH NUMBERS are shown in the margin in black rectangles below the route grade. On the photographs the route numbers are marked and the lines of ascent indicated. Some routes or parts of routes may be visible on more than one photographs, and where this occurs, these additional photo numbers appear at the end of the introduction to the route. A dashed line signifies that this section of the route is not visible. Not all routes described in the text have necessarily been marked on the photographs in order to avoid overcrowding. In such cases reference is only made to the photograph in the introductory text to the route.

HEIGHTS quoted for the whole climb refer to the vertical interval from the base of the route to its top and not to the amount of climbing involved, which may be much longer. The final TIME gives a good indication for a rope of two climbers, competent at that standard and experiencing no delays due to other parties, weather etc. It may also aid the decision as to whether bivouac equipment should be carried on longer routes.

ABBREVIATIONS are used for points of the compass and for left and right. Others frequently used are Aig (Aiguille), Mt (Mont) and Pt (Point where this refers to a spot height or Pointe used in a name).

## EQUIPMENT

With so many manuals now available on the craft of alpinism, there is little point in dwelling on the subject here. When it comes to equipment, most parties tend to use a single 11mm rope on middle-grade climbs where long rappels are not involved. They will carry a few hexentrics, wires, slings for spikes and plenty of karabiners for the in situ pegs. On modern rock routes 50m ropes and a full rack of hexentrics, wires, Friends etc are considered de rigueur. On the less frequented climbs, difficult pitches may require blade pegs, RPs or a very bold approach)

## OTHER GUIDEBOOKS TO THE AREA

At the time of writing there are no longer any definitive guidebooks to the range. The French Guide Vallot series 'La chaine du Mt Blanc' in 4 volumes is more than ten years old and is out of print. It has been replaced by a selected climbing guide in two volumes (Francois Labande, 1987). Similar comments apply to the Italian guides, though a recent Swiss Alpine Club publication covers the Swiss end of the range including parts of France.

There are a number of large hardback publications, in several languages, with a 'Selected Climbs' format. These generally contain a superb photographic coverage. Perhaps the most well-known is Gaston Rébuffat's The Mont Blanc Massif – The 100 Finest Routes. Unfortunately the English edition is presently unavailable. For pure rock climbing, the excellent topo guides by Michel Piola cover many of the modern creations. There is also available a valley crags guidebook using topo diagrams – Grandes Ecoles d'Escalade de la Vallée de Chamonix by François Burnier and Dominique Potard.

## VALLEY BASES

CHAMONIX VALLEY. Although pleasant and often much quieter bases can be found in the small villages from Les Houches to Le Tour, convenience ensures that most parties will stay close to either Chamonix or Argentière.

CHAMONIX is situated on the main road and railway line between Le Fayet and the Franco-Swiss border with numerous shops, hotels, 'bunkhouses' and camp sites of all standards. The Montenvers rack railway lies across a bridge just beyond the main station and téléphériques are clearly marked on the map. Recorded weather forecasts can be heard by dialling (50) 53 01 31 40 or Geneva (022) 98 24 24. Rescue services are in the hands of the Peloton de Gendarmerie de Haute Montagne (PGHM). See the note about the Office de la Haute Montagne.

    The main tourist information centre opposite the office provides details on trains, buses and téléphériques. The Mont Blanc tunnel connects Chamonix to Courmayeur in Italy and is a toll road. There is a bus service and officially passports are necessary although alpinists having descended on the Italian side of the range can normally get back with some other form of identification.

ARGENTIERE is served by a very regular bus and train service from Chamonix. This small village 8km up the valley from Chamonix has a good selection of shops, hotels and camp sites. The guides' bureau and the Tourist Office, both near the centre of the village, provide detailed weather forecasts etc.

VAL MONTJOIE is a picturesque and somewhat quieter valley on the W side of the massif and has several small resorts. Le Fayet at the entrance to to the valley is reached easily by regular train or bus service from Chamonix. Onward bus connections reach St Gervais-les-Bains and Les Contamines where shops and accommodation are available. The roadhead is at Notre-Dame de la Gorge and a large car park and camp site are situated 2km before this point.

COURMAYEUR is quickly reached from Chamonix by road through the Mont Blanc tunnel. A popular resort with a wide selection of shops, accommodation etc. The Office du Val Veny in the rue du Mont Blanc Tel (0165) 84 10 21 offers information on routes, weather forecasts etc. A weather forecast is also posted in Toni Gobbi's sports shop in the main street. Rescue services are in the hands of the Cosmacini di Alto. Most parties use the various camp sites in either the Val Veni or Val Ferret. Roadheads in these valleys are reached from Courmayeur by a very regular bus service during the summer months. Unfortunately the incidence of theft from unattended vehicles in these valleys has risen alarmingly in recent years.

SWISS VAL FERRET. A tarmac road runs from Orsières as far as Ferret at 1700m. The main village at Praz de Fort can be reached throughout the year by bus from Orsières and has a good selection of shops etc. The bus continues to the simple villages of La Fouly (large camp site) and Ferret during the summer months only. A side road reaches the picturesque resort of lakeside Champex at the entrance to the Arpette valley (bus service from Orsières in the summer). Rescue services are governed by the Gendarmerie d'Orsières Tel (026) 4 11 06.

## GRADING COMPARISONS

| UIAA | UK | France | | USA | DDR | Australia |
|------|-----|--------|-----|------|-----|-----------|
| III | | III | | 5.4 | III | |
| IV– | V Diff | IV– | | | | |
| IV | M Severe | IV | | 5.5 | IV | |
| IV+ | | IV+ | | | | 12 |
| V– | 4a | V– | | 5.6 | V | 13 |
| V | 4b | V | | | VI | 14 |
| V+ | | | 5a | 5.7 | VIIa | 15 |
| VI– | 4c | V+ | 5b | 5.8 | VIIb | |
| VI | 5a | | 5c | | | 16 |
| VI+ | 5b | 6a | | 5.9 | VIIc | 17 / 18 |
| VII– | | | | 5.10a / 5.10b | VIIIa | 19 / 20 |
| VII | 5c | 6b | | 5.10c / 5.10d | VIIIb | 21 |
| VII+ | | 6c | | 5.11a / 5.11b | VIIIc | 22 |
| VIII– | 6a | | | 5.11c / 5.11d | IXa | 23 |
| VIII | | 7a | | | IXb | 24 |
| VIII+ | 6b | 7b | | 5.12a / 5.12b | IXc | 25 |
| IX– | | | | 5.12c / 5.12d | Xa | 26 |
| IX | 6c | 7c | | | Xb | 27 |
| IX+ | | | | 5.13a / 5.13b | Xc | 28 / 29 |

20

# Huts

**H1**  **Col du Midi Hut (Abri Simond)**  3600m. A disused and derelict wooden structure with one usable room giving an adequate, though often overcrowded, bivouac shelter. Reached in 15–20min from the Midi Téléphérique Station by descending the NE ridge for 100m or so, until steep snow slopes (several crevasses) lead back underneath the S face of the Aig du Midi to the upper section of the Vallée Blanche. F

    Care must be exercised in this region, indeed in the whole summit area of the Midi, as fatal accidents have occurred due to contact with apparently 'disused' electrical cables. In 1989 one room had been refurbished but was being used by workmen reconstructing the Cosmiques Hut. It is rumoured that the Abri Simond will be removed when this work is completed.

**Cosmiques Hut**  3613m. This was the Alpine Glaciology Laboratory situated close to the Abri Simond and which provided accomodation until it was destroyed by fire. In 1989 work was in progress to rebuild a large hut for alpinists. Completion date is set for summer 1991.

**Aiguille du Midi Téléphérique Station**  3795mSituated on the N summit of the Aig du Midi, this is a popular starting and finishing point for many expeditions. A rock tunnel and gallery lead to the start of the NE ridge which in turn gives access to the Vallée Blanche. Difficulty can be experienced in winter if the snow tunnel leading onto the NE ridge has not been excavated. Entry and exit is then made via a small metal door in the wall on the S side of the ridge. Officially climbers are not allowed to stay here but in emergencies it is often possible to bivouac in the tunnel.

**H2**  **Requin Hut**  2516m. Property of the CAF. Situated below the Dent du Requin on the L bank of the Tacul glacier. Warden in late spring and summer. Room for 118. Restaurant service. Tel 50 53 16 96

From the Aig du Midi Téléphérique Station descend the Vallée Blanche to the Col du Gros Rognon (3415m) and continue under Mt Blanc du Tacul until level with the Pyramide du Tacul. Go round in a wide arc to the N and descend the glacier to just above the Petit Rognon. Weave a way down through the Géant icefall (both the route and difficulty varying from year to year – some danger of serac fall) and just below the base, traverse horizontally L to the hut. A good track is usually to be found in summer. 2hr. F

**H3** Because of a land slip the start from Montenvers has changed. Walk S on a good path above the glacier following signs to 'Les Refuges'. Descend ladders to the Mer de Glace. At the point at which the glacier is reached there are cairns indicating the route on the glacier. However, it is usually better to ignore these and instead follow the edge of the glacier over moraine, ice and boulders (there is usually a track with some waymarks) as far as l'Angle. From there it is fairly easy to work out into the middle of the glacier. (If the cairns are followed, work out towards the centre through the very crevassed region of the glacier then go up the middle to easier ground). Trend R below the Trélaporte promontory (c2000m). (In reverse, keep to the middle of the glacier until level with a conspicuous white square printed on a large slab at the point where the path from Montenvers meets the glacier. Then head directly for the square and so reach the ladders, or before reaching the very crevassed region of the glacier move over to the L bank about level with l'Angle and follow the edge of the glacier to the ladders. Melt streams on the glacier can be difficult to cross.

Keep on the R side and reach a steeper more crevassed section followed by a longer easier-angled section that leads to the Géant icefall. The correct route on the glacier is usually well-marked with painted stones and oil drums. Reach the moraine on the L side of the Envers de Blaitière glacier. Don't climb the moraine, which is very unstable, but instead continue up the R side of the Tacul glacier to the rock knoll on which the hut stands (large green and white marker). Ladders and stanchions lead up to a zig-zag path up rocks to the hut. 3hr

**Plan de l'Aiguille Hotel** 2203m. Privately owned. Situated about 10min below the Téléphérique Station. Room for 30. 2–3hr from Chamonix using the path starting opposite the Aig du Midi Téléphérique Station.

**Montenvers Hotel** 1909m. Privately owned (by the Commune de Chamonix). Situated just below the terminus of the rack railway. Room for 120. Tel 50 53 00 33. 2–2½hr on foot from Chamonix, 1½–2hr from Le Praz. Some 15min walk along the lower track to the Plan de l'Aiguille is the 'Chalet Austria', a small and disused wooden hut for those requiring a 'comfortable' bivouac free of charge.

**H4** **Envers des Aiguilles Hut** 2523m. Owned by CAF. Situated at the
**45** base of the SE ridge of the Tour Verte below the Aig de Roc. Warden and restaurant service throughout the summer. Room for

46. No telephone. Immediately below the hut there is good rock climbing on slabs and buttresses that are well-equipped with pegs and bolts.

From Montenvers follow Route H3 until level with l'Angle. Continue up the R side of the glacier which is fairly flat and waymarked. Leave the glacier at the foot of the N spur of the Tête de Trélaporte (yellow paint flashes) and climb ladders to reach a good path that traverses L below the Trélaporte glacier. Go round the SE ridge of the Aig de Roc and zig-zag steeply up to the hut. 2½hr

In winter the best method is to start from the Midi Téléphérique Station. Descend the Vallée Blanche, Géant icefall etc. until roughly level with the hut which at this point is visible from the glacier. Reach the moraine on the L and from its top go diagonally up R (avalanche potential; path in summer) to the hut.

**Grands Montets Station** 3295m. The terminus of the Argentière-Lognan-Grands Montets Téléphérique which operates from the end of June until the beginning of September, and from December to Whitsun. One is no longer officially allowed to bivouac inside the station and there is no available running water.

**Dru Rognon Bivouac** c2663m. The Dru Rognon lies at the top of the moraine on the L bank of the Nant Blanc glacier. There is no hut but an area of excellent bivouac sites in caves adjacent to the Dru glacier and walled enclosures atop the Rognon. It is the accepted starting point for routes on the Nant Blanc face of the Verte, N and W faces of the Dru.

Normally an approach is made via the Grands Montets. However it is useful to know the route from Montenvers when the téléphérique is closed or the Nant Blanc glacier is too crevassed. It is also the normal route of descent.

**H5**
**86**

Summer: From the Col des Grands Montets go towards the shoulder on the NW ridge of the Petite Aig Verte. Traverse below the rimaye and cross the ridge at c3270m. Slant down mixed ground to a steep narrow and enclosed couloir leading onto the Nant Blanc glacier. Climb down this or the rocky spur on the R, cross the glacier and follow the L side down to the Dru Rognon. 1hr

It is possible to cross the NW ridge of the Petite Aig Verte much lower at c3170m and slant down L across the base of a huge snowfield. Reach a rocky ridge on the edge of a line of cliffs overlooking the Nant Blanc glacier. Up to the L an obvious weakness leads down onto the glacier at the same point as before. PD−

**H6**

**82**

Winter: Descend the Grands Montets glacier to c3000m. On the L (S) of the spur culminating in Pt 3009m is a couloir of average angle 40° leading down to the Nant Blanc glacier. Descend this and cross the glacier, ascending slightly to reach the Dru Rognon. 1½hr

Easier but longer is to continue down the Grands Montets glacier and descend the slopes to the R of the spur 3009m to the Nant Blanc glacier. 2hr

**H7**

**86**

From Montenvers follow the path S, descend the ladders to the Mer de Glace and cross it to the bottom of the Dru Torrent (1885m). Follow the moraine N until, just before the Bayer Torrent, a faint track rises up to the R above a wet rock barrier 30m above the moraine. The path slants L passing below more large rock barriers then zig-zags up to the R side of the Nant Blanc glacier. Follow the moraine to the Dru Rognon. 3hr

**H8**

**80**

**Charpoua Hut** 2841m. Also called the Refuge Charlet. Privately owned but administered by the CAF. Situated below the S side of the Drus near the top of the Rognon de la Charpoua. Room for 12. Always open with a warden in summer.

From Montenvers follow Route H3 until opposite Pt 2082m. Reach the large ravine that lies between this point and the long moraine coming down from the Rognon de la Charpoua. Go up this (paint flashes) and reach the moraine on the L (cables) via a well-marked path. Follow the crest to the rognon and climb this, working L (cables and cut steps) to reach a gully leading up to the hut on the R. 3hr

**H9**

**Couvercle Hut** 2687m. A large hut and excellent viewpoint situated below the SE ridge of the Moine. Room for 137. Warden in summer. Tel 50 53 16 94. Locked in winter but the old hut situated under a large tilted slab of granite 100m NE of the new hut remains open. Room for 30.

From Montenvers follow Route H3 to below the Trélaporte promontory then cross the glacier and moraine crests (faint track, cairns, painted boulders etc) towards the foot of the Egralets cliffs. Keep going up the moraine and ice parallel to the cliffs until directly opposite a series of ladders (2230m, 1½–2hr)

A steep but easy path well-adorned with ladders and cables reaches the top of these cliffs. Follow the path over grass and moraine to the L side of the Talèfre glacier. Directly below the hut the path forks. Take the L branch which zig-zags up to the hut in a few minutes. 2½–3½hr from Montenvers.

In winter the slopes above the Egralets cliffs can be threatened by avalanche and the true path difficult to locate. A far safer approach uses the old path ascending the rib of the Pierre à Bérenger (2466m) on the R side of the Talèfre seracs (there is a rope in place to ascend the moraine). At the top traverse L onto the flat section of the glacier, head N towards the rocky Jardin de Talèfre, then cross the glacier to the SW in order to reach the hut.

**Argentière Hut**  2771m. Property of the CAF. A fine large hut and magnificent viewpoint situated on the R bank of the Argentière glacier at the foot of the SW (Jardin) ridge of the Aig d'Argentière. Room for 140. Restaurant service and warden from 15 March to 15 September with the exception in most years of the month of June. Part of the hut always remains open outside of these dates as a winter refuge (Room for 60). Places need to be reserved in advance for spring weekends. Tel 50 53 16 92

**H10**

**93**

From the Aig des Grands Montets Téléphérique Station descend the Rognons glacier, passing just L of a small rognon (3000m) and continue almost to the top of the Moraine des Rognons before turning SE and crossing the S branch of the Rognons glacier to reach the L bank of the Argentière glacier. Follow this until close to the Pyramide d'Argentière 2866m. Cross the glacier diagonally and the moraine that follows until a good track on the lateral moraine leads directly to the hut. 1½hr, F

**H11**

The bottom terminus of the Argentière-Grands Montets Téléphérique lies at the end of a minor road coming from Les Chosalets where there is a car park. From here take the wide path cutting steeply through wooded slopes on the R side of the glacier. Higher, steep zig-zags lead to the Chalet Militaire de Lognan (2032m, 1½hr).

Above, the path reaches the crest of the moraine (this point can also be reached from the Croix de Lognan 1975m, the intermediate téléphérique station, in ½–¾hr). Follow it to above the icefall then take a well-marked track that traverses around the slope of the moraine to reach the glacier. Follow the R side (crevasses) to the Moraine des Rognons and cross these slabby rocks (chains etc) to a platform on the SE end from where it is possible to descend to the glacier over large blocks (1½–2hr). Generally, when there is plenty of snow cover, it is quicker to remain on the glacier below this moraine. Continue up the R side of the glacier, joining Route H10, and so reach the hut (1hr). 4–4½hr

In summer the normal approach utilises the téléphérique from the Grands Montets terminus. Descent is usually made reversing Route H11 or via the Croix de Lognan.

**Albert Premier Hut** 2702m. Property of the CAF. Situated on the R bank of the Tour glacier. Room for 130. Warden and restaurant service in summer. Closed in winter but the old wooden hut just below remains open (room for 30). It is essential for individuals to pre-book bed space and meals. Tel. 50 54 06 20

There are a number of ways to reach this hut, the choice depending largely on the season.

**H12** From the upper téléphérique terminus (2186m) S of the Col de Balme follow a good path to the S, passing below the Charamillon Lake. After a rising traverse around the shoulder of the Bec du Picheu the path bears E to reach the moraine on the R bank of the Tour glacier (2484m). Follow this to the hut. 1½hr

**H13** From the intermediate station of Charamillon (which can also be reached in ¾hr from Le Tour by a wide track) take a path on the R that slants up to the crest of the Vormaine ridge. Cross a plateau to join the route above, near the lake. 1¾hr to the hut.

**H14** A direct but more arduous route begins near the téléphérique station in Le Tour and follows a good track E to the foot of the lateral moraine on the L side of the Tour glacier. Zig-zag up the slopes and cross the stream above the Cascade du Picheu. Gain the crest of the moraine at the 'Fenêtre du Tour' and follow it all the way to the hut (2hr). This route is generally used in descent.

In winter: The means of access above become impracticable and two alternatives are offered. The latter is becoming the most popular especially to those on ski.

**H15** From Le Tour head E towards the snout of the Tour glacier passing to the R of the Vormaine ski-lift station and keeping S of Route H14. Cross the moraine to reach a sort of open ravine and follow this for a little way until a second ravine on the L can be used to reach the foot of the steep section (yellow plaque). Ascend this steep section on the lateral moraine using a line of fixed chains. Reach the crest of the moraine above and follow it all the way to the hut.

**H16**    From the Grands Montets descend by Route H10 to the Argentière glacier. Cross it immediately and make a gently rising traverse to the NW below the SW buttress of the Chardonnet, the Adams Reilly glacier, and so reach the top L corner of the cwm containing the tiny Passon glacier. Take the Rhand branch of a double couloir and follow it directly to the Col du Passon. The hut lies on the far side of the Tour glacier.

**Trient Hut** 3170m. Property of the CAS. Situated on the R bank of the Trient glacier under the Pt d'Orny. Room for 155. Restaurant service and warden in spring and summer. Tel (026) 4 14 38

**H17**    From the Orny Hut follow the path on the R side of the Orny glacier, then along the glacier itself to the foot of the Col d'Orny. If snow conditions are good it is possible to cross the col then turn N climbing the rocks to the hut. Otherwise turn R before the col, passing below the remains of the old hut and follow a good stony track (red paint marks) to the hut. 1hr

**H18**    From Champex follow the footpath up the Arpette Valley, finishing on scree and snow, to a point just below the Col des Ecandies (3½hr). Turn sharply L and climb a couloir, or the rocks on the R, to reach the Fenêtre du Chamois (2985m). Cross the ridge between the two Lmost gendarmes in a group of 3. The fenêtre is unnamed on the map but lies SSE and above the Col des Ecandies (1hr).

  Cross a short steep slope to the SSW and a snowy shoulder below the Petite Pt d'Orny to reach the Trient Plateau. Follow the edge of this to the hut (1hr). 5 – 5½hr from Champex.

**H19**    From Trient it is best to take the path through wooded slopes on the L side of the Trient River. Pass the Chalet du Glacier (1583m) and Vesevey Chalets (2096m) and reach the little ablation valley behind the lateral moraine of the Trient glacier. Follow this to the Col des Ecandies (3½ – 4hr) then traverse E to the Fenêtre du Chamois couloir where Route H18 is joined. 5½ – 6hr to the hut.

In winter and spring the hut is generally reached from the Grands Montets via the Col du Chardonnet and the Fenêtre de Saleina.

**Orny Hut** c2850m. Property of the CAS. Situated on the L bank of the Orny glacier, above and to the E of the upper Lake Orny. The hut is used as a training centre for rock climbing by the CAS, several climbing areas having been developed at all standards around the hut. Ask at the hut for details. Room for 80 (30 in the winter room). Warden in summer. Tel (026) 4 18 87

**H20**  From La Breya (2188m), reached by télésiège from Champex, a good path traverses SW across the rocky flank of the hillside to the middle of the Combe d'Orny. Follow this valley then moraine on the R to the hut. 2–2½hr

It is possible to walk from Champex via the Arpette Chalets (1688m) and the Col de la Breya (2401m) to join the previous route though this is hardly done these days. 4½hr to the hut.

**H21**  From Praz de Fort it is possible to drive on a small surfaced road to c1470m where the track to the hut begins. Flow of traffic is often controlled and the best tactic is to use the good carpark at c1250m walking the last 30min. Follow the path up the R side of the Vallon d'Arpette de Saleina which zig-zags wearily to join the previous route near the lower lake. 4hr

In winter the approach to be recommended follows the 'Tour de Mont Blanc' path till it forks at 1319m. Take the path on the R into the Combe d'Orny and follow it to where it joins Route H20. 4½hr in summer to the hut.

**H22**  **Saleina Hut**  2691m. Property of the CAS. Situated above the R bank of the Saleina glacier below the Pts des Planereuses. Room for 43. Restaurant service and warden most of the summer. No telephone.

From Praz de Fort either use the same approach as Route H21 or follow the track on the L side of the river, parking at c1300m. The path slants up the hillside above the river and climbs the rocky buttress that forms the terminal moraine on the L side of the Saleina glacier using cables, cut steps etc. Once on top, follow the crest of the moraine until it is possible to work up to the S into a cwm below the Clochers des Planereuses. Cross the cwm to the promontory where the hut is situated. 3½hr.

It is worth noting that in winter one can generally only get into the hut through the roof.

**H23**  **A Neuve Hut**  2735m. Property of the CAS. Situated under the Pts des Essettes to the E of the A Neuve glacier. Room for 26. Warden in summer. Tel (026) 4 24 24

From La Fouly go through L'A Neuve to a parking place at the end of a driveable track in the forest (1592m). Follow the track on the L through the forest. Continue along moraine until the track crosses the river on a small footbridge (c2100m). Above is a large block inscribed 'Bloc Javelle'. Zig-zag up a ravine, finally making a wide detour to the NW. Reach the hut on the R via a rocky chimney with fixed chains. 3hr

In winter the slopes below the hut can be prone to avalanche after snowfall. However it is easy to reach the A Neuve glacier directly. Don't cross the footbridge but continue along the moraine and climb the icefall onto the upper plateau immediately below Pt 2661m.

At a pinch the hut could be reached on ski via the Grands Montets, Col du Chardonnet and a short though possibly tricky crossing of the Col de la Grande Lui.

**H24**    **Saleina-A Neuve Huts Connection**    Three closely linked passes give a direct passage with little difficulty. From the Saleina Hut head S to the Col des Planereuses and pass through the gap on the R (1¼hr). Descend the Planereuses glacier for a short distance then bear R to cross the Col Sup de Crête Sèche 3024m. Contour the Treutse Bô glacier then gain the Col Sup des Essettes (3113m) (1hr). Descend a long snow couloir to the A Neuve glacier and so reach the hut (¾hr). About 3hr, in total, either way. F

**H25**    **Dolent Bivouac Hut**    2667m. Property of the CAS. Occasionally called the Cabane de la Maye and constructed in orange polyester. Situated just below the tip of the Dolent glacier on the L bank. Room for 14. There is sometimes a warden in summer and gaz stoves are provided. The access described is indicated by red paint flashes.

From La Fouly go through L'A Neuve and reach a parking place at the end of the road leading into the Combe des Fonds. After crossing the river follow a track W to the cliffs that lie on the corner between Grand Lui and the Combe des Fonds. The path climbs to the top of these (fixed handrails etc) until at about 1900m one can cross the grassy slopes of 'Sur La Lys' to the SW. Go around the base of La Maye to c2150m then head up towards 2731m. The hut is situated on the moraine below this point. 2½hr

In winter there is really no safe approach to this hut.

**H26**    **Triolet Hut**    2590m. Rifugio Dalmazzi. CAI property. Situated on the L bank of the Triolet glacier under a rock wall at the base of Pt 3228m of Mts Rouges de Triolet. Room for 30. Always open with a warden resident much of the summer. Good cooking equipment, gaz stove etc.

From the Arnuva Restaurant in the Val Ferret (1769m) continue along the unmade road for about 20min to a sharp bend level with the moraine on the R side of the Triolet glacier opening. Follow a well-marked path across the river and up the moraine till just past spot height 2267m a large grassy gully appears on the R. The path goes up the L side of the gully, then crosses it to zig-zag up the R side until the upper terraces lead horizontally back L across the top of the gully to the hut. (The gully can be climbed direct via large blocks and an easy finishing chimney). 2–2½hr

In winter the slope between the hut and the upper plateau of the Triolet glacier can be avalanche-prone and the approach just plain hard work. It is often possible to ascend the L side of the glacier quite easily, between the icefall and the rocks of Mt Rouge de Gruetta (stonefall). This gives an avalanche-free and rapid means of access to the upper plateau and is worth considering as a summer possibility for routes on Mt Gruetta, Aig de Leschaux etc.

**Fiorio Bivouac Hut** 2724m. Property of the CAAI. Bivacco Cesare Fiorio al Dolent. Situated on the rocky flanks that form the L bank of the Pré de Bar glacier. Room for 20. No warden. Always open. The old hut 30m lower has room for 5.

**H27**  From the parking place at the end of the road in the Italian Val Ferret, continue along the track for ¾hr to reach Pré de Bar (2062m). Follow a vague track, behind the moraine, leading towards the Petit Col Ferret. Between two streams (cairn) take a very steep track going up to the R (avoid going into the obvious gully where the path seems to go). Just before reaching the col a track heads W then NW across moraine and slabby rock (cairns) to reach the hut. 3hr

**H28**  From La Fouly follow the main road S along the Swiss Val Ferret for about 1km to where a good path crosses a footbridge over the river at 1614m. Follow this path, taking the R fork through the forest, where it turns sharply SE and contours round to the chalets of Léchère-Dessus (1877m). These chalets can also be reached by a good track from Ferret. A vague path now follows the river to a small lake (La Gouille, 2141m). Reach the upper section of the Combe des Fonds and cross the Petit Col Ferret to join H27. 3hr

In winter follow the Combe des Fonds directly from L'A Neuve. Large avalanches can reach this from the W flanks after heavy snowfall.

## Col du Midi 3532m

The broad snowy saddle near the head of the Vallée Blanche can easily be reached from the Midi Téléphérique Station. Descend the NE ridge for 100m or so until steep snow slopes lead back underneath the S face of the Midi (rimaye) to the flat upper plateau of the Vallée Blanche.

## Aiguille du Midi 3842m

N summit: A Malczenski with J Balmat and 5 other guides, 4 Aug 1818. Winter: F Burnaby with A and E Cupelin, Jan 1883

The highest point of the Chamonix Aiguilles. Capped by its characteristic radio-television mast and lightning conductor, the internal structure of the 2 summits has been radically altered by the restaurants, workrooms and associated tunnels of the station. As a viewpoint it is breathtaking, and its various faces offer a host of quality climbs in all grades.

**1**
PD+

**SOUTH-SOUTH-WEST (COSMIQUES) RIDGE**
G and M Finch, 29 Aug 1911

*A pleasant little route and good introduction to Alpine mixed climbing. It is best avoided in the early morning rush-hour when numerous other parties congregate. Although very short and safe, the technical difficulties are high for the grade.*

From the Abri Simond Hut follow the ridge, passing below and R of the first summit. Regain the crest and continue to a second smaller summit where some awkward climbing, just below the crest on the R side, leads to the gap before the first prominent gendarme. Climb down or rappel 20m on the R side and regain the crest beyond the gendarme via a shallow chimney (III+), a platform and a short snow slope. Continue to a second gendarme and either turn it on snow on the R or climb a crack on the L and descend a split in the tower to the snow crest beyond. Reach the final step and climb a short wall (IV, or an aid crack on the R) to a narrow ledge. A chimney on the L, or a crack on the R leads to a platform. Climb a large corner/chimney (III) on the L side of the ridge to a snow shoulder and the viewing platform. c260m, 2½–3hr

## Aiguille du Midi: Cosmiques Spur

Reached in 20min from the téléphérique station. An attractive little piece of granite leading to the Cosmiques Ridge. One should beware when climbing on the R side of the face of live supply cables (15,000V!)

**2**
V/V+
2

**SOUTH FACE**
B Pierre and G Rébuffat, 13 Aug 1956

The classic route and very popular. It is well-equipped for a rappel descent. 120m, 3½hr to the station.

**3**
V/A1
2

**EAST FACE**
P Chavasse with P Leroux, 23 July 1971

Another nice little climb with a short aid section over the roof. Watch out for one or two loose blocks. 120m, 4hr to the station.

## Aiguille du Midi: South-East Pillar

This wonderful piece of granite, often referred to as the S face, is now the scene of many high-standard free rock routes. It is deservedly very popular and being well-bathed in sunshine can be climbed almost immediately after bad weather. Unfortunately in busy periods large queues can develop at the base of the climbs. From the summit a short descent on the N side and a snow crest lead to the station but several routes have fixed rappel points down their length.

**4**
VII
46
3

**LA DAME DU LAC**
G and R Vogler, 30 June 1982

A direct line up the steep grey walls on the L of the face that gives some excellent crack climbing. 180m

**5**
VIII–
46
3

**MAZEAUD ROUTE**
P Lafond, P Mazeaud and A Tsinant, 27 and 30 Aug 1963

After the initial pitches of strenuous crack climbing the difficulties ease and the Rébuffat Route is followed to the top. There are numerous in situ aid points but the climb is now generally accomplished free. 190m

**6**    **MA DALTON**

IX–    G Hopfgartner and M Piola, 9 July 1984

`46`
`3`

A monumental roof crack, climbed with 1 rest point by T Renault.
Combined with a finish up the open dièdre R of the Rébuffat
Route, it provides the hardest technical climbing on the face. 180m

**7**    **REBUFFAT**

VII    M Baquet and G Rébuffat, 13 July 1956

`46`
`3`

A magnificent classic on exposed open slabs. It can still be easily
ascended in its original form at V and A1 and an increasingly
popular start via the Contamine gives a more homogenous climb
with the crux on the S-shaped crack (VI/VI+). 190m

**8**    **CONTAMINE**

VIII–    M Bron, C Bozon, A Contamine, J Juge and P Labrunie, 1 Sept
1957

`46`
`3`

A very strenuous crack climb with a hard crux pitch just below the
top. There is still a considerable quantity of in situ equipment
which allows an ascent at the original grade of V and A1. 190m

## Aiguille du Midi: North-West Face

Together with the N face this is reached from the Plan de l'Aiguille
Téléphérique Station in 1–1½hr. A good path leads to the Pélerins
glacier which is crossed to the foot of the face. Due to the easy
access and descent from the top of the route by téléphérique, routes
here feel less serious than perhaps they ought. It has become a
popular venue for winter climbing, though at that time of year the
final slopes can be prone to wind slab.

**9**    **VOGLER COULOIR**

D    F Burnier and R Vogler, 11 May 1980

*A nice little ice climb that in snowy conditions is a useful inclusion to
routes that can be achieved from the Midi Station. It rises to the
Cosmiques Ridge from the main couloir on the SW flank.*

The foot of the couloir can be reached by following the main SW
couloir from the Bossons glacier but this makes for a lengthy
undertaking. The most convenient approach is to rappel from the
bridge connecting the 2 summits of the Midi and descend the broad

snowy couloir for 300m (45°) until it widens. A narrow couloir
breaks through the walls of the L bank. The first pitch is 80° and is
followed by 250m of 50° to the foot of a gendarme 60m below the
Cosmiques Ridge. Climb up a narrow icy chimney on the R side
(70°). c300m, 4hr

**10**     **WEST COULOIR**
D/D+    J Chassagne and E Schmutz, Dec 1977

This couloir, which rises from the top of the Rond glacier, is
guarded at its base by a large serac. It is exposed to frequent
stonefall and provides a suitable winter expedition when it is about
the same standard as the Gervasutti Couloir on Mt Blanc du Tacul.
Finish with mixed climbing on the upper section of the long NW
ridge. 900m, 8hr

**11**     **1st SPUR**
TD     G Perrin with Y Seigneur, 1969. Winter: J Dumery and Y Seigneur,
     27–29 Feb 1976

*This is very well-defined in the upper section below the point where it*
*joins the NW ridge. It is probably the steepest of all the spurs on this side*
*of the mountain and gives fine free climbing on sound granite.*

By starting in the couloir on the L, climb the spur and turn the first
buttress on the L (IV). Avoiding an overhanging section on the L,
continue up the crest to a buttress below a grey rockfall scar. On the
L climb 2 pitches on snow then come back R to the grey scar (V).
Climb cracks to the top (V+). Climb up to the third buttress (IV)
and traverse R to an icy couloir. Reach a dièdre after 3 pitches and
climb it (V/V+) to regain the crest. Climb up this on the R (IV+)
then slant back L (IV+) and so reach on easy ground the top of the
third buttress. Continue up snowy rocks, joining the NW ridge,
until it is possible to move L onto the steep ice slopes which are
followed to the summit ridge. 1000m, 12–14hr

**12**     **NORTH-WEST COULOIR**
D+     M Hugonnot and J Marjoux, 24 June 1964. Winter: D Haston and
     G Neithardt, Jan 1974

The long narrow couloir immediately to the L gives an elegant
mixed climb where very cold and snowy conditions are essential to
minimise the objective dangers. 1000m, 8hr

**13**     **2nd SPUR**

AD+     C Dent, J Oakley Maund with J Jaun and K Maurer, Aug 1879

**48**

*A classic mixed climb on varied terrain which is both long and serious for its grade and a fine achievement for its era.*

Climb the easy rocks on the R side of the spur until they steepen and form a distinct ridge. Climb on the R side of this to reach a secondary couloir which leads back up L to a col on the crest of the spur. Continue up the mixed slope above to a shoulder and climb steep ice slopes to an exit on the NE ridge just L of the station. 1000m, 6–8hr

## Aiguille du Midi: North Face

**14**     **3rd (CENTRAL) SPUR**

TD     O Mossaz with Y Seigneur, 31 Aug 1963. Winter: G Perrin and J Delsirer with Y Seigneur, 5–6 Jan 1969

**48**

*Although overshadowed by its neighbour, this is a direct and interesting climb with difficulties on both rock and ice.*

Climb easily up the spur (III) to the first steep gendarme and turn it on the L. Just below the second gendarme, climb up R in an icy chimney (IV+) followed by slabs and reach the L side of an icy couloir by a delicate traverse (V) or diagonal rappel. Slant L on a ledge to reach a snowy shoulder and climb up the spur above via an overhanging dièdre (V+) and the Rhand of 2 chimneys to reach the top of the second gendarme. Climb across to a couloir on the L. It overhangs at the top and leads to a ridge. Follow this to a steep buttress and slant up R on a snowy ledge (V at the start). Reach the base of a second buttress which is again avoided, this time on the L, by a snowy couloir. Climb steeply through the gully to the R of the great serac barrier and reach the upper ice slopes. Follow these to the NE ridge close to the station. c1200m, 10–12hr

**15**     **FRENDO SPUR**

D+     E Frendo and R Rionda, 11 July 1941. Winter: J Martin, E Stagni and R Wohlschlag, 21–22 Jan 1964

**48**

*A magnificent and well-established classic. It is one of the finest mixed climbs in the Aiguilles with gradually increasing difficulties all the way to the top. If the lower rock buttress is fairly dry, the route can easily be completed in a day from the first téléphérique to the Plan de l'Aiguille.*

*However many parties climb the buttress in the afternoon and bivouac below the ice crest. This ensures good conditions in the upper section early next morning.*

Reach the base of the lower rock buttress and on the L side climb a snowy ramp that slants up R to the top of the first step. Go up slabs and broken rock trending slightly L for about 100m then go straight up a series of broken icy chimneys (III) to gain the crest of the spur and follow it to a small col on a level shoulder. Climb cracks and chimneys on good rock, keeping slightly L (IV) to reach another shoulder at the foot of the ice crest (good bivouac sites, 3–4hr).

This ice crest, which steepens at the top (55°), is followed to the L side of the rock rognon. The most elegant finish takes the rock rognon. It has been climbed just about everywhere, but the best solution is: Go up some cracked slabs to the foot of 2 parallel cracks on the R of the steep ice couloir splitting the rognon. Climb these (IV and V) to a small shoulder below the final headwall. Traverse horizontally L to the ice couloir (V–) and climb it to an abrupt finish. A short snow crest leads to the NE ridge and the entrance to the Midi station.

An increasingly popular and often quicker finish is to avoid the rognon by the steep ice on either side, the R side being more amenable. Scottish 3, 1100m, 9–12hr from the Plan de l'Aiguille.

**16**  **E H M SPUR**

D    M Feuillarade and Y Seigneur, 8–9 Jan 1966

**48**

*A mixed route that involves crossing a difficult serac barrier to reach the upper hanging glacier. See also Photo 49.*

Go diagonally Rwards from the base of the spur to reach the first step and climb it on the L side. Continue up mixed ground to the second step and avoid it on the R by climbing up ramps to a small amphitheatre dominated by the hanging glacier. Slant up to reach the crest of the spur through a hole and continue up the L flank on bands of snow or ice to the serac barrier. This is usually the crux and the hanging glacier is ascended to reach the NE ridge at a level section. 900m, 8–12hr to the Midi station.

**17**  **TOURNIER SPUR**

D    J Morin with C Tournier and A Caux, 13 Aug 1944. Winter: W

**49**  Cecchinel and C Jager, 1–3 March 1969

*This is probably the second most popular route on the N face although, compared to the Frendo, ascents are still relatively scarce.*

Reach the base of the spur at 2779m and climb it on broken rock to the foot of a steep step. Traverse L along a ledge and climb the R side of the Col du Plan hanging glacier (ice fall danger). Take a secondary rock buttress overlooking the ice slope above and follow it back to the crest of the spur. Continue to the last rocks, cross a rimaye on the R and climb the ice slopes for 100m to the Midi-Plan ridge. Follow this to the Midi station in 1hr. 800m, 10hr from the Plan de l'Aiguille.

The spur can be climbed direct at V and A1.

**18**     **MIDI-PLAN TRAVERSE (NORTH-EAST RIDGE)**
PD     G Young and J Knubel, 10 Aug 1907

**49**

*A splendid snow ridge and an outstandingly popular classic. Combined with a descent of the Mer de Glace via the Requin Hut it makes an excellent introduction to the range for a suitably acclimatised party. This is now the normal route to the summit of the Aig du Plan and to ensure a modicum of solitude, start before the rush hour which begins with the arrival of the first téléphérique. Short sections of II/III. See also Photo 48.*

From the tunnel exit of the Midi station, follow the ridge NE over Pt 3626m and descend steeply to the rocks of 3518m. A thin crest leads to the Col du Plan. Climb rocks and a snowy couloir on the Chamonix side to reach the Rognon du Plan. Follow the rocky crest then descend a system of couloirs and ledges on the R side to the snow. Traverse under the rocks to reach the Col Sup du Plan. Climb the snow ridge and easy rocks to the summit of the Aig du Plan. 3–4hr

# Col du Plan 3475m

The lowest point on the Midi-Plan Ridge.

**19**     **NORTH FACE**
D–     R Aubert, R Dittert, P Demarchi, F Marullaz and R Mussard, 14 Sept 1941. Winter: W Cecchinel, 7 Feb 1971

**49**

*There are a number of routes on this side though only one has gained classic status. Once established on this excellent mixed climb it is objectively safe (but may be subject to rockfall in the lower part from parties above) though the approach could be threatened by a large serac*

*fall from the hanging glacier to the R of the start. It has gained a certain popularity and is regularly ascended in winter.*

From the Plan de l'Aiguille follow the path to the SE and where it splits into 3 branches take the central one which leads to the upper part of the moraine on the L side of the Pélerins glacier. Follow the moraine onto the glacier and go up it to the rock spur below the col (1½hr).

Climb onto the spur from the L and keeping on the L side go up the easy rock until at half-height an icy couloir on the R side of the spur can be followed to the hanging glacier (III). This is not too steep (50°) and leads to the col. By keeping on the L side of the hanging glacier it is possible to obtain rock belays throughout. The gradually steepening couloir to the L of the spur is exposed to stonefall but in cold and icy conditions it allows the Col du Plan to be gained entirely on ice (D, crux is Scottish 3). 600m, 3–5hr

Descent: Normally the most practical method of escape is to follow the NE ridge to the Midi station in 1hr. However it is possible to descend due E from the col, keeping close below the rocks of the Rognon du Plan to reach the Envers du Plan glacier and the Requin Hut. This is very crevassed and can only be recommended early in the year (PD, 1½hr).

# Rognon du Plan 3601m

**20**
D

**49**

**WEST FACE DIRECT**
A Parat and J Paris, 7 July 1968

Although predominantly a rock climb, it is easy to wander back and forth across this face on straightforward mixed ground and most of the difficulties are avoidable. IV with 2 pitches of V. 800m

**21**
TD–

**45**

**FIL A PLOMB**
D Radigue and S Tavernier, July 1984. Winter: E Escoffier and D Lacroix, 20 Jan 1985

A modern ice climb in a couloir hidden on the N face. 600m, 6–8hr

**22**
V/A1

**45**

**SOUTH-EAST RIDGE VIA SOUTH FACE OF POINTE 3462m**
R Bozon and C Marin, 11 Sept 1977

*This is a delightful little rock climb of some 250m followed by an easy snow crest to the summit. It clears quickly after bad weather and is suitable for a short day.*

Approach either from the Requin Hut or from the Aig du Midi via the Midi-Plan Ridge and a descent from the Col du Plan (see Route 19).

Climb up the rib on good rock (IV and V with a little A1) to the top of Pt 3462m and continue up the snow crest to the summit. 4hr

The various obvious crack lines to the L give hard and strenuous climbing with pitches up to VII+/VIII.

# Aiguille du Plan 3673m

J Eccles with M and A Payot, 4 July 1871

The second highest and one of the most interesting peaks in the Aiguilles, the Plan has 4 faces and these give a wide variety of routes on rock, snow and ice that encompass all levels of difficulty.

**23**
**PD**
**45**

### SOUTH-EAST FACE
First ascent party

*Although the traditional route of ascent, it is now used almost exclusively as a means of descent to the Requin Hut after reaching the summit by the 'normal' route via the Midi-Plan Ridge. It is a glacier expedition and conditions vary enormously from year to year. The upper slopes can deteriorate badly in the afternoon.*

From the summit descend the snow ridge easily to the Col Sup du Plan then find the best line down the Envers du Plan glacier to reach the base of the SE ridge of the Requin. Climb down a rocky barrier (stonefall later in the day) onto the snow slopes below the E face of the Requin. Reach the top of the moraine on the R and follow the path down to the Requin Hut. c1100m, 2hr

*Aiguille du Plan continued on page 42*

# Aiguille du Plan: West Face

This huge and complex rocky wall, seamed with couloirs, is reached in 1½hr from the Plan de l'Aiguille. Despite a number of fine routes, it is rarely visited.

**24**
ED2
50

**SYLCHRIS**
C Profit, D Radigue and S Tavernier, 26 June 1985

*Though not as sustained as the next route, the difficult climbing lies in very steep and thinly-iced corners. It should be attempted during and after a night of hard frost in spring or early summer season when the mountain is well-endowed with snow and ice,*

The first 150m are straightforward 55°. There then follow 4 pitches with fixed belay anchors whose difficulty increases to a final 40m of vertical ice. More 55° climbing leads to the final 200m which gives sustained climbing on 70°–90° ice before easier ground leads to the Col Sup du Plan. 700m, 15hr

**25**
ED2
50

**GRAND WEST COULOIR**
P Gabarrou and J Picard-Deyme, 10–14 Dec 1975, although much of the lower couloir had previously been climbed by L Lachenal and L Terray in 1947. Winter: J Nezerka and J Rakoncaj, 6–7 Feb 1982

This is the most direct line on the W face and follows the thin chimney/gully immediately R of the Central Spur. It is rarely in condition and being seriously exposed to stonefall has almost always been repeated in winter months. Several sections of icy rock have generally required aid climbing and the route has not gained the popularity of other steep couloirs in the range. The easiest start takes a ramp on the R that slants steeply up L to below the first narrows. Scottish 5, 700m

**26**
TD–
50

**CENTRAL PILLAR DIRECT**
J Brown and T Patey, 18 July 1963

*Although several parties have considered this to be one of the better rock climbs of its class in the Aiguilles, the route has been surprisingly neglected. In dry conditions it gives a superb free climb on excellent granite.*

Climb easy broken rock on the R flank of the spur to a shallow-angled zone of blocks and, usually, a snow patch. Slant L across the snow and climb a chimney for 60m followed by easier rocks until it is possible to traverse R across an icy couloir which is itself on the R of a small ridge. Continue above, climbing another long chimney followed by a thin crack in a steep wall. Easier rocks lead to another steep wall which is climbed by a ledge slanting up to the R. Cross an icy couloir on the R and reach a little spur. The first section of this can be avoided on the R (short rappel) but once regained it should be followed directly to a small snowy col at the top. Descend a little on the L and traverse across slabs and ledges (V, with 1 short tension traverse) for 50m to a chimney of poor rock. Climb it (IV) to an amphitheatre of easy snowy ledges and go up them on the R to a shoulder below the headwall. Slant up to the L for a pitch in an easy ledge and chimney line leading to a good platform below a huge dièdre. Climb it for 120m (V+, sustained). A final snow crest and a couloir on the far side lead to the summit ridge. 700m, 10hr from the Plan de l'Aiguille.

---

*Aiguille du Plan continued*

**27**  **NORTH-WEST RIDGE INTEGRAL**
TD+   This demanding expedition was achieved in a most direct form by L Audoubert, J Dumery and Y Seigneur, 12–13 July 1973

This route involves climbing the Peigne by its SW ridge, the most reasonable combination being the Papillons Ridge followed by the Chamonix face, and continues to the summit of the Pélerins via the Carmichael Route. Climb along the ridge over Pt Migot to the W face of the Deux Aigles where Route 62 is followed. Rappel the N side to the Col des Deux Aigles and continue to the summit of the Plan. 1100m

**28**  **NORTH FACE DIRECT**
TD−   P Dillemann with A Charlet and J Simond, 19 July 1929. Winter: M
47    Feuillarade, J Martin and Y Seigneur, 8–9 Feb 1966

*Threading its way up a steep hanging glacier in the upper half of the face, this route has become an established classic and one of Charlet's greatest mixed climbs. The bottom rock spur is quite lengthy (400m) and most parties climb it in the afternoon to a bivouac near the top. The difficulties of the hanging glacier will of course change from year to year and there is variable objective danger from ice falling off the serac barriers. However in recent years a fairly clear line up the L side has appeared and the climb has become quite popular, with regular winter ascents. See also Photo 55.*

From the Plan de l'Aiguille station take the path on the L that leads to the little lake. Take the L branch which goes N of the lake and crosses the moraine to the Blaitière glacier. Go up this to the foot of the huge spur coming down from the hanging glacier of the N face (1½hr). Follow the glacier L of the spur and climb easily to the gap between the first and second gendarmes. Turn the second gendarme on the R and follow the crest until it is possible to traverse round the third on a ledge to the R, and reach the base of the fourth. Climb this by chimneys (IV) to a horizontal ridge and continue to the hanging glacier (3hr; good bivouac sites in the vicinity of the fourth gendarme). Climb the glacier choosing the line of least resistance and also one most protected from falling ice. The middle section is usually quite sustained at 55°–60°. In the upper section traverse R and reach easy slopes that lead to the summit rocks. 1000m, 7–12hr from Plan de l'Aiguille.

## 29   LAGARDE-SEGOGNE COULOIR

TD/TD+   J Lagarde and H de Ségogne, 24–25 July 1926. Winter: W
**62**   Cecchinel and C Jager, 27–29 Dec 1971

*This hidden couloir on the N face of the Dent du Caimen was an incredible ascent for its time and not repeated for nearly fifty years. Today it is recognised as a magnificent ice route that is very much in the modern idiom. It is a serious and committing undertaking and more so if the direct starts are taken. See also Photo 47*

From the Plan de l'Aiguille reach the Blaitière glacier and follow it to the foot of the Blaitière hanging glacier (1½hr). Climb the large snowy couloir on the W face of the Blaitière for 1 pitch then slant R across ledges (IV, mixed) to the hanging glacier and bypass it on the L via a steep ice pitch. Climb up and across the snow slope to cross the rimaye directly below the Col du Caimen (4hr).

Two direct starts have been added. The first climbs a very thin icy runnel just R of the serac barrier (Scottish 4/5) and the second climbs the couloir to the L of the huge rock spur taken by the N Face Direct of the Plan. At about half-height on this, traverse diagonally L across mixed ground to reach the snow slopes (Scottish 4).

Climb steep mixed ground towards the Col du Caimen for 120m before traversing R to the base of the impressive couloir that slants across the N face. 7 difficult and sustained pitches (Scottish 4, average angle 64°) lead to the Brèche du Caimen.

It is possible to rappel down the S side and so gain the Envers de Blaitière glacier, but more logical to continue over the summit of the Plan. Either make a rising traverse across the northern slopes of the Crocodile or, safer but harder, traverse the Crocodile and reach the summit of the Plan by the main ridge. 900m, 13–15hr from the Plan de l'Aiguille.

| | |
|---|---|
| **30** | **EAST COULOIR** |
| ED1/ED2 | C Dale and P Thornhill, 5–7 Feb 1986 |

The big couloir between the E ridges of Plan and Crocodile. The main difficulties occur on mixed ground in the last 400m where the granite was found to be of good quality. Scottish 5, c500m. See Photo 51.

| | |
|---|---|
| **31** | **EAST RIDGE** |
| D/D+ | V Ryan with F and J Lochmatter, 20 June 1906 |

**51**

*A marvellous climb in traditional mode. Although of great classic status, there has been a decreasing number of ascents in recent years due to changing fashion. The climbing is sustained, though not exposed, taking a succession of strenuous cracks separated by big stances. The granite is excellent throughout. In dry years, crossing the several rimayes and establishing oneself on the ridge can often be the crux of the route. See also Photo 45.*

From the Envers Hut go S over scree to the N branch of the Envers de Blaitière glacier. Cross this going first below the SE ridge of the Pts des Nantillons then the long SE ridge of the Blaitière heading for the Dent du Requin. Reach the much bigger S branch of the glacier and walk up it, crossing one or two rimayes until below the E ridge and alongside the N face of the Pain de Sucre (1½–2hr). Cross the rimaye beneath the snow gully on the L and traverse R onto the ridge about 80m above its base. If this is impossible climb the bottom of the ridge via cracks (IV), providing one can reach these from the glacier, or cross on the R near the Plan-Crocodile Couloir (stonefall) and slant up L on a snowy ledge line.

Climb up directly for 30m to a large ledge system with good sheltered bivouac sites on the L. Gain a second ledge above and follow it Rwards to where it narrows into a dièdre (III) and leads to the couloir. Climb the L side of the couloir for 80m and reach a prominent shoulder on the L; this point can also be reached from the first ledge by climbing the L flank of the spur close to the couloir leading to the Col du Pain de Sucre (IV+ at the end but maybe the easiest alternative in very snowy conditions).

The climbing now begins in earnest and the route-finding becomes easier. Follow the crest to the first step and climb it by 2 cracks (IV) leading to a deep chimney (IV). Now follow the crest directly climbing a series of cracks and chimneys, one of which, a slightly slanting corner, is the famous Grand Mère Crack (IV+). A little before the final step avoid a vertical Y-shaped crack by the overhanging crest of the ridge on the L (IV). The step above is climbed entirely on its L side. Climb a crack (IV+) to a ledge that slopes down to the R, then take a chimney that leads up to the ridge. In the upper section of this chimney move L (IV+) to easier ground and follow it for 3 pitches to a Y-shaped crack in the upper part of the step. Reach this by a chimney system on the L with 2 jammed blocks (IV+). Take the L branch of the Y (IV+) and follow easy ground to the summit. 550m, 8–10hr from the hut.

**32    ENVERS BARBARE**
TD    Winter: L André, P Gabarrou and T Pasture, 10 March 1985. A
**51**    summer ascent had been made prior to this date.

The ice gully immediately L of the E ridge. The difficulties are short but sustained with 1 section of 90° ice. 500m. See also Photo 45.

## Col du Pain de Sucre 3556m

The SW side of this col is very easy and can be reached by a short traverse from the upper section of Route 23.

**33    NORTH-EAST FACE**
D+    P and P Dalmais with G and M Charlet, 13 Aug 1931. Winter: M
**51**    Batard and M Leclanché, Feb 1975

This is short but quite steep and in good conditions has minimal stonefall danger. c440m. 5hr. See also Photo 53

## Pain de Sucre 3607m

G Mayer with A Dibona, 18 Aug 1913

The highest of the subsidiary peaks between the Plan and the Requin and a short ascent from the Envers du Plan glacier.

**34** **NORTH-WEST RIDGE**

PD First ascent party in descent

*A short rock ridge with a pitch of III.*

Reach the Col du Pain du Sucre and follow the ridge to a large gendarme. Drop down on the R side and follow ledges to cross the couloir coming down from the far side of the gendarme. Slant up a series of chimneys on the R side to the NW ridge and climb slabs on the R flank to the summit. 1hr from the col.

**35** **SOUTH FACE**

PD L Brincard and M Michaud with A Couttet and R Simond, 13 July

**45** 1926

*This is the most popular descent route. See also Photo51.*

From the summit descend the SE ridge to the flat section (2 rappels) and follow it to a snowy saddle before a pinnacle on the ridge. Descend a couloir of broken rock on the S side to the glacier and join Route 28. c200m, about 3hr to the Requin Hut.

**36** **NORTH FACE**

D Direct route: R Greloz and F Marullaz, 13 Aug 1931. Usual route:

**53** R Gréloz and A Roch, 4 July 1937. Winter: M Berreux and R Flematti, 12 Jan 1975

*Although tucked away in an unlikely position on the S side of the Aiguilles, this is one of their classic ice climbs and perhaps the most popular. The sun hits the face at dawn so a very early start is essential. On the first ascent a more difficult line was taken direct to the summit (D+). This is hardly ever climbed nowadays and most parties follow the Pain de Rideau ice slope to an exit on the E ridge. A good introduction to the bigger and more serious ice faces.*

Follow Route 31 to the foot of the face and bear L up the large snow slope. Cross the middle rock band on snow-covered slabs and, working L on the upper slopes, exit onto the E ridge which is followed (Route 36) to the summit. The original finish slants R below the final rock wall of the Pain de Sucre and finishes up a steep couloir to the gap between the summit and the large gendarme on the NW ridge. Average angle 56°, 7–9hr from the Envers Hut.

**37**     **EAST RIDGE**
D+     G Rébuffat and L Terray, 2 Aug 1944

**53**

*A long and reasonably interesting rock route with some mixed climbing higher up. It is similar in standard to the E Ridge of the Plan though not nearly as good.*

The lower section of the ridge is broad and on the L side is a huge pear-shaped buttress. Climb couloirs on either side to the gap behind it and continue directly above up a series of chimneys and cracks to a zone of terraces in the centre of the spur (IV and V). Slant up L then back R, passing under an enormous block to reach the crest of the ridge. Climb it, mainly on the L side (IV and IV+) to reach the upper snowy section wich is followed to the foot of the final pyramid. 2 pitches now lead to the summit. Go up cracks on the R (III) then slant L, passing a flake, to the ridge (III). Climb it by a short dièdre on the L side (III) and continue up the R side (IV) until a slab on the L (IV) leads to the final cracks (III). 750m, about 9hr from the Envers Hut.

    Above the central terraces the conspicuous dièdre has been climbed direct to the upper ridge (V+ and A1).

---

# Grand Gendarme d'Envers du Plan 3520m

**38**     **EAST COULOIR**
D     R Baumont and G Gaby, 20 June 1976

**53**

This is the long couloir on the L of the E ridge of the Pain de Sucre. It is very exposed to stonefall and although the average angle is only 45° there is a 100m rock wall at half-height giving some very difficult climbing on icy granite. 700m

**39**     **NORTH-EAST SPUR**
TD     L Berardini and R Paragot, 9 Aug 1957

**53**

Difficult free climbing with 1 short aid pitch following a line mainly on the L side of the spur. Reaching the base is severely exposed to stonefall and the route has seen very few ascents. VI and A1. 600m, 8hr

## Col du Requin 3304m

Under very cold and icy conditions the N side of this col offers 3 very worthwhile ice/mixed climbs.

**40**
TD
`53`

**RIGHT BRANCH**

T Eastman and T Sorenson, 1977

This follows the couloir immediately L of the NE spur of the Grand Gendarme. The average angle is 70° and it is obviously exposed to stonefall. The main difficulties occur on steep mixed ground where the gully narrows at ⅔ height. 600m, 9hr

**41**
TD+
`53`

**NOVEL HORIZON**

B Cormier and D Radigue, 22 Feb 1985

The line of discontinuous runnels and ice smears between the 2 branches. c550m, 7hr

**42**
TD
`53`

**LEFT BRANCH**

R Baumont and G Gaby, 26 June 1976

Similar to the R Branch but leading directly to the col. 550m, 9hr

A descent is effected very easily down the short couloir on the S side.

## Dent du Requin 3422m

G Hastings, A Mummery, N Collie and W Slingsby, 25 July 1893

One of the most popular peaks in the Chamonix Aiguilles offering a varied selection of climbs on sound granite. Small satellite peaks in close proximity to the hut now sport a considerable number of short hard modern climbs which are very much in vogue.

**43**
AD–
`45`

**SOUTH-WEST FACE**

E Fontaine with J and A Simond, 25 July 1898

*This is the normal route and still a worthwhile ascent. Above the shoulder the granite becomes excellent and the climbing quite exposed.*

From the Requin Hut follow the footpath W to the top of the moraine. Cross the glacier to the R and then work up L crossing a slabby rock barrier to a small snow patch beneath the SE (Chapeau à Cornes) ridge (stonefall). Contour the base of Pt 2977m and reach the Envers du Plan glacier. Go up this, passing through a very crevassed section until opposite the Col du Requin (Route 23 in reverse).

Climb rocks on the R side of the couloir (to avoid stonefall in the bed) leading up to the col. After 100m traverse steeply across the face to the R on ledges and mixed ground until a little chimney, slanting to the L, leads up to a gap in the SE ridge. On the far side is a good platform known as the 'Shoulder'. (2½hr)

Descend a little and reach ledges crossing the E face towards the summit tower. Follow these to a couloir which is climbed for 5m before traversing R to reach the 'Colonnes', a steep wall split by parallel cracks below the overhanging prow of the 'Nez du Requin'. A short chimney followed by the middle of 3 vertical cracks leads to a good stance on the R. Climb a crack and traverse R below an overhang to another good ledge (III+). A deep chimney on the R (III) leads to a third ledge and another leads to the fourth. Climb chimney cracks for 20m (III+) to the foot of the summit block.

Traverse R to a chimney on the N side. Climb this and follow flakes Rwards onto the W side turning a smooth block on the R to reach the summit. 3–4hr from the hut.

Descent: Climb down the flakes on the W side again and reach a ledge at the top of the Fontaine Chimneys on the SW flank. Make an airy rappel down the chimneys and slabs below. Traverse round to the L and regain the ascent route fractionally below the 'Shoulder'. 2½hr to the hut.

**44**
AD
53

## SOUTH-EAST (CHAPEAU A CORNES) RIDGE

R Mayor, C Robertson and G Young with J Knubel and a porter, 3 Aug 1906

*This is a delightful excursion which joins the normal route at the shoulder. It is reasonably sustained and forms a far more interesting route to the summit, albeit at a higher technical standard. A pleasant introduction to Alpine rock with several delicate pitches of IV. See also Photo 45.*

Follow Route 43 to the Envers du Plan glacier and after a short distance reach a small cirque on the R lying below 2 prominent gendarmes on the ridge (1½hr). On the extreme L cross the rimaye and climb a steep wet wall (IV). Follow big ledges diagonally Rwards and reach a series of slanting dièdres which are climbed (II+) to Pt 2977m on the ridge. One arrives on the crest at a gap between 2 pinnacles. Turn the higher on the R and follow the crest to the prominent gendarmes. Turn these on the R again and regain the crest after the second gendarme by a deep chimney (IV). Continue along the ridge to the Chapeau à Cornes (3320m). Turn this on the R crossing a smooth slab (IV) to reach a system of dièdres slanting to the R. Follow these (III) to easy ground and go up R to the shoulder where Route 43 is joined (2–2½hr. Equipment left here can be picked up on the descent). Continue to the summit by the normal route. 500m, 4½–5hr from the Requin Hut.

*Dent du Requin continued on page 51*

## Dent du Requin: East Face

Excellent granite and some classic lines make this a regular venue for aspiring rock climbers. On the routes described the first 200m are very straightforward leaving c400m of difficulties to the summit.

### 45 EAST PILLAR
V+
M André, F Bonniot and S Mendola, 4 April 1964

**52**
**1**

This is a very good free route on the excellent granite of the pillar immediately to the L of the central dièdre. Unfortunately it is not homogeneous in difficulty being mainly III and IV with some strenuous sections of V and V+. 6–8hr. See also Photo 45.

### 46 CENTRAL DIEDRE
VV+/A1
R Mazars with G Bettembourg and H Thivierge, 16 Aug 1974

**52**
**1**

The most direct line on the face. This is largely a free climb that at present contains 2 easy aid sections. 570m, 8hr

### 47 RENAUDIE DIRECT (CENTRAL SPUR)
V
J and J Renaudie, 1946 (not in this form). As followed today: L Lachenal and G Robino with an ENSA party, Aug 1948

**52**
**1**

*This is the classic route on the E face with sustained climbing of medium difficulty. It is arguably one of the finest routes of its class in the Aiguilles. See also Photo 45.*

Cross the little glacier to the foot of the E face and slant up L on steeper snow heading for a couloir which comes down from the Chapeau à Cornes Ridge (1hr). Just before reaching this slant up R on easy ledges and continue up terraces above, to reach their high point directly below the central dièdre. The wall now steepens.

Traverse L a pitch and climb an easy couloir to a large terrace which can be followed to the R past the foot of the dièdre (1hr). Follow the terrace and slant up R in the cracks above to reach the central spur (III/IV). Climb up it for a pitch until it is possible to traverse back L to a good terrace below some fine red slabs. Climb these for 3 pitches (IV and V) working L towards the top where the spur becomes very steep. Climb 2 successive cracks (IV and V) and continue up the centre of the spur for 3 pitches (IV+) to the base of a gendarme that forms the top of the spur. Turn it on the R regaining the spur after 2 pitches (IV+). From the shoulder below a black overhanging dièdre in the summit block, slant up R in a chimney (IV+) to reach the NE ridge and climb this to join the normal route just below the summit.570m, 5–6hr from the hut

---

*Dent du Requin continued*

**48**
**V+**
**45**

**SOUTH FACE OF CHAPEAU A CORNES**
C Jager and M Martinetti, 17 Sept 1963

*This used to be climbed quite regularly and was thought to give some fine though strenuous crack climbing on very steep rock with one 10m section of A1/A2. The line is fairly complex and the principle difficulties lie in the first 180m. Unfortunately modern development around the base of the Requin has has rather overshadowed routes such as this, leaving it as perhaps a quieter alternative. From the base of the summit block of the Chapeau one can easily continue to the top of the Requin by Route 44.*

Follow Route 43 to the rimaye and move L to the steep smooth walls of the Chapeau. There is a huge dièdre just to the R of a nose but on the L side of the prominent pillar on the lower part of this face. 5m to the L of this climb 2 successive cracks to good terraces (V). Take the R hand of 2 deep chimneys (IV+) and continue for another pitch up cracks and a strenuous overhang (V+) to a pile of blocks. Slant L in a groove (V+) to a terrace at the base of a huge dièdre topped by a yellow overhang. Traverse L for 10m (A1/2) then climb straight up on flakes before moving L to another terrace. Climb the dièdre above (V+) then the R wall (IV+) to reach a big couloir. Climb up for several pitches (IV with a slanting crack of V) to a wall. Traverse R and climb cracks and chimneys (IV and V) to the SE ridge. Continue up this and climb the summit block of the Chapeau on the S side (V−). 300m, 6hr from the hut.

**49**     **NORTH-EAST (MAYER-DIBONA) RIDGE**

AD+/D–    G Mayer and A Dibona, 23 Aug 1913. Winter: R Guillaume and G Tek, 15 Feb 1959

**52**

*This is a fairly popular climb which largely follows the L flank of the ridge. It is not sustained although route-finding in the lower section can be tricky, but the situation is splendid with impressive views across the N and E faces. See also Photos 45 and 53.*

Follow Route 43 to the little glacier below the E face and go up to the N corner where a couloir comes down from a notch near the base of the ridge (1hr). Climb the couloir which has 3 overhanging chockstone pitches. Climb each on the L side (IV and IV+) and continue up the rocks on the L side to the notch. Climb a short chimney to a system of ledges that run just L of the crest for quite a long way to where the flanks of the ridge steepen and gendarmes begin to appear on the crest. Traverse L below the first gendarme on yellow slabs to a shoulder below the pointed gendarme – the 'Fer de Lance'. Climb several vertical cracks (III+) to the foot of a narrow fault coming down from a small gap in the ridge. This gap lies above the deep notch after the 'Fer de Lance'.

    Climb down or rappel (10m) into the big couloir on the E face and go up the R wall to where a series of ledges lead L across the face. Climb a dièdre (40m, IV) to the crest of the NE ridge and follow this in an airy situation to a buttress about 50m high. Climb grooves on the L (IV+) then slabs (IV) to the top and follow the crest. Turn a little gendarme on the R, to reach the horizontal shoulder at the foot of the terminal block where the normal route is joined. 600m, 6–8hr from the hut to the summit.

**50**     **NORTH FACE DIRECT**

ED3    P Gabarrou and A Long, 15–16 Aug 1983

**53**

*A very steep climb and an eliminate line on the classic route, leading directly to the summit. The difficulties are primarily those of hard technical free climbing on very sound and compact granite in an austere environment.*

Climb 4 pitches on snow and ice up to the R of the spur and take a series of parallel cracks R of the huge chimney line to a large terrace atop the spur (3 pitches, VII). Some delicate climbing up the ridge above leads to the steep upper wall. Climb it directly in a series of splendid cracks and dièdres (VII/VII+) working close to the couloir of the classic route in the upper section. Cross the snowy terraces, move up R and climb the headwall by a steep crack (VII) leading to a conspicuous narrow ledge. Follow it R and make difficult moves into a dièdre (VIII). Follow this and cracks above to the summit.700m, 18hr

**51  NORTH FACE ORIGINAL ROUTE**
TD J Couttet and G Rébuffat, 22 July 1945. Winter: W Cecchinel and C
53 Jager, 22–24 Dec 1974

*The classic line but still infrequently ascended. It is a far more serious proposition than its situation or low altitude would suggest, and a cold night is required for the route to be well frozen. The climbing is quite sustained, steep and sunless but appears to be objectively safe.*

From the Envers Hut traverse S to the Blaitière glacier and cross it to the foot of the face (1hr). Climb the snow just R of the lower spur and slant L to gain a steep and icy section of mixed ground leading up to the gap behind the spur. A high wall split by 3 crack systems leads up to a secondary ridge on the R and has on its L a prominent couloir. Follow a ledge line towards the central system but before reaching it climb a vertical wet chimney (IV+) to reach the cracks on the L and climb them (III and IV, poor rock) to the icefield. Parties have also climbed the prominent couloir and reached the icefield by a difficult headwall with some aid moves.

Climb the ice slope to a narrow buttress sandwiched between 2 thin gullies. Get onto the buttress from the R and climb a dièdre for 10m (A1) before moving onto the L side and following slabs and walls to the top (80m, V. Excellent climbing). Climb the ice funnel above and slant L up the obvious ledge line to the NE ridge which is joined just below the 50m buttress. Follow Route 49 to the summit. 700m, 8–10hr from the hut.

The funnel can also be climbed directly to the W ridge.

**52  WEST RIDGE**
V A Crampé, A Deschenaux, A Dagaud, G Joubert and L Perramon
53 with K Gurékian, 27 Aug 1947

From the Col du Requin it is possible to follow the ridge fairly directly over the various gendarmes until the final tower before the summit. One must now traverse R below it and struggle with the Fontaine Chimneys before gaining the highest point. 1 pitch of V+. 6hr from the hut.

## Dent du Requin: Satellites

The small rock peaks at the base of the Dent and close to the Requin Hut give many short modern climbs that are often bolt-protected. Most pitches are of very high quality and the atmosphere more akin to a somewhat bigger version of a British crag. Despite this, some of the harder climbs can give bold and serious runouts.

**53**    **POINTE 2977m SOUTH FACE**
VIII    J Boivin and M Moioli; D Lacroix and A Sebatti, 5 Aug 1984

**45**
**5**

The steep little face of this Pt which lies at the end of the Chapeau à Cornes ridge can be reached in ¾hr from the hut. It gives very sustained 'thin crack' climbing with unavoidable moves of VII. Either descend by reversing Route 44 or make 6 rappels back down the route. 170m

## Dent du Requin: Capucin du Requin 3047m

There are several climbs on the very steep pear-shaped face overlooking the Envers de Blaitière glacier. Originally climbed with many long artificial sections, they are currently not in vogue.

## Dent du Requin: Pointe 2851m East Face

A direct line up the centre of this magnificent slender slab gives one of the finest and most difficult routes in the massif.

**54**    **FOLIES BELGERES**
IX–    M Armand, M Piola and P Steiner during June and July 1985

**53**
**4**

350m, with unavoidable moves of VIII. Descend by rappeling the route.

## Dent du Requin: Pointe 2784m South-East Face

Reached in ¼hr from the Requin Hut this face is now laced with top quality modern rock climbs. Most routes can be rappeled to regain the base.

**55**    **LAISSEZ BRONZER LES CADAVRES AU SOLEIL**
VI+    D Radigue and R Vogler, 9 June 1985

`52`
`9`

An excellent crack climb on the L side of the face. 200m, 4hr

**56**    **CENTRAL CHIMNEY LINE**
V+    J Brown, R Moseley and D Whillans, 20 July 1954

`52`
`9`

The original route and most obvious line on the face giving a crack climb of medium difficulty. 250m

**57**    **TOUCHE PAS MON PILIER**
VIII    R Ghilini and partner, date unknown

`52`

The thin crack line on the wall immediately R of the previous climb requires some extremely difficult and strenuous work to overcome the first long pitch (unavoidable moves of VII). After that the grade is maintained at a steady VI to VI+. 250m. Seealso Photo 58.

**58**    **CONGO STAR**
VII–    M Piola and P Steiner, 30 June 1985

`52`
`9`

A very fine crack and wall climb giving sustained climbing all the way to the summit. It is probably the best of the routesdescribed here. Unavoidable moves of V+. 300m

## Col des Deux Aigles 3453m

**59**    **SOUTH-WEST SIDE**
D    G Hastings, A Mummery, J Collie and W Slingsby, 7 Aug 1893

`50`

The N side of the col overlooks the hanging glacier on the N face of the Plan and the route up this very often deviates onto the col. The SW side is a steep ice couloir that is severely exposed to stonefall. However when well-iced in winter conditions it becomes a useful addition to the number of relatively accessible routes available from the Plan de l'Aiguille station. 550m. Seealso Photo 56.

## Aiguilles des Deux Aigles 3487m

H Beaujard with J Simond, 15 July 1905

A spectacular peak situated on the NW ridge of the Plan. It is one of the most inaccessible summits in the Aiguilles and is seldom visited.

The easiest method of approach is to climb the Aig du Plan and descend the snow slopes of the NW ridge (c40°) to the Col des Deux Aigles. The top is in the form of a trident with the N point considered to be the highest.

**60**     **FROM COL DES DEUX AIGLES**
V+    Traverse round all 3 points on the N side until a col is reached at the foot of the N point. Follow an ascending ledge on the Pélerins side and climb a crack (V+) to the summit. 1hr

**61**     **NORTH SPUR**
TD    B Pierre and G Rébuffat, 13 August 1949

**54**

*This magnificent spur, rising out of the hanging glacier on the Plan, has seen very few ascents. The route as a whole gives difficult climbing on both rock and ice in a serious location. See also Photo 47.*

Follow Route 28 until just above the first steep section of the hanging glacier, then traverse R to the foot of the spur (5hr). The spur is steep and smooth at the base so climb the couloir on the R side to about half-height where it becomes steep and narrow. Move L on to the spur and climb a series of cracks and chimneys, at first on the R side (IV and V) then on the L side (V and V+) of the crest. Finish by a slightly ascending traverse L to the col at the foot of the N point and join Route 60. 800m, 12hr from Plan de l'Aiguille.

**62**     **NORTH-WEST FACE**
TD    L Audobert, J Dumery and Y Seigneur, 13 July 1973

**54**

*Included in the Integral Traverse of the NW ridge of the Plan, this can also be approached via the Col Sup des Pélerins and gives a steep climb on excellent rock which the first ascent party compared to the E face of the Grand Capucin. See also Photo 47.*

From the NW brèche at the foot of the face climb straight up the crest of the ridge in a series of cracks (sustained V and A1) working R to a detached flake. Then climb thin cracks, a dièdre and a wall to a platform on the ridge crest. Make a diagonal rappel into a couloir on the L and climb it (V+ then IV) to join Route 60 below the N summit. 6hr

## Col Supérieur des Pélerins 3278m

Between the Migot and a 15m high gendarme on the ridge to the SE. The N side is a short steep ice couloir first climbed from the hanging glacier on the N face of the Plan by P Dillemann with A Charlet and J Simond in 1929 (200m, D). The SW side is an easy snow couloir (PD).

## Pointe Migot 3311m

M and M Damesme, A Migot and M Parat, 31 July 1927

Also referred to as the Pt des Pélerins. This is a rather undistinguished summit on the ridge between the Aigs des Pélerins and Deux Aigles.

**63** · **NORTH SPUR**

TD–/TD  J Brown and T Patey; C Bonington and R Ford, 21 July 1964

**54**

*A surprisingly good route which takes an interesting and unrelenting line but has not become popular. There is some loose rock at the base and the lower section is very slow to clear of verglas.*

Follow Route 28 to the Blaitière glacier and go up to the R of the lower rock spur of the N face of the Plan until below the couloir leading up to the Col des Pélerins. This area is exposed to serac fall from the hanging glacier. 30m L of the couloir climb up easy rocks to a chimney-crack. The first 5–6m overhangs (VI or A1). Continue straight up (V) until it divides then climb the overhanging corner on the R (IV) and the groove above to the snowfield. From the top L corner climb a conspicuous diagonal ramp, running from R to L, in 4 pitches (V and V+, a little loose at first) to the upper part of the face. Climb up R and continue on the W flank of the spur in a chimney line (IV+) and up easier slabs to the summit. 600m, 7–9hr from the Plan de l'Aiguille.

Either descend the SW couloir of the Col Sup des Pélerins or take the normal route down the Aig des Pélerins. 2–3hr to the Plan de l'Aiguille.

# Aiguille des Pélerins 3318m

A Brun and R O'Gorman with E Charlet and J Ravanel, 9 July 1905. Winter: J Quenin-Puget with A Couttet, 29 Feb 1928

One of the more popular summits in the Aiguilles, offering a wide variety of rock climbs to suit most tastes.

**64**
PD
**56**

### SOUTH FACE (NORMAL ROUTE)
H Beaujard with J Simond and 2 porters, 10 July 1905

*An easy, popular excursion which is a very good outing for novices. It is the standard descent for parties completing routes on the other faces of the peak. Pitches of II. See also Photo 50.*

From the Plan de l'Aiguille station follow the path to the end of the moraine on the L side of the Pélerins glacier and reach the couloir descending from the Col Sup des Pélerins. Climb the couloir until a large area of broken ledges slants up L to the gap below the fourth and final step in the SW ridge of the Aig des Pélerins. Follow these ledges for c100m then climb up R in a rocky couloir that runs parallel to the main couloir. About 40m below the Col des Pélerins, slant up L to reach the ESE ridge about halfway between the col and a prominent 10m pinnacle. Go up the ridge, turning the pinnacle on the R, to the summit. About 4hr from the Plan de L'Aiguille.

In descent: From the summit follow the ridge ESE towards Pt Migot turning a 10m pinnacle on the L and when about halfway between the latter and the Col des Pélerins, go down a rocky couloir on the S flank parallel to the main couloir on the L. Reach an area of broken ledges coming down from the fourth and final step on the SW ridge and slant L down these for 100m to the main couloir where it widens. Descend it to the moraine on the R side of the Pélerins glacier and follow this down to the Plan de l'Aiguille. 2½hr
    The upper section of the main couloir below the Col des Pélerins is rather loose and dangerous.

**65**
V
**56**
**8**

### SOUTH-WEST (GRUTTER) RIDGE INTEGRAL
First complete ascent: E Frendo, G Rébuffat and L Terray, 10 Oct 1943

*A quite long and very worthwhile expedition. The ridge can be reached and left easily at various points and is thus an ideal choice when the weather is doubtful. The first step contains the hardest climbing though the rock is not altogether sound. The climbing on the fourth step is excellent and is often reached by following the Normal Route. 600m*

From the Plan de l'Aiguille station follow the path to the end of the moraine and reach the foot of the SW ridge in 1hr.

# Aiguille des Pélerins: North-West and North Faces

Routes on the NW face begin about 50m above the triple fork in the Peigne couloir (Route 74) and are generally combined with an ascent of one of the routes on the Peigne, thus giving 2 summits in one excursion.

**66** **CARMICHAEL ROUTE**
IV   E and Y Carmichael with A and G Charlet, 10 Sept 1925

**56**

*A very popular classic of medium difficulty. There is 1 pitch of V*

From a point about 50m above the triple fork in the Peigne Couloir, cross to the R side and climb up to some terraces at the base of a huge chimney. Climb grooves on the L (III) followed by easier ledges. Reach the foot of the face where an obvious line of cracks slants up R to a gap in the upper part of the Grutter Ridge. Follow these for 2 pitches turning a large overhang on the R. Traverse L on a ledge and slant up R for a further 2 pitches to the gap in the ridge (sustained IV). Climb the ridge keeping slightly on the L side (IV) to within 20m of the top then traverse L on a ledge and climb a slab (V) to the summit. (It is possible to avoid this last slab by traversing R to the ESE ridge.) c200m, 2hr

**67** **CHARLET ROUTE – DIRECT FINISH**
V+   A Charlet, 29 July 1925

**56**

*This combination offers fairly sustained free climbing on the L side of the face. Charlet traversed R along the huge platform below the final pyramid (which is often a snow patch) and finished via the Grutter Ridge. The Direct Finish is part of a route climbed in 1967 with several artificial sections below the platform.*

Follow the Carmichael Route to the foot of the face then continue up L for 20m and climb a chimney (IV). An easy pitch above and a slanting crack (IV) leads to an overhanging section containing some large flakes. Climb the overhang and the crack above (V+) to a ledge below some huge roofs level with the large platform on the R. By descending slightly on the R climb up a crack and move across to the platform (IV). On the L of an enormous niche in the upper wall, climb up some flakes and the steep crack above (V+) before a couple of peg moves lead R to a ledge. A series of cracks rise vertically to the summit. Climb these directly to the top (IV and V). c200m, 3hr

| | |
|---|---|
| **68** | **NORTH FACE** |
| ED2 | In winter: R Carrington and A Rouse, 7–8 Feb 1975 |
| **54** | |

This follows the line of the open couloir dropping from the Col des Pélerins. The upper section lies at an easier angle and is not that well defined and an exit can be made almost anywhere on the ridge between the col and the summit. In summer conditions it is a poor climb on verglased rock (V and A1) (first ascended by G Rébuffat and L Terray, 10 Aug 1944). However in winter it often forms a succession of superb white ice runnels and in this condition has almost reached modern classic status with a number of ascents. Scottish 5. The approach and initial easy ground are somewhat threatened by serac fall from the Plan hanging glacier. 540m

| | |
|---|---|
| **69** | **NORTH FACE DIRECT** |
| ED1/2 | L Dard and J Reppelin, 28–29 Aug 1967 |
| **54** | |
| **10** | |

*At the time of its inception this was considered one of the more demanding rock routes in the Aiguilles. There is certainly a serious atmosphere on this cold icy wall, and the line has only rarely been repeated.*

The bottom of the face has 2 light-coloured dièdre/chimney lines and the climb takes the line of the L one and continues on easier ground to the huge and often snowy terrace. The substance of the route is contained in the enormous dièdre on the R which is followed to an exit on the ESE ridge just below the summit. The wide detour near the top can probably be avoided. VI and A2. 600m, 16hr

| | |
|---|---|
| **70** | **NORTH PILLAR – NOSTRADAMUS** |
| ED2 | M Piola and P Sprungli, 10–11 Aug 1980 |
| **54** | |
| **10** | |

Subsequent ascents have confirmed that in its completely free state this is one of the very best of the modern hard routes, giving sustained open face climbing (VII+). It was certainly a breakthrough in a new style of 'big wall' climbing in the Aiguilles. At over half-height but below the crux, the route crosses a snowy gully/terrace, which in a fairly dry season can be managed without crampons. It is possible to bivouac here or escape Rwards to the Col du Peigne but fast parties should reach the top before dark. RPs or blade pegs must be carried. By using aid the difficulties can be reduced to VI/VI+. 600m, 12–15hr

## Col du Peigne 3121m

First traverse: J Deudon, R Gaché, R Gréloz and L Valluet, 4 Aug 1932

Between the Aigs des Pélerins and du Peigne. The SW side of this col used to form the normal route to the summit of the Peigne. It is loose, unpleasant and notorious for stonefall. It can and should now be avoided at all costs. The NE side is a difficult and uninteresting rock climb in summer but due to its low altitude forms good white ice in the winter months, and gives 3 thoroughly recommendable routes.

**71**
TD+
**NORTH-EAST FACE LEFT-HAND ROUTE**
In winter: R Carrington and A Rouse, March 1978

`47`

This is the most obvious line on the NE face and is best approached by a rising traverse from the easy ground at the base of the Col des Pélerins. 400m

**72**
ED2
**DIRECT START**
A Bailey and A Nisbet, March 1982

`47`

The first 2 pitches provide very hard climbing after which the difficulties progressively ease to the upper couloir. 400m

**73**
ED1
**RIGHT-HAND ROUTE**
In winter: A Nisbet and N Spinks, Dec 1979

`47`

The main difficulties are shorter and give access to an exposed ramp leading L to the upper couloir. 400m

## Aiguille du Peigne 3192m

G Liégard, R O'Gorman with J Couttetand J Ravanel, 23 July 1906

One of the most classic and frequented summits in the Aiguilles. It gives an enormous selection of first-rate rock climbs which due to their low altitude and ease of access have become extremely popular. Most routes dry fairly quickly after bad weather. The

Peigne Couloir achieved a certain notoriety for accidents caused by stonefall and should only be used in winter. The summit area is a well-known attracter of lightning and the normal decent is reasonably involved. Unlike the Pélerins it does not allow height to be lost rapidly.

Rock routes have been described with a technical grading, as many are short and finish well below the summit. However an ascent or combination ascent of the harder climbs to the top of the mountain would be worthy of an overall grading of at least TD.

## 74 NORMAL ROUTE

AD

**55**

*Described in both ascent and descent as the easiest and safest route to and from the summit. It is still a worthwhile ascent for novices with interesting route-finding and some exposed pitches in the upper section.*

From the Plan de l'Aiguille follow the path along the moraine to reach the Peigne snowfield below the S flank of the mountain and slightly to the L of the base of the main Peigne Couloir (1hr). Go up the L side for about 60m then slant L on a ledge line, crossing a small gap to reach the SW Couloir on the R of the Papillons Ridge. Climb this easily to where it steepens, then climb up to the R in a smooth crack before a traverse back L leads to the top of the Papillons Ridge (III). Follow the ridge, mainly on the L side, and turn Pt 3009m by a rocky couloir on the R. Reach the col behind the gendarme then trend up R on poor rock to a gap in the SW ridge just above the red gendarme 3078m (2hr).

On the other side descend a ledge to the triple fork in the Peigne Couloir and climb easy rocks on the L side towards the summit pyramid. Level with the Col du Peigne trend Rwards and climb an open chimney (IV+) to reach the ESE ridge at a little col just below the summit. Reach the E summit in 10m by the exposed ridge (III/IV) and continue along the crenellated ridge (from where the Peigne gets its name) to a small notch. Make a short rappel to the gap and climb out to the main summit. 5hr from the Plan de l'Aiguille.

Descent: From the summit descend a chimney on the Chamonix side for 5m or so and rappel 20m down a steep wall to a large terrace. Go down the SW ridge for 10m and cross onto the Pélerins side. Descend open chimneys (rappels) at first near the ridge and then more towards the couloir and reverse the ascent route to the gap above gendarme 3078m. Go down broken rock on the Chamonix side, passing one subsidiary couloir on the L, to reach the col SE of Pt 3009m and descend the easy couloir (the second subsidiary couloir on the L) below the Pt. After a short distance traverse across the R wall (facing out) and reach the upper section of the Papillons Ridge. Go down this easily on the Chamonix side. (In the vicinity is the top of 'Le Ticket', Route 86 on the NW face. Well-equipped rappel anchors allow a speedy descent of this route to the bottom of the face.) When the ridge narrows make a long rappel on the L side into the SW couloir and reverse the route of ascent to the Plan de l'Aiguille. c600m, 3–3½hr

| 75 | **SOUTH-WEST RIDGE** |
|----|----------------------|
| V+ | G Devouassoux and Y Mazino, 1965 |

*This climbs the crest of the pillar on Gendarme 3078m and although it has not gained the popularity of the neighbouring Vaucher Route, it is thought by many to be even better. It is possible to descend the Normal Route after reaching the summit of the gendarme but the continuation ridge to the top of the Peigne contains some fine climbing.*

It is possible to climb the ridge directly, alongside the Peigne Couloir (III and IV) but better to reach it via the lower section of the Vaucher Route. In the central steeper section one must reach and climb some strenuous cracks on the L side of the pillar. After that the crest is climbed directly up the front face over a prominent overhang (short section of A2) bearing R to the summit of the gendarme.

From the large ledge below the summit block of the Peigne, climb the Lépiney Crack which slants up to the L (V) and continue via a chimney (IV), a steep crack of 6m on the L (VI or A1) and a corner (IV+) to the summit. c600m, 8hr from the Plan de l'Aiguille.

| 76 | **SOUTH-WEST FACE (VAUCHER ROUTE)** |
|----|-------------------------------------|
| VI | P Labrunie and M Vaucher with A Contamine, 12 Aug 1957 |

A fine free rock route which has become an established classic and is therefore very popular. The climbing is sustained and interesting on magnificent granite, and it is well worth continuing up the excellent slabby crest of the SW ridge to the summit of the Peigne. 400m (600m to the summit of the Peigne), 4–0 5hr

| 77 | **MINETTES RIDGE** |
|----|--------------------|
| IV | A de Chatellus and R Merle d'Aubigné with G Charlet, Aug 1943 |

*This is the ridge immediately to the R of the SW (Papillons) Couloir leading to Pt 3009m and has become quite popular in recent times.*

Start as for the Normal Route but instead of completely crossing the ridge climb up its centre (pitches of IV) to the top. c400m, 2–3hr.

**78**    **PAPILLONS (WEST) RIDGE**

V

55

First complete ascent by ropes led by K Gurékian, L Pez and A Subut, 10 Sept 1948

*A classic and most enjoyable little route on perfect rock. It can be used to give a better start to the N Face and Ridge routes, thus providing more continuous climbing from the foot of the mountain to the summit; or as a route in its own right for a short day.*

Reach the foot of the ridge from the Plan de l'Aiguille in ¾hr. Go up to the first step and climb it on the R via a crack to the R of a flake. Finish by a short double crack (III). After a short horizontal section climb a step (IV) and continue to a second which is climbed delicately by a cracked slab (V). Continue up the ridge until it steepens and climb a groove (IV) to an easier-angled section. Follow this, turning a block on the L and a pinnacle on the R, to a steep section climbed by cracks (III and IV). The ridge narrows and leads to a small gap below a prominent steep tower. Climb cracks on the L for 15m (III) then go R into a letter box (jammed block). Gain a chimney on the R and climb it passing an overhang on the R and reaching the top of this tower by a system of flakes (V).

    Descend a little chimney and cross a couloir to reach the gap in front of the last tower. Climb it by the thin crack in a slab (V) and slant up L to reach the top via detached flakes (2817m). Follow the horizontal ridge for 25m to a gap. Here is the rappel point into the Papillons Couloir on the R by which one can descend. Alternatively continue along the ridge (II and III) and follow the Normal Route to the col behind Pt 3009m. 480m to Pt 3009m, 4hr from the Plan de l'Aiguille.

**79**    **NORTH SPUR OF THIRD TOWER OF PAPILLONS RIDGE**

V

55

R Bozon, F Obert and J Verdier, date unknown

*Although a little chilly in the morning and somewhat lichenous, this crack climb has rapidly become a little classic of medium difficulty.*

Start on the R side of a huge detached flake leaning against the lower crest of the spur. Climb the crack (V) to the top and continue more or less on the crest for another 2 pitches (V) taking the Rhand of 2 wide cracks. Another pitch up the crest leads to some loose blocks (V). Above is a large roof so slant up L to avoid it, via a wide

crack (IV+) and chimney (V) to a good ledge below the red
gendarme. Turn this on the L (IV+) and climb dièdres for 2 more
pitches (IV) to reach the gap between the third and fourth towers on
the Papillons Ridge. 300m, 3–4hr

*Aiguille du Peigne continued on page 68*

## Aiguille du Peigne: Upper North-West Face

This is the front face of the Peigne above the central snowfield just
L of Pt 3009m. It can be combined with the Papillons Ridge or one
of the many routes on the Lower NW Face but is not climbed
nearly as frequently as these lower routes.

**80**
V
**55**
**12**

**WEST-NORTH-WEST FACE**
R Ferlet and L Terray, 2 Aug 1943

This is the concave wall with an obvious crack system on the R,
rising from the ground leading up to the gap above gendarme
3078m. Traditionally referred to as the 'Chamonix Face'. Short
brutal cracks and a strenuous layback. c140m

**81**
VII/VII+
**55**
**12**

**NORTH-WEST PILLAR**
R Mazars with G Rébuffat, 16 Aug 1967. Completely free: M Moran
and M Vesely, 26 July 1985

*This separates the WNW face on the R from the true NW face, and is
20m L of Route 80.*

This follows the approximate line of the first ascent party – a route
which contained several aid sections and appears rarely to have been
repeated. c170m

**82**
VI/VI+
**55**
**12**

**NORTH-WEST FACE – PASCAL MEYER ROUTE**
J Massenet, P Meyer and B Perrin, 13 July 1959

The most direct route on the face with some quite bold and serious
climbing. The route is done completely free but several aid points
here and there will reduce the technical grade to V+. c180m

**83**
VI
**55**

**NORTH RIDGE**
F Aubert, J Martin, J Menegaux and M Schatz, 2 Aug 1947.
Winter: L Griffin and A Nicollet via the Papillons Ridge, March
1973

*The substance of this route lies in the huge monolithic dièdre cleaving the final 200m of the ridge and gives superb crack climbing. Many still consider this to be one of the finest classic rock climbs in the Aiguilles. Being deeply cut and largely sunless, the dièdre may clear slowly after bad weather. The lower section is easy and rather disjointed and is often avoided by traversing L from Pt 3009m to gain the dièdre. However it does give a direct line and the complete route is described below.*

From the Plan de l'Aiguille station follow the path to the little lake and go up to the foot of the ridge (1hr).

Turn the first step by a couloir on the R (III) and regain the crest. Several pitches lead to some blocks below a white slab at the base of the triangular step in the ridge. Descend L then climb a crack (IV−) and continue on the L flank by slabs and cracks (III) to a final steep wall which is climbed in a chimney (IV). Climb the huge slab above in a dièdre sloping to the R (III) and go back L to a terrace. The route becomes a little vague but generally one climbs diagonally Lwards until it is possible to go up to the col between a small pointed tower and the upper section of the N ridge. Traverse R on easy ledges to below the col behind Pt 3009m. Follow a broken rake back L to reach the ridge at a good platform below the final dièdre (2–3hr).

Starting slightly L of the obvious wide crack in the corner, climb the chimney-dièdre for 60m to a stance under a roof (IV). Climb this on the R (V) and above make a rising traverse across the wall (V+) to a superb open groove and climb it to a roof (V). Turn this on the R (V) and follow a steep crack (V+) to an overhanging corner. Climb across the R wall and take a slanting crack (VI) to an easier crack which leads to a large crevice behind an enormous flake (V−). Passing behind the flake go L and climb an open groove for 20m (V). Go up L then back R to a niche (IV). Climb up the L side and go over a small bulge (IV+) to the notch just L of the summit block. 600m, 5–8hr from the Plan de l'Aiguille.

# Aiguille du Peigne: Lower North-West Face

This is the steep smooth wall below gendarme 3009m. In recent years it has become an extremely popular arena for technical open face climbing. There is very little mountaineering commitment as the wall is only 250m high and can be descended rapidly by rappel, but some routes involve bold leads. Generally however climbs tend to be well-endowed with essential bolt and peg protection and some offer quality that ranks with that found anywhere else in the Aiguilles. A rappel descent is usually made via Route 85 or 86 but will not be appreciated on a crowded afternoon.

One can reach the ledges at the base either easily on the L across the snow or by a pitch of IV− on the R which avoids the snow (1hr from the Plan de l'Aiguille).

**84**    **LES LEPIDOPTERES**
V−

M Armand and M Piola, 28 July 1986

`55`
`13`

A delightful little climb up the cracks and walls on the R side of the face. 180m

**85**    **VERDON MEMORIES**
VII+

D and M Piola, 25 July 1986

`55`
`13`

A top quality modern route that could well rival the 'Ticket' for popularity. There are unavoidable moves of VII− in the upper half and the route can be conveniently descended by rappel starting from the notch at the top of the Papillon Ridge. 240m

**86**    **LE TICKET, LE CARRE, LE ROND ET LA LUNE**
VII+

G Hopfgartner and M Piola, 18 July 1983

`55`
`13`

This is generally thought to be the finest route on these walls. It became an instant modern classic and has seen many ascents. It involves some sustained open face climbing with unavoidable moves of VI+. This climb is normally chosen for a rappel descent of the wall, and has well-equipped belay points. 250m

**87**    **DIMANCHE NOIR**
VIII

M Armand, G Hopfgartner and M Piola, 27−28 July 1985

`55`
`13`

The best of the wall's super-difficult routes. The crux moves are bold and unavoidable. 250m

**88**    **LA PASSE MONGOLE**
VII

D and G Long, G and R Vogler, 5 July 1982

`55`
`13`

This follows more or less the line of an old aid route and finishes up the prominent Lward facing dièdre high on the face. Difficult climbing in dièdres with unavoidable crux moves on open faces. 250m

**89**    **AQUAPLANING**

VI+    G and R Vogler, 13 Aug 1981

**55**

When dry this offers some very fine pitches. Unfortunately it is often wet as drainage is slow to clear. The route begins with some vertical cracks leading to the base of an easy Lward sloping ramp and finishes up the large V-shaped depression. 200m

---

*Aiguille du Peigne continued*

**90**    **NORTH-EAST FACE DIRECT**

TD/TD+    R Porta and J Reppelin, 22 Aug 1967

**47**

*Of the several routes here, this is probably the best, though none have gained popularity. The main difficulties, open face and crack climbing, are concentrated in the last 300m and can also be reached by descending the easy snowy ramp Lwards from below the final dièdre on the N ridge. The hard pitches were originally climbed with aid reducing the technical grading to V+ and A1.*

Go up the Blaitière glacier passing the foot of the N ridge. Before reaching the start of Route 73 to the Col duPeigne, climb a narrow snowy couloir on the R until blocked by an overhang. Climb the L wall to a small notch and continue working L for several pitches to the snow ramp that slants up R towards the pointed tower on the N ridge (III and IV). Climb a vertical chimney (IV+) and continue for 2 pitches to a small dièdre below a large and distinctive crack (IV). Reach the top of the dièdre by first climbing out R then back L (V) and slant up R to some small snowy ledges (V). Slightly to the L climb a crack (V) then continue straight up a series of cracks and corners, parallel to the large distinctive crack mentioned above, to reach a large snowy ledge (V and V+). Starting on the L climb up and reach (V/V+) the huge Lward slanting dièdre that cuts the upper part of the NE face and begins lower down on the N ridge. Climb this (VII). It becomes easier and near the top somewhat looser. A difficult exit (VI/VI+) is made up R to the summit ridge. 500m, 8–10hr from the Plan de l'Aiguille.

# Dent du Crocodile 3640m

E Fontaine with J Ravanel and E Charlet, 31 May 1904. Winter: M Galley with R Lambert, 13 Jan 1937

A large rock tower on the ridge, N of the Aig du Plan.

**91**    **SOUTH-SOUTH-WEST RIDGE (NORMAL ROUTE)**
PD    First ascent party

**45**

This summit is quickly reached by descending its NNE ridge from the top of the Aig du Plan. Turn a small step on the W side and cross an icy couloir to the foot of the SSW ridge which is easy scrambling. ¾hr. See also Photo 51.

**92**    **NORTH-NORTH-EAST RIDGE FROM BRECHE DU**
D−    **CAIMAN**

**45**    E Fontaine with J Ravanel and L Tournier, 20 July 1905

*An integral part in the traverse of the Aiguilles and described in both ascent and descent. See also Photo 51.*

From the Brèche climb up to some chimneys on the L side of the ridge and follow them back to the crest. Cross to the R side and climb a very open chimney (40m, IV) to the top of the first step in the ridge. Climb the second step slightly on the R side (30m, IV). A ledge and chimney line on the R side of the last step leads round the N top to the main summit. c240m, 4hr

In descent: Rappel the second step directly and the last step down the W side reaching the Brèche by a descending traverse. 3hr

**93**    **EAST RIDGE**
TD−    P Allain, J and R Leininger, 29–30 July 1936

**51**
**6**

*The classic climb on the Crocodile which being relatively remote sees few ascents nowadays. The last 300m give typically strenuous crack and chimney pitches in the traditional mould. At the time of its ascent this was considered the hardest rock climb in the Aiguilles. See also Photo 45*

Follow Route 31 and continue across the Plan-Crocodile Couloir. Slant up R to the base of an obvious red tower on the E ridge and turn it on the L. Slant up R to the foot of the second tower where the main difficulties begin. The first grade V chimney pitches are generally considered the crux. Parties often descend by the same route making 10 rappels to the foot of the second tower. 525m, 8–10hr from the Envers Hut.

# Brèche du Caiman 3498m

Lying between the Crocodile and the Dent du Caiman, the N side of this col is taken by the Lagarde-Ségogne Couloir (Route 29). The SE side has no real merit as a route of ascent being a rocky couloir (IV with 1 pitch of V) that is seriously exposed to stonefall. However it is the only practical means of escape from this section of the ridge.

Descent: 2 rappels down the couloir lead to a zone of easy terraces. Descend these and make 3 more rappels to a second zone. Cross these, rising slightly to the Plan-Crocodile Couloir and reverse Route 31 to the Envers Hut.

# Dent du Caiman 3554m

E Fontaine with J Ravanel and L Tournier, 20 July 1905. Winter: M Galley with R Lambert, 13 Jan 1937

This rather inaccessible summit is a striking pyramid of yellow granite that in the first half of this century was a classic expedition in its own right. Nowadays it is hardly ever reached and is generally crossed only during a complete traverse of the Aiguilles.

**94**
D–

**45**

**SOUTH-WEST RIDGE**
First ascent party

*This is a long, interesting and surprisingly varied route.*

From the Requin Hut reach the Brèche du Caiman by Routes 91 and 92. On the L side climb a short chimney and steep wall to a terrace below a shoulder on the ridge. Slant up L and come back R along a horizontal ledge until it is possible to climb directly to the summit via a detached flake (IV). ½hr

The ridge can be descended in 2 rappels.

**95**
D

**45**

**EAST FACE**
P Allain and R Leininger, 17–18 July 1935

*An excellent little route and a traditional classic. It has a lengthy and rather disagreeable approach via Route 31, a traverse of the Crocodile-Caiman Couloir, and an ascent of the couloir leading to the Col du Caiman. Nowadays it forms an integral part of the traverse of the Aiguilles and only appears to be ascended during that expedition. 200m of difficulty.*

About 50m below the Col du Caiman work up L to a double line of chimneys on the E face, to the R of an obvious pillar. Start in the Rhand chimney (V−) then work up and L to a platform (IV). Traverse L to a couloir and use it to reach the SE spur of the Caiman. Follow this crest easily then climb a chimney on the L (IV) to a terrace level with the Brèche du Caiman. Climb a steep wall (6m. IV+) and reach the base of a groove. Traverse L overlooking the Crocodile-Caiman Couloir for 5m and climb up for 10m on the R of a thin crack to the top of the groove (IV). Above, a few delicate moves (V−) lead to easy ground and the shoulder mentioned in the description of the SW ridge.Follow this to the top. 4–5hr

**96     NORTH-EAST RIDGE**
First descent: P Allain and G Poulet, 4 Aug 1945

*Described in descent as a link in the traverse of the Aiguilles. In ascent it is a difficult free and artificial climb in a very exposed situation.*

From the summit descend 10m on the R side of the ridge to a ledge. Rappel diagonally down this face for 35m and follow a ledge back to the top of the second step (move of V). A few mdown on the Chamonix side make another rappel (40m) to a snowy ledge. Descend a chimney to a large block and traverse R to a ledge near the top of the first step. Make 2 rappels down this to the Col du Caiman. c250m, 3–4hr

## Col du Caiman 3392m

First Traverse: J Grieve and K Spence, 1969

The SE side is an unpleasant rock couloir with a difficult 50m final wall (IV). The N side is a steep and sombre mixed climb that has probably only received 2 ascents.

**97     NORTH SIDE**
TD     G Rébuffat and L Terray, 26 Aug 1942
**62**

Follow the steep mixed ground above the Blaitière hanging glacier and L of Route 29 to finish up the extremely steep ice corner about 50–60m high (Scottish 5). Average angle 60°, 600m. See also Photo 47.

## Col de Blaitière 3352m

This lies between Pt Chevalier (3418m), a small hump on the ridge NE of the Caiman, and the Pt de Lépiney.

**98**
D
**62**

**NORTH SIDE**
First traverse via an ascent of the N side: P Fallet and R Tézenas du Montcel, 19 July 1927

This gives 250m of mixed climbing above the Blaitière hanging glacier taking a diagonal line R then back L to the col. It is exposed to stonefall and has little merit. See also Photo 47.

## Pointe de Lépiney 3429m

J and T de Lépiney, 9 Sept 1920

A minor and relatively inaccessible summit on the main ridge with a magnificent rock face on the Envers side. Despite the low altitude all routes to the summit have a certain degree of seriousness as there is no easy way off. Traditionally an ascent from the E was completed by a traverse of the Fou and Blaitière to descend the Nantillons glacier. Nowadays it is more usual to rappel though this is still quite involved.

**99**
**57**

**DESCENT**
a) From the summit make 15 rappels (some of a tricky diagonal nature) to the Envers glacier via Route 102.
b) Make a short rappel to a terrace on the Chamonix face and go down to a series of large ledges level with the W shoulder. Follow an easy ledge round to the N ridge above a step overlooking the Col du Fou. Rappel to the Col (½hr). From there see Route 104.

**100**
TD–
**57**
**7**

**EAST FACE CLASSIC ROUTE**
M Bron and E Gauchat, 6 Sept 1953

Good climbing that is often more delicate than strenuous despite following a line of chimneys. The granite is generally sound though the approach to the route in the Fou Couloir is exposed to stonefall. It is normally combined with an ascent of the SW ridge of the Fou. 450m from the rimaye, 7hr from the hut.

**101**    **SECURITE ET LIBERTE**
ED1/2    P Cordier and E Decamp, 16 Aug 1981

**57**
**7**

This is the modern classic of the E face and considered one of the best free climbs in the Chamonix Aiguilles. However it is not that frequently climbed. Despite its name, belays and protection in the upper half are not that good and a retreat from this area would be quite difficult. The crux sections are difficult traverses on compact and very exposed slabs. VII, 500m, 8hr. See also Photo 45.

**102**    **LES VACANCES DE MONSIEUR HULOT**
ED2    P Camison and D Suchet, 13–14 and 30 Aug 1984

**57**
**7**

A direct and sustained eliminate on the previous route. There are unavoidable moves of VII+ on compact slabs but each stance is equipped with a good rappel point. VIII, 500m. See alsoPhoto 45.

**103**    **SOUTH-EAST RIDGE**
TD    J Collaer, P Cordier and J Ramouillet, 26 July 1975

**45**
**7**

Although not often ascended there are some superb pitches on this route. It is however easy to avoid the upper half of the great dièdre by cracks (IV) 40m to the L, and higher, the ridge runs close to the rocky couloir below the Col du Blatière into which it is easy to escape at several points. 500m

To the R of 'Securité' a 14–0itch route joining it 5 pitches below the summit has unavoidable moves of VII protected by a total of 61 bolts. It has instantly gained considerable popularity! Climbed by D Anker, M Piola and P Strappazzon, Aug 1988. ED1, 500m

# Col du Fou 3365m

**104**    **TRAVERSE**
AD    First traverse: C Authenac with F Tournier, 19 July 1938

Situated on the main crest below the SW ridge of the Fou, the col can be reached on the W side from the Nantillons glacier by a long and tedious approach. Follow the Fontaine Ledges (Route 117) across the upper part of the W face of the Blaitière and cross a huge snowy couloir leading down to the Blaitière hanging glacier. Slant up under the W face of the Fou on a series of discontinuous ledges (pitches of III) to the col.

The E side is quite often rappeled for 200m to the snowy couloir below the S face of the Fou, after an ascent of the latter or a route on the Lépiney. Continue down the R side and rappel the rocks at the base of the Lépiney to the glacier. Apart from being unpleasant, this is very exposed to stonefall and can hardly be recommended. See Photos 55, 57 and 62

# Aiguille du Fou 3501m

E Fontaine with J and J Ravanel, 16 July 1901

One of the most attractive summits in the Aiguilles. The Normal Route, best combined with an ascent of the Aig de Blaitière, is nowadays rather unfrequented.

**105**    **NORTH-NORTH-EAST RIDGE (NORMAL ROUTE)**
AD+    First ascent party

*A long and varied climb with continuous interest. See Photos 55, 60 and 62*

From the Plan de l'Aiguille reach the Brèche de Blaitière preferably by Route 113. Go up the ridge towards the central summit of the Blaitière for 1 pitch then traverse R along a system of ledges to the Blaitière-Ciseaux gap. Go onto the Envers side and descend 40m before slanting up towards the gap between it and the following gendarme. Reach this gap by a strenuous chimney (III). Continue along the L side of the ridge, climbing an easy chimney slanting to the L. Cross a short slab (III+) into a gully. Follow it up to the summit block of the Fou. This is 10m high and can be ascended by throwing a rope over the top or climbing the NE ridge (V). 6hr from the Plan de l'Aiguille.

**106**    **SOUTH-WEST RIDGE**
TD−    P Allain and R Latour, Aug 1933

**57**
**15**

Although short, this is a traditional classic that gives sustained and strenuous jamming on excellent granite. It is best combined with an ascent of the E face of the Lépiney. c135m, 2–3hr

**107**    **SOUTH FACE**
ED2/3    T Frost, J Harlin, G Hemming and S Fulton during July 1963

**57**
**15**

A magnificent and exceptionally sustained climb with a seriousness out of all proportion to its length and situation. On the very rare occasions that it has been ascended completely free (ED5, IX), it has provided the most demanding climbing in the range. however most parties will use aid on the hard pitches to make the ascent more reasonable; VI/VI+ and A2. With the present in situ gear a fast party will complete the route in a day; otherwise there is only one possible bivouac site on the route. The approach couloir is seriously exposed to stonefall and the foot of the difficulties should be reached shortly after dawn. 600m from the rimaye, 350m on the final wall.

On the L side of the face a mixed free and aid route put up by P Colas and P Grenier on 19–21 June 1988 (VII–, A2) was well-equipped at each stance with good anchor points. It now offers the best existing rappel descent on this side of the peak!

| 108 | **SOUTH FACE – BALLADE AU CLAIR DE LUNE** |
|-----|-------------------------------------------|
| ED3 | E Bellin, J Boivin and M Moioli, 18–19 Aug 1983 |
| **57** | |

A direct route up the R side of the face. It gives good free climbing with several pitches of VII but has 1 demanding aid pitch above the diagonal crack on skyhooks and copperheads (A3/4). 600m. See also Photo 60.

| 109 | **WEST FACE DIRECT** |
|-----|----------------------|
| TD+ | M Boysen and J Jordan, Aug 1966 |
| **55** | |

The face is split by easy diagonal ramps, one of which is taken by the Normal Route, on this side, to the Col du Fou. The climbing is therefore not homogeneous in difficulty despite the steepness of the face, and the route is probably unrepeated. VI+, c500m. See also Photos 47 and 62

## Aiguille des Ciseaux 3479m

M Berthelot with J and E Ravanel, 22 Aug 1906

This takes its name from a resemblance to a pair of open scissors when seen from Chamonix. The summit can be easily reached from Route 105.

Two climbs of medium difficulty have been created on the SE Spur which, in its lower section, forms a steep slabby wall of excellent granite. Both have become quite popular. Although it is possible to continue to the summit via a secondary couloir just R of the crest (c200m, II and III) most parties rappel back down the Troussier Route.

**110**
VI
**LE FIL A COUDRE**
E Bellin and P Camison, 30 July 1984

`60`
`14`
Reach the foot of the face in 1½hr from the Envers Hut and start up a wide curving crack running up the R side of a flake. 600m, 5hr. See also Photo 47

**111**
V
**ORIGINAL ROUTE**
G Prioreschi and J Troussier, 25 July 1978

`60`
`14`
A modern classic. 600m, 4–5hr. See also Photos 45 and 57

# Aiguille de Blaitière 3522m

E Whitwell with C and J Lauener, 6 Aug 1874 (although the N and lowest peak had been climbed the previous year)

One of the most popular peaks in the Aiguilles with a considerable variety of climbing. There is even a choice of normal routes and in recent years numerous short rock climbs have been developed around the base of the W face. There are 3 summits with the central point fractionally the highest.

**112**
AD
`59`
**ROCHER DE LA CORDE**
*The original ascent route to the central peak. Interesting, delicate, and probably the nicest route to the summit.*

Follow Route 133 or 134 to the upper part of the Nantillons glacier. Cross the rimaye and go up the snow slope to a gap in the ridge just R of 2 pointed gendarmes. Follow the ridge to the top of the rocky buttress of the 'Rocher de la Corde' and make a short rappel down the wall on the R to a narrow snow/ice crest. Follow it R to the point where it merges into the steep slope, then work up L on the rocks directly below the central peak. Climb a 10m chimney (III) to a niche below an overhanging block. Work up L via a crack and some slabs to the couloir leading up to the gap between the Central and S Pts. It is possible to reach this gap from the ledges on the SW side (Route 105) via a chimney and crack line (IV+). Traverse onto the SW face from the gap and climb a 6m chimney. Pass through a letter box onto the N side and gain the summit. c200m from the rimaye, 6hr from the Plan de l'Aiguille.

### 113 SPENCER COULOIR
AD/AD+ S Spencer with H Almer and C Jossi, 7 Aug 1898

**59**

*This is the quickest means of reaching the summit and is very popular. It is a suitable, though lengthy, introduction to the general mountaineering routes of the range.*

Climb the couloir to the Brèche de Blaitière in 1hr. Average angle 51°. It is now possible to traverse L and gain the Rocher de la Corde Route but a more direct line is as follows: traverse L and climb an icy couloir and ramp for 70m to a platform on the N ridge of the central peak. Climb a steep crack on the L (10m. III+). Traverse R and climb a groove for 30m (III) to the summit. 200m from the rimaye, 5–5½hr from the Plan de l'Aiguille.

  2 rappels lead back to the brèche.

### 114 BREGEAULT RIDGE
PD+ H Bregeault and T Thomas with A and P Blanc, 7 Aug 1906

**59**

A rocky scramble up the broken crest on the R side of the Spencer Couloir. It is the easiest route to the summit and the safest in descent.

### 115 NORTH-EAST COULOIR
D P Labrunie and M Negri with A Contamine, 27 Aug 1961

**59**

The steep ice couloir immediately R of the Bregeault Ridge. c300m, 5hr

### 116 NORTH-NORTH-EAST COULOIR
TD– F Audibert and C Mollier, 30 June 1965

**59**

The even steeper ice couloir R of the previous route which has 2 converging branches in the lower section. Climb the narrow L branch into the main couloir. 300m to the NW ridge, several pitches of 70°, 6hr

### 117 NORTH-WEST RIDGE POINTE DE CHAMONIX (NORTH SUMMIT)
D V Ryan with F and J Lochmatter, 1906

**59**

*The classic expedition, though not often climbed in its entirety. It is notoriously difficult to follow and there are so many variations that the description below is given more as a rough guide. The lower part of the ridge can be avoided by taking the Nantillons glacier but this misses the very best of the climbing. See also Photo 62*

From the Plan de l'Aiguille, follow Route 134 to the large scree terraces on the R edge of the glacier. Go up the glacier slopes for 100m then climb back up to the ridge and follow it to the first gap below a steep step (III and IV). Work up slanting cracks on the R flank to a big wall. Start climbing this on the L (V) and where it becomes vertical, traverse delicately L to the ridge (V). On the Nantillons side, reach the second gap from where the 'False Fontaine Ledges' lead R onto the W face. Turn the next tower on the L side to a third gap and the start of the true 'Fontaine Ledges'. Go onto the L side and climb a 25m chimney back onto the ridge (IV). Go down a chimney on the N side to a jammed block. Slant up L across slabs (IV) to a snow-filled couloir and follow it to the fourth gap. Climb the ridge more or less directly to the fifth gap (V) and the top of the NNE Couloir (Route 116). Turn a tower on the R to the last gap and the top of the NE Couloir (Route 115). On the L side, slant up easy mixed ground to a huge mixed chimney and climb it directly (IV+, icy) to the N summit. c750m, 9hr from the Plan de l'Aiguille.

| 118 | **NORTH-WEST RIDGE DIRECT – JAPANESE ROUTE** |
|-----|----------|
| TD | Y Kato, T Nakano and M Suzuki, 6–7 Sept 1972 |
| **62** | |

Below the first gap, gained from the Nantillons glacier in the previous route, the ridge splits with the NW branch falling towards Pte 2475m on the moraine. The lower section of this takes the form of a steep red pillar 300m high. This route climbs just R of the crest – a succession of exceptionally varied pitches on perfect granite that have seen very little traffic, mainly due to an inability to locate the correct line (which would appear to coincide with 'L'Eau Rancé d'Arabie' in several sections). Other starts on the pillar are now preferred and a fast party should be able to complete the route to the summit and descend the same day. c800m

*Aiguille de Blaitière continued on page 82*

# Aiguille de Blaitière: Red Pillar

Almost a dozen routes have been climbed on this pillar and are usually terminated after the major difficulties, where a quick rappel descent is possible down Route 122. Climbs are generally well-equipped with essential in situ protection and belays. The quality of these routes is very high and some have now even seen winter ascents.

**119  L'EAU RANCE D'ARABIE**
VII     M Piola and P Steiner, 2–3 Aug 1985

62
16      One of the best of the harder routes with unavoidable crux moves and a couple of off-width cracks. 250m

**120  DALE-SIMMONDS**
VI      C Dale and D Simmonds, 17 July 1984

62      This takes the central open groove system on the L of the Crook-Penning Route. Start 6m L of the latter and slant L up slabs to gain the groove. 250m

**121  CROOK-PENNING**
VI+     M Crook and T Penning, 18 Aug 1982

62
16      On the L side of the 200m subsidiary pillar in an open depression. Although not at all homogeneous in difficulty, the climbing is better than it looks. 250m

**122  MAJORETTE THATCHER**
VI+     M Piola and P Steiner, 17 July 1984

61
16      Thoroughly recommended, giving steep crack climbing with a difficult roof pitch. This is the line normally used for descent – 5 rappels from good in situ anchors. 200m, see also Photo 62

**123  LA GAULOISERIE**
VIII    C Carli and J Chassagne, Autumn 1984

61
16      This takes the obvious huge red dièdre on the R side of the pillar. 200m

**124  NABOT LEON**
V/V+    T Cerdon and M Piola, 18 Sept 1985

61      This is an excellent little route of sustained medium difficulty, taking the extreme R edge of the pillar. A series of Rward-facing dièdres leads to the conspicuous rampline slanting back L to the top of Majorette Thatcher. 180m

A huge complex face with a number of pillars in the lower half leading to a system of ledges. Above these lies the steep terminal wall. It is now common to finish the climbs at the Fontaine or False Fontaine Ledges and generally rappel back down the route to equipment left at the base. It is also easy but much longer to traverse these ledges Lwards to the NW ridge and descend this and the Nantillons glacier to the moraine. An ascent of one of the harder routes to the summit is a more involved expedition and would warrant an overall grading of at least TD+ and a time of 10hr or more.

One can approach the face directly, crossing the Blaitière glacier and scrambling up the lower rock barrier to terraces at the foot of the route or, as is more popular these days, by the moraine below the NW ridge and a traverse below the red pillar on the same terraces that lead into the centre of the face (c2hr from the Plan de l'Aiguille).

| | | |
|---|---|---|
| **125** | **SEIGNEUR ROUTE** | |
| V+ | A Parat and Y Seigneur, 15 July 1964 | |

**61**
**17**

This climbs the R side of the depression on the L flank of the central pillar finishing on the False Ledges quite close to the NW ridge. The lower section can provide an alternative start to the middle ledge system on the pillar. There are one or two short sections of A1 in the upper section. 350m

**126** **FIDEL FIASCO**
VII+ M Piola and P Steiner, 22 and 30 July 1984

**61**
**17**

Hard sustained and strenuous climbing up the L side of the central pillar. There are some unavoidable moves of VII high on this route and it is considered one of the better climbs on the face. 350m

**127** **CENTRAL PILLAR – TROUSSIER ROUTE**
V+ R Ghilini, P Grenier, G Thomas and J Troussier, Aug 1978

**61**
**17**

This was the original route on the front face of the pillar and gives a very good crack climb of medium difficulty on excellent granite. Despite being one of the easiest routes on the face, it has not had that many ascents. 350m. See also Photo 62

### 128 WILLIAMINE DADA
VIII+  M Piola and P Steiner, 18–19 Aug 1983

This is an excellent route with a variety of free climbing problems and has become quite popular. Although there are one or two very hard pitches, a little aid will reduce the overall difficulty to give a homogeneous route of VI/VI+. Each stance has a well-equipped rappel point giving the most popular descent line from the False Ledges. 350m. See also Photo 62

### 129 BRITISH ROUTE
VII  J Brown and D Whillans, 25 July 1954. Winter: F Audibert and M Martinetti, 19–21 Jan 1964

The established classic on the face following a series of difficult cracks just R of the huge rock scar. The famous 'Fissure Brown', a wide and awkward offwidth/chimney, is still rarelyclimbed completely free (many parties avoid it by easier cracks to the L). One or two large wooden wedges here and on other sections of the climb can reduce the difficulty. The original finish above the Fontaine Ledges has little in situ gear and can take 3–4hr to the N summit. 750m. See also Photo 62

### 130 WEST PILLAR
VI/A1/2  M Galbraith and A McKeith, 26–27 July 1966

This takes the obvious line of grooves on the L side of the huge rib overlooking the Grand Couloir and has been repeated more often in recent years with a number of variations. The climb begins in the central and easiest-looking of 3 dièdres and the first 3 pitches can form a less demanding alternative start to the British Route. The upper section is very exposed. 350m

The crest of the rib on the R of the W pillar has been climbed by V Couttet and F Laroche, 28 July 1985; 'Cacou'; 350m; V/VI. The Grand Couloir, first climbed in 1980 and used as an abseil descent from time to time (fixed anchors) is not to be recommended in either direction!

*Aiguille de Blaitière continued*

**131**  **SOUTH-EAST RIDGE**
D+  J and R Leininger, 8 Aug 1937

**60**

*The classic ascent from the Envers side. In order to popularise this route in the 1950's, 3 ropes were fixed on the hard pitches. These still remain and being of 8cm diameter rotting hemp detract from an otherwise delicate, interesting and very worthwhile excursion. The overall grading applies to the route as described below (in hope of future restoration). See also Photo 45*

From the Envers Hut reach the Envers de Blaitière glacier and climb up the basin between the SE ridges of the Blaitière and Pt des Nantillons. Reach a rocky spur on the L projecting up the glacier from above the foot of the ridge. Traverse L across the tongue of snow behind it and climb up to the ridge by a series of parallel cracks (IV, 1½hr).

Turn the first gendarme and climb an exposed slab to a step. Climb a short wall (IV) then traverse R to a dièdre slanting up to the L. Climb it finishing on the slab to the L (V). Follow the ridge to a block forming a roof, climb it on the L (IV) and go up to a second step. On the L side climb a dièdre (V) and the chimney above (IV) to the top of the step and continue on the exposed crest for 70m to the third step. Follow a ledge on the L flank for 15m to a gully and climb it (IV) finishing L up the slab (V). On the R climb a slab (IV) to gain a small col below the large fourth step. Climb this by a long slanting weakness on the L flank (IV at the start) and regain the ridge near the Blaitière-Ciseaux Col from where cracks on the R are climbed to the S summit. 550m, 8hr from the hut.

**132**  **EAST FACE**
D−  V Ryan with F and J Lochmatter, July 1914

**60**

*An old and established mountaineering route that is nowadays almost totally neglected despite offering sustained and extremely fine climbing in the upper section. See also Photo 45*

Continue up the glacier basin of Route 131 and climb onto the rock spur coming down from the Rocher de la Corde at its lowest point. This is just R of the large icy couloir coming down from the brèche. Slant up L to the crest and follow it (pitches of IV) to the smooth upper walls. Traverse L across the couloir and climb a chimney system (IV) on the E face. Turn a vertical buttress on the R when level with the top of the Rocher de la Corde and slant up L via walls and chimneys (IV) to the summit. 500m, 6hr from the hut.

# Col des Nantillons 3292m and 3310m

A double col whose gaps are separated by the Pt des Nantillons. The NW side is entirely covered by the Nantillons glacier and forms the normal approach to many climbs on the Charmoz, Grépon and Blaitière summits.

**133** **NORTH-WEST SIDE**
PD/PD+ First traverse: H Seymour Hoare with J von Bergen and U Almer,
13 Sept 1875

62

*The condition of the icefalls above and alongside the 'Rognon' varies from year to year but will generally threaten the route with serac fall. Recently this situation has become more serious and an alternative approach via the lower buttress of the Blaitière NW ridge gives a much safer access to the upper basin. See also Photo 59*

From the Plan de l'Aiguille station follow the path towards the little lake, passing N of it and crossing the moraine to reach the Blaitière glacier. Traverse the dry, level glacier and reach the crest of the far moraine at 2475m. The path continues across the next moraine (good bivouac sites at the top, 2525m) to the Nantillons glacier which is crossed almost horizontally to the base of the Rognon (1¼hr. This point can also be reached from Montenvers in 2hr).

Generally the 'Narrows' to the L of the Rognon is a chaotic icefall though occasionally it can be a straightforward ice slope which allows the Rognon to be bypassed completely. Get onto the Rognon from the L and climb steep but easy rocks reaching the crest at about half-height. Follow it to the 'Salle à Manger' at the top – a traditional resting place but exposed to serac fall from above (¾hr). Climb up and bear L under the serac barriers heading for the Charmoz-Grépon Couloir. Close to the base of the couloir slant up R to the upper plateau and so gain the col. 3½hr from the Plan de l'Aiguille.

**134**
PD+
62

*The alternative approach though technically more difficult avoids the dangers in the vicinity of the Rognon and is especially recommended late in the day for descent. See also Photo 59*

From Pt 2525m at the top of the moraine climb snowfields on the L side of the NW ridge of the Aig de Blaitière until it is possible to trend back R up broken rock to reach the crest at the foot of a smooth prominent step. Climb this (30m, III+) exiting on the R, then continue up the easier-angled slabs on the ridge (III) for 70m to reach large scree terraces on the R edge of the Nantillons glacier (good bivouac sites). Go up snow/ice slopes for 150m close under the ridge and turn the seracs on the R. Trend L into an easier-angled basin and continue up a steeper snow/ice ramp above the cliffs, passing under the NE couloir (Route 115). Traverse the slope below the Spencer Couloir to reach the upper plateau and so gain the col. 4hr from the Plan de l'Aiguille, 3hr in descent. See also Photo 59

## Pointe des Nantillons 3359m

An insignificant point on the crest between the two Cols des Nantillons which offers a tremendous selection of high-quality rock climbs above the Envers Hut.

**135**
D−
60

**SOUTH FACE**
F Gros, A Roch and E Stagni with R Lambert, 26 Aug 1937

*A pleasant route of medium difficulty on excellent granite. See also Photo 45*

From the Envers Hut follow Route 131 up the glacier basin until just below the projecting rocky spur on the L, where a prominent snow ramp leads R onto the S face (1½hr). Follow it, crossing a subsidiary spur, to a rocky couloir which is climbed taking the L branch (IV) to the crest of a spur. Easy ledges on the L lead to some cracks. Climb these (40m, IV+) to reach another spur on the R. Follow it, turning a gendarme on the R and higher climbing a chimney with loose blocks to a large gendarme. Make a diagonal rappel L and traverse to a huge slab (IV). Make a 10m tension traverse L to an easy couloir and follow it to the summit. 450m, 6hr from the hut.

**136**  **SOUTH-EAST RIDGE**
D+  L Dugit, K Gurékian and M Lenoir, 21 Sept 1947

**60**

*The main difficulties of this route lie in the first 320m to the summit of the first Pt on the ridge (2921m). The climbing is good but the line is poor, starting in a large couloir-chimney on the L of the face. See also Photo 45*

Climb the couloir (IV) with a traverse L near the top to the crest of the ridge. Follow this for 4–5 pitches (IV and V) until a long traverse R is made across the E face to a secondary spur. Climb this a little way then come back L passing behind a big flake until slabs and walls lead to the summit of the first Pt (V and IV). From here follow the ridge to the foot of the second Pt and make a long, slightly descending, traverse to a huge couloir which is followed to join Route 135 near the summit (pitches of IV). 750m, 9hr from the hut.


## Pointes des Nantillons: First Pointe 2921m

There are numerous better lines to the summit of this Pt than the 1947 route. They can be continued at a much easier standard to the summit via the SE Ridge Route but most parties tend to rappel down the line of Amazonia which is well-equipped for this purpose. The bottom of the face is reached in 20min from the Envers Hut.

**137**  **AMAZONIA**
V/VI  G Hopfgartner and M Piola, 2 Sept 1984

**63**
**18**

In the category of the short and unserious rock route, this has almost reached the status of a modern classic with excellent open face climbing that sees many ascents. The crux second pitch gives committing yet well-protected moves. 320m, 4hr. See also Photo 45

**138**  **DIRECT START – GUY-ANNE**
VI+  M Piola and P Steiner, 3 Aug 1984

**63**
**18**

This gives a much harder start up the steep walls to the L and the first few pitches give especially interesting open face and crack climbing. 320m, 4–5hr

**139    U C P A**
V/V+    An U C P A party, Aug 1984

The conspicuous dièdre line immediately to the R of Amazonia. 320m

**140    BIENVENUE AU GEORGES V**
VI/VI+    M Piola and P Strappazzon, 3–4 Sept 1986

This takes the steep compact slabs to the R of U.C.P.A. and the difficulties, although not of an exceptionally high order, are unavoidable. It is considered by many to be one of the best routes of its type in the range. 320m

## Pointes des Nantillons: Second Pointe 3128m

Routes here, on the E face are not so populated but still offer high quality ascents.

**141    SPARK IN THE RAIN**
VII+    C de Bode and P Camison, 21 July 1984

This climbs thin red slabs to gain the long dièdre on the E face. A little aid can reduce the difficulties to VI+ and makes the climbing more homogeneous in standard. 350m. See also Photo 64

**142    TROUSSIER DIEDRE**
V+/VI    P Grenier, R Nicod, L Ruyssen and J Troussier, 9 Aug 1977

The most elegant line on this side of the ridge and generally rappeled to regain the glacier. It begins about 50m to the L of the base of the couloir leading up to the Col des Nantillons and is reached in ½hr from the Envers Hut. 350m. See also Photo 64

**143    BRABANT-MEYER ROUTE**
D+/TD–    M Brabant and P Meyer, 23 Aug 1961

Although not the most aesthetic line on the face, this gives surprisingly good climbing on sound granite. From the notch where the route joins the SE ridge, traverse L for a pitch then climb up 2 or 3 pitches to rejoin it below a 40m high gendarme. Starting with a crack on the L climb up the ridge (V) to a second gendarme. Climb short cracks on the L (V) to reach the top of this and continue up the crest turning a huge block on the R to the summit. 600m, 8–9hr from the hut. See also Photo 64

# Bec d'Oiseau 3417m

An insignificant pointe halfway down the SW ridge of the Grépon with a superb pillar on the Envers side.

**144**  **SOUTH-EAST PILLAR**
TD/TD+  P Bodin and P Meyer, 2 Aug 1959

**60**

*This gives a brilliant day's outing from the Envers Hut. It takes the crest of the spur characterised by the huge and pointed monolithic wall which is clearly visible from afar. The climbing is highly recommended, being interesting, varied, more delicate than strenuous and still uncrowded. See also Photo 58*

From the Envers Hut reach the foot of the couloir coming down from the NE gap of the Col des Nantillons (½hr). Traverse R to reach a large block at the base of a 20m high pillar and climb a crack on the R side (V) followed by a short dièdre on the R. Climb a little wall on the L (IV) to an easy grassy ramp. Follow this up R to below smooth walls and slant up L easily on broken rock to the L side of the spur. Slant up R and rejoin the crest by a 25m dièdre (IV and V). Continue up slightly L of the crest for 1 pitch (V) then 2 easy pitches on the R to reach the L side of the monolithic wall. Climb easily up on this side until directly below the top of the slab. There are 2 dièdres separated by a spur. Start in the L, traverse into the R (IV) and climb it and the flake above (VI and A1).

Climb a small pillar on the R then a wall (V+) followed by 2 successive dièdres to the crest (V). Continue up the crest for 15m (V and VI) then 2 more pitches (III and IV). Climb a bulge on the R (V) then continue for 2 more pitches, at first on the R then the L side of the crest (IV) to a triangular gendarme 30m high. Climb it on its L side via a short dièdre (V+ and A1). Follow the horizontal ridge for 30m then reach the foot of the final tower by a short rappel. Climb a dièdre followed by a wide crack on the R (IV). Go up a white slab using flakes on the L then traverse R under a very loose block and climb a short dièdre (IV+). Follow a dièdre formed by the flake above (V−) which leans to the R and becomes a ledge. Climb up to a second ledge then slant L on poorish rock (IV+) to the base of a giant 'ear' and layback it (V). A crack on the R leads to the S summit. The N summit is reached by a short jump across a crevice. 650m, 10–12hr from the hut.

Descent: Make 1 rappel on the Chamonix side then scramble down to the Col des Nantillons.

87

**145**    **EAST-SOUTH-EAST SPUR**

TD    B Chrétien and J Jérôme, 16 July 1976

**58**

The spur immediately to the R of the monolithic slab, approached via the lower walls of the Aig du Roc and finishing up the final tower of the SE pillar. V and V+, 650m, 9hr.

## Aiguille du Grépon 3482m

A Mummery with A Burgener and B Venetz, 5 Aug 1881. Winter: R Lambert and E Poget, 7 Feb 1932

Probably one of the most popular and certainly the most famous of the Chamonix Aiguilles. The highest point is at the S end of a thin crenellated crest. The mountain is usually traversed and is best combined with the Grands Charmoz.

**146**    **TRAVERSE BY NORTH AND SOUTH-SOUTH-WEST**

D−    **RIDGES**

**62**    First ascent party; though the ascent and descent of the SSW ridge was not done until 1885 by H Dunod with F and G Simond and A Tairraz

*This is the normal route and one of the great Alpine classics. It is an excursion of incomparable variety and magnificent exposure on perfect granite. The technical difficulties are not high and the stances and belays more than sufficient. See also Photo 64*

From the Plan de l'Aiguille follow Route 133/134 to the base of the Charmoz-Grépon Couloir (3¼hr). Climb the couloir by the rocks on the L side, then slant back into it at a point just before it deepens. Climb the couloir or cracks on the L returning to the R side to reach a balcony where the couloir forks (¾hr). Take the R branch and after 45m climb a dièdre on the L (IV) to the col between the Charmoz and the Grépon.

     Follow a ledge on the Mer de Glace side for 20m then ascend diagonally on steeper ground for 30m to a small gap in the N ridge. This is the top of the R branch of the Charmoz-Grépon Couloir. Descend this couloir for a few metres and traverse (IV) into the Mummery Crack, a wide smooth crack that is climbed (IV) to a good stance. A short chimney leads up R to the 'Trou du Canon' – a hole through which one gains the Mer de Glace side. Slant up L and climb a chimney (III) then pass through a letter box to the

Nantillons side. Climb the 'Rateau à Chèvre', a splendid flake crack rising across the sheer face on the R (IV). Reach the gap beyond the N summit and climb the Grand Gendarme by its N ridge (III+). Rappel 20m to the gap below, mainly on the Nantillons side to avoid a nastypendulum that could land a climber in difficulties on the Mer de Glace side. Follow a ledge on the Nantillons side, then the ridge itself until a remarkable horizontal ledge, the 'Vire aux Bicyclettes', can be reached in a few metres down on the Mer de Glace side. From the far end climb a short chimney to a gap below the summit tower. Climb this directly by the Venetz Crack (IV) or on the Nantillons side by a Z-shaped crack, reached through a letter box (IV). 6hr from the Plan de l'Aiguille.

Rappel from the Madonna 20m alongside the Knubel Crack on the E face and gain the Brèche Balfour along a series of detached flakes. Follow ledges and chimneys that slant down the W face at 45° to a terrace, near the ridge. Rappel down a smooth groove on the W flank and reach a block wedged in a narrow 'neck' in the ridge. Descend this 'à cheval' (sharper at the base!) then ascend a short wall (III) to the 'C.P. Terrace' – a large sloping ledge. Go down the ridge turning a small tower on the R and reach the col between the Grépon and the Bec d'Oiseau. Scramble down to the Col des Nantillons (1hr).

*Aiguille du Grepon continued on page 90*

# Aiguille du Grépon: West Face

2 routes are worthy of consideration on this face, although the difficulties are quite short and end a long way below the summit where the huge diagonal couloir line, first climbed in 1914, splits the face.

**47**
**V/VI**

**65**
**20**

**WEST FACE**
R Duchier, R Gabriel, G Livanos and C Magol, 25 July 1947

On the R of the base of the Charmoz-Grépon Couloir is a huge curving chimney line. The climb starts in a crack 8m to the R of this before slanting back into the chimney after 1 pitch. It continues this line, climbing dièdres and smooth walls to join the couloir. The direct exit to the gap on the R of the flat topped Gendarme (3473m) is a more interesting finish. 200m of difficulty, 5hr. See also Photo 62

**148**

VII

**DIRECT**

M Crook and C Dale, 21 Aug 1985

Spectacular climbing on excellent granite. 250m of difficulty, 5hr. See also Photo 62

---

*Aiguille du Grepon continued*

**149**

D

**MER DE GLACE FACE**

H Jones, R Todhunter and G Young with J Knubel and H Brocherel, 19 Aug 1911

*Another well-established classic of the region which is safe and well-protected on good rock. For many years it remained technically the hardest climb in the range although the true finish, the Knubel Crack, is easily avoided. Nowadays it is rather neglected due to the increasing popularity of the shorter, harder climbs available on the Envers side of the Aiguilles. Route finding on the lower section is tricky. See also Photo 45*

Cross the spur just behind the Envers Hut and descend a steep grassy gully to the Trélaporte glacier. Cross this, passing under the Tour Rouge, and reach the rimaye of a little snowy bay directly below the two-pointed Cornes de Chamois. Cross the rimaye or climb rocks on the R side (IV). Climb up the slope then traverse L onto the Grépon by way of a sloping terrace. Above and L of the terrace climb a chimney (IV) or the slab to the R (IV) and follow a ledge L into a couloir. Climb it to the top where, about 30m to the R, lies a small wooden hut in very poor repair – the Tour Rouge Bivouac (2822m, 2hr).

Climb up L in a chimney line (III) to reach the large scree terraces on a level with the col behind the Tour Rouge. Slant up L to the main spur coming down from the N summit of the Grépon. Go up this to a squat tower then traverse L crossing a chimney and descending some slabs to a platform on the edge of a couloir (avoid the tendency to go too high before traversing L towards the couloir). Make a short diagonal rappel into the couloir, climb it for 20m then take ledges on the L to a large terrace on the second spur which comes down from the region of the S summit. Climb up above, avoiding a steep chimney on the R, to a second terrace where the difficulties begin and the route-finding becomes easier (3hr).

Climb a dièdre (15m, IV) then a chimney with a chockstone (IV) and continue in cracks and chimneys (III/IV) to a small shoulder. Climb up the R flank of the ridge to another shoulder below the final wall (1½hr). On the R climb a short crack to a ledge (IV+). Follow it L beneath a high chimney and after 30m slant R on easy ground to a platform at the top of the chimney. Go up the chimney above (35m, IV), climb slabs on the R and a strenuous crack (IV+) and follow the chimney to the Brèche Balfour (1½hr). Traverse R along a series of detached flakes to a 20m crack, the Knubel Crack. Climb it to an overhang and large chockstone, then move onto the L wall and reach the top (V/V+). 800m, about 8hr from the hut.

| 150 | **EAST PILLAR** |
| TD− | Probably H Fraedris and W Korner, 22−23 July 1935 |
| 64 | |

This is very rarely climbed but goes more or less up the crest of the spur above the squat tower reached on the previous route. The crux occurs in the central section with 4 pitches of V in a long dièdre. Otherwise it is fairly sustained at IV and IV+ offering crack and chimney climbing on very sound granite. 800m, 9hr. See also Photo 45

| 151 | **VIA AIGUILLE DE ROC** |
| VI | E Frendo, J Carrel, R Faure and R Grière, 18 Aug 1938 |
| 64 | |

*This is a very fine finish to any route reaching the summit of the Roc. When combined with routes on the S or E faces it becomes a long and excellent excursion of TD to ED2 standard. See also Photo 45*

From the summit make 2 rappels down the NW side to the Roc-Grépon Col. Go up L for 10m and climb the gently overhanging Frendo dièdre (VI or A1). Reach a niche on the L, then a second above, via a deep chimney (V). Climb the vertical crest on the R (V) to easy slabs. From here there is an easy line of cracks and chimneys escaping L to the SW ridge of the Grépon (II/III) but just above is the L end of the large ledge that lies below the high chimney mentioned in Route 149. Follow this route to the summit. 3−4hr

# Aiguille de Roc 3409m

M O'Brien with A Couttet and G Cachat, 6 Aug 1927. Winter: L Lachenal and L Pez, 6 Feb 1949

This beautiful rock spire is situated below and to the E of the summit of the Grépon and now offers an enormous selection of first-class rock climbs. There are many modern classics, most of which join traditional routes well below the summit. Most parties descend from this point by rappel but an ascent to the spectacular summit and continuation to the Grépon is a magnificent expedition which is highly recommended.

**152**    **EAST FACE**

D    First ascent party

**64**

*Nowadays the modern lines, with their superior climbing, take pride of place and this classic means of access to the summit is rarely followed. However it remains a good route with varied and interesting climbing of medium difficulty. See also Photo 45*

From the Envers Hut follow Route 149 to the large scree terraces level with the col behind the Tour Rouge. Traverse L to the Roc-Grépon Couloir and climb up the L side to a prominent shoulder on the E ridge of the Roc. Traverse L again descending slightly, then zig-zag up to the base of a huge couloir (not visible from below) which leads up to the highest col on the E ridge. Climb it on its L side, then in the bed, to the col (4hr).

     The climbing now becomes steeper. Follow a ledge diagonally L wards and just before reaching the vertical crack at its end, climb a cracked slab (IV) and another steep slab above (IV+) slanting L to a platform (it is possible to avoid this on the L of the vertical crack (III)). Follow the ledge up to the R for 20m then climb up L in a slanting dièdre passing over 2 overhangs (IV). Climb up R to a small couloir (IV at the start) and go up it for 5m before traversing L to the SE ridge. In 25m reach the final rock pinnacle and climb a narrow chimney on the E face (25m, IV+) finishing on the R. Either free climb (VI/VI+) or lasso a knob on the L and swing across to reach the top. 700m, 6hr from the Envers Hut, 800m and TD to summit of Grépon.

**153**    **DESCENT VIA EAST FACE**

**64**

From just below the summit make 3–4 rappels down to the col on the E ridge then climb down the route of ascent until the huge terraces that mark the top of the routes on the steep lower walls of the E face. Follow the terraces down towards the SE ridge and reach a sort of small shoulder which is the point where 'Children of the Moon' finishes. Descend this in 8 long rappels off well-equipped in situ anchors.

### 154 SOUTH (CORDIER) PILLAR
VI

P Cordier and J Remouillet, 13–14 July 1974

58
21

The forerunner of the many modern rock routes climbed on the S side of the Aiguilles. This is a top quality free climb and although many parties will descend the lower SE ridge, the exhilarating finish along the upper SE ridge and a continuation to the summit of the Grépon will extend this into a long, demanding and highly recommended mountain route. 500m, 8–10hr to Roc summit, 800m and TD to Grépon. See also Photo 45

### 155 DIEDRE DES MOUSQUETAIRES
V+/VI–

M Afanassieff, J Fabre and L Ware, 29 Aug 1978

58
21

This gives some excellent and quite sustained crack and corner climbing on the prominent dièdre splitting the upper part of the S face. There is little in situ gear and as yet it has not gained the popularity of adjacent routes. 500m, 6–7hr to junction with SE ridge. See also Photo 45

### 156 SUBTILITES DULFERIENNES
VI

C Dellamonica, M Batard and M Piola, 9 Sept 1982

58
21

More excellent crack and corner climbing, which is both harder and more sustained than the S pillar, has ensured modern classic status for this interesting route. Some of the moves of VI cannot be aided. 450m, 6–7hr to SE ridge. See also Photo 45

### 157 DESCENT BY SOUTH-EAST RIDGE
*This is the most practical means of descent when it is necessary to retrieve equipment left at the foot of the routes on the S face. See Photos 45, 58 and 64*

From the summit climb down and rappel the upper section of the SE ridge until the top of the S pillar. Make 5 rappels down the SE ridge to easier ground and go down this on the NE side until about 50m above the gap before the Tour Verte (cairn). Cross onto the S side and go down easy ledges until a few rappels lead to the glacier quite close to the start of the S Pillar. 3–4hr

## Aiguille de Roc: East Face

The lower section of the E face is a steep wall overlooking the Trélaporte glacier about 20min from the Envers Hut. At the time of writing there are well over a dozen routes of which many have gained instant popularity and have already become noted modern classics. Descent is usually effected by rappeling the 'Children of the Moon' but an ascent to the summit of the Roc via the line of the E ridge direct is highly recommended.

**158    AU SOLEIL DES ILES**
VII
X Carraro and M Piola, 8–9 July 1986

24

A short route on the very L side of the face. The difficult moves take place on compact steep walls and cannot be avoided. 120m. See Photo 64

**159    SONAM**
V
M Batard, J Moinet, F Pichon and M Preteseille, 12 July 1984

64
24

A pleasant little climb on the zone of excellent white granite towards the L side of the face. 200m

**160    CHILDREN OF THE MOON**
VI
M Piola and N Schenkel, 22 Aug 1982

64
24

The original route on the face and still the most popular, giving a good introduction to the modern rock climbs on the Envers side of the Aiguilles. Although not at all sustained, nor as fine as neighbouring routes, it has quickly become a modern classic. It provides delightful open climbing on steep slabs with a few tricky moves over the roof. 300m

**161    GEMINI**
VII+
G Hopfgartner, D and M Piola, 4 and 5 Sept 1983

64

A much harder direct start, joining the original route at end of pitch 6. 180m, Bolt protected.

**162    PYRAMIDE**
VII–
M Batard and M Piola, 25 Aug 1982. Winter: M Piola and P Steiner, 16 March 1984

64
25

This is a brilliant piece of climbing and is considerd by some to be the best of the modern climbs on this side of the Aigs. The first 350m on the crest of the beautiful red pillar are very sustained and lead directly to the E ridge. Continuing to the summit of the Grépon via the E Ridge Direct of the Roc gives a very elegant line of 850m, ED2, which will possibly require a bivouac. 350m. See also Photo 45

**163** **PANNE DES SENS**
VIII  M Piola and P Steiner, 19–20 July 1984

After climbing the first pitch of the previous route, the L edge of the pillar can be followed directly to a junction with Pitch 8. 250m. See Photo 64

**164** **EAST RIDGE DIRECT**
TD  J Dessaux and R Fournier, 28 Aug 1968

`64`
`25`

Excellent climbing in an exposed situation keeping within a few m of the crest all the way to the summit. It is the logical continuation of Pyramid. V+, c350m. See also Photo 45

## Tour Rouge 2899m

This squat pinnacle reached in 20min from the Envers Hut has numerous fine lines on its sunny SE face. The climbs have an unserious atmosphere and are most enjoyable. That described below is considered to be one of the best rock routes in the range and has received over 1000 ascents.

**165** **LE MARCHAND DE SABLE**
VII–  G Hopfgartner and M Piola, 19–20 July 1983

`64`
`22`

A modern and very popular classic giving varied climbing on excellent granite. Although most of the route could be climbed at V/V+ using a little aid, the penultimate pitch gives unavoidable VI/VI+ moves on a steep compact slab. Descent by rappel. 280m, 5hr. See also Photo 45

## Tour Verte 2760m

The small tower immediately behind the Envers Hut offers many short routes.

**166** **LE PIEGE**
VI/VI+  M Piola and J Schenkel, 25 July 1984

`45`
`23`

A short and strenuous direct line on the E face generally following a series of cracks and dièdres broken by big ledges. Descent by rappel. 200m, 3–4hr

## Pointe Elisabeth c2850m

The E face of this pointed tower on the R side of the Trélaporte glacier below Pt 3038m has about 10 short routes.

**167**    **GRENIER-TROUSSIER ROUTE**
VI+    P Grenier and J Troussier, 11 July 1982

**45**
**29**

The most popular ascent follows the central crack line on the SE face reached in ½–¾hr from the Envers Hut. 250m

## Aiguille des Grands Charmoz 3445m

H Dunod and P Vignon with J Desailloux, F Folliguet, F and G Simond, 9 Aug 1885. Winter: C Sauvage with J Ravanel, 11 Jan 1910

The narrow and pinnacle-studded crest of this mountain is generally traversed, more often than not in conjunction with the Grépon. Some of the best routes in the Aigs, on both rock and ice, lie on its various flanks and ridges.

**168**    **SOUTH-WEST FACE AND MAIN RIDGE TRAVERSE**
AD+    T Jose with F Simond and P Burnet, 10 Sept 1887, although the N
**62**    summit had been reached in 1880 by Mummery's party.

*Although the easiest and traditionally the normal approach to the summit utilises the Charmoz-Grépon Couloir, nowadays this is almost universally used in descent after a traverse of the mountain. The classic route, described below, is very oftencontinued to the summit of the Grépon and provides interesting and delicate climbing along the eroded crest. It is very popular and rightly so.*

Follow Route 133/134 to the Charmoz-Grépon Couloir and climb it to the point where it deepens (3½hr). Traverse L across the top of the last section of broken rocks for about 100m and reach the base of a diagonal line of weakness slanting L across the SW face to Brèche 3421m, just R of the NW Pt on the summit ridge.
     Start by climbing a deep chimney-groove on the R of a small buttress (III+) avoiding the overhang on the R (IV). Continue up the chimney above (III) then the slab on the R (III) returning L by an easy chimney to reach the base of 2 deep chimneys. Climb the one on the R, the Burgener Chimney (IV), over 2 jammed blocks (icy). Above, go through a letter box to a large platform of blocks

and follow a line of easy chimneys for a couple of pitches to Brèche 3421m (1hr).

Now follow the summit ridge climbing the first gendarme directly by lassoing the top, or by the wall on the Nantillons side (IV/IV+). Climb the second gendarme directly or turn it on the R side (IV) and turn the third, the 'Carrée', also on the R (IV) to reach a platform in front of 'Baton Wicks'. Rappel 15m down a chimney on the R side to the gap beyond and turn the following gendarme on the L to reach the most distinctive gap in the ridge. Follow the crest over 2 gendarmes and climb cracks (III) in the final wall to the summit. 5¼hr from the Plan de l'Aiguille.

Go back down the final wall then slant L on broken rocks overlooking the Nantillons glacier to reach the L branch of the Charmoz-Grépon Couloir. Go down this easily, keeping close to the L wall until it joins the main couloir and Route 146 which can be reversed to the Nantillons glacier. 3–4hr from summit to Plan de l'Aiguille.

*Aiguille des Grands Charmoz continued on page 99*

# Aiguille des Grands Charmoz: West Face

At the time of writing there are at least 8 routes on this splendid wall. Only one has become classic although two of the finest routes were destroyed in 1980 by the partial collapse of the central pillar. The continuity of the face is unfortunately broken at two-thirds height by a zone of easy terraces by which it is possible to effect an escape R into the Charmoz-Grépon Couloir. There are only 2 independent finishes on the final wall and that taken by the Desmaison Route is rarely done. The foot of the face can be reached easily via Route 133 in 1½hr from Plan de l'Aiguille.

**169**
TD+
65

**HAGENMULLER-MARX ROUTE**
J Hagenmuller and G Marx, 1979

A difficult route towards the R side of the face which apart from a short pendulum was climbed completely free with 2 pitches of VII. The N summit is reached via the upper section of the Cordier Route. 550m, 10–12hr. see also Photo 62

## HAGENMULLER-BERNERON ROUTE
J Hagenmuller and J Berneron, 3 July 1982

Another line parallel to and immediately R of the Cordier Pillar. The start of this and the previous route involves crossing complicated crevassed ground towards the icefall.

**170**
TD

65
26

## CORDIER PILLAR
G Addison, P Cordier, T Fagard and S Jouty, 6 July 1970. Winter: T Nakano and M Susuki, Feb 1976

An established classic which gives one of the finest rock climbs in the Aigs. The climbing is generally open and delicate on excellent granite and can be very well protected. The face clears quickly after bad weather and attracts many parties. Although it has become fashionable to escape at ⅔–height, this can hardly be recommended as it misses the best climbing which lies above, on the exposed summit buttress.
  Many parties nowadays rappel the route from the summit ridge which does have the merit of allowing easy retrieval of sacs left at the foot and avoids the tortuous descent of the Nantillons glacier at a bad time of day. 600m, 9hr. See also Photo 62

**171**
TD–

65
26

## GHILINI ROUTE
R Ghilini and L Giacomini, 8 July 1976

This climbs the crest of the thin pillar just L of the previous route. Approaching via the original route to the snow patch, the crest of the pillar is gained and climbed for 2 pitches (V+). Now follow a deep couloir-chimney on the L (IV and V) and return to the crest via an easy chimney/crack (III+) leads to the upper section of the Cordier Pillar. 600m, 6–8hr. See also Photo 62

**172**
IV+/V

65
26

## ORIGINAL ROUTE
M Lenoir and P Leroux, 14 July 1947

The easiest route on the wall taking a line of cracks and chimneys. The climbing is interesting though often strenuous but certain sections can remain quite wet for a long time and the route is rarely ascended. 350m to the terraces. See also Photo 62

**173**
TD

65

## DESMAISON ROUTE
R Desmaison and P Mazeaud, 4–5 Sept 1959

*This takes the huge dièdre on the L side of the prominent pointed pillar, partially destroyed by rockfall, in the centre of the face. The line is very direct but needs a prolonged dry spell to render it climbable with a modicum of enjoyment. It has seen very few repetitions though the upper section would provide an alternative finish to many of the routes on the lower wall. See also Photo 62*

Climb the dièdre directly (cracks and chimneys IV and V) with an exit R to the top of the pillar from where the terraces are easily reached. Climb up the terraces on the L to their apex at the foot of some overhanging walls. Climb a widening jamming crack on the L (V) then slant R up a rampline for 2 pitches to a flake on the L (V). Traverse R to a big chimney-dièdre coming down from the NW ridge. Climb it to the upper section of the ramp (V). Follow this up and R, eventually moving round a corner to gain a steep cracked slab (IV+) above the overhanging walls of the buttress. Now climb straight up, following a series of cracks, dièdres and chimneys (IV, V and 1 pitch of VI with a few aid moves) to join the upper section of the Cordier Pillar, 2 pitches below the N summit and Brèche 3421m. 600m, 12hr

**174 NORTHERN PILLAR**
TD   Y Mathelin and E Schmutz, 16 July 1976

`65`

*This takes the L flank of the pillar and as with the previous route many of the pitches may be wet or icy unless climbed after a prolonged dry spell. When this occurs, the climbing becomes both interesting and enjoyable. See also Photo 62*

Begin at the point where the glacier climbs highest onto the face and go up a succession of grooves and chimneys (IV and V with a little aid) to a series of easy ledges below the pillar. Ascend these, then climb a wet chimney (IV) on the pillar to a zone of ledges that lead up L to the steep gully flanking the pillar. Traverse R to the crest and climb it via a series of cracks (V and A1) moving L to the final chimney (IV+) above which, easy ground leads to the central terraces. Continue up the Desmaison finish. 600m, 14hr

---

*Aiguille des Grands Charmoz continued*

**175 NORTH-WEST RIDGE**
TD   P Allain and M Schatz, 28 Aug 1950

`66`

*A long serious route in a fine and exposed situation. Similar in character to the S ridge of the Noire but harder and more sustained in its upper*

*section. It does not appear to have gained the popularity that it deserves.
See also Photo 65*

From the Plan de l'Aiguille follow Route 186 to the Col de l'Etala.
Start up the ridge, first on the L then back to the Ron slabs facing
the Mer de Glace, until a short awkward crack (IV) leads to a long
level section. Continue to a small col below a small tower and climb
easy slabs, then a gully on the R, until a second smaller tower forces
one to turn it on the R (poor rock). Continue along the crest to a
second deeper col then rappel or climb down on the L side and
traverse on this flank below the 2 prominent towers immediately
after the col. Continue, crossing ribs and couloirs until a line of
chimney-cracks slant up easily to the R for 50m to gain the gap
behind the second tower (4hr).

On the ridge above is a step with a fine vertical chimney
containing 2 huge chockstones. Ignore it and climb round the step
on the R making a short hand traverse (V) to a dièdre which is
climbed to the top (20m, IV). Follow the ridge for 10m to a little
gap and climb out by a strenuous crack (V). Climb easy slabs on the
L side to a spear-shaped gendarme.

Either cross the ridge below this and follow an exposed ledge
on the Nantillons side for 30m where one can climb up a series of
cracks and blocks to the gap behind the gendarme (IV−),or climb
directly up slabs on the N flank to the gap, negotiating a small
overlap (IV/V−).

Now make a rising traverse on the N flank for 40m to a large
chimney that leads back to the ridge (III). Climb a cracked wall (IV)
and descend slightly to a narrow stance on the Nantillons side.
Cross the vertical and exposed R wall (V) to a small foothold and
pegs, then rappel and pendulum into the bed of a couloir which is
climbed to a stony terrace. Climb steeply up cracks and chimneys to
the R (IV, poor rock) to below the final buttress. On the N side, but
close to the crest, climb a crack to a niche (35m, V). A short pitch
leads up R to the crest (V−) and a sloping stance below a smooth
and exposed slab which is undercut at the base. Using a rurp or
shoulder to start, climb boldly up and over a smooth bulge until a
terrace is reached after 12m (VI. exposed). Go up R over easy slabs
to the NW summit tower which can be turned on the R or climbed
(III) to reach the normal route. 8–10hr from the Col de l'Etala.

**176**    **NORTH FACE**

TD

**66**

W Merkl and W Welzenbach, 30 June–1 July 1931 (lower half),
5–9 July 1931 (upper half). Direct Route: A Heckmair and G

Kroner, 31 July–1 Aug 1931. Winter: G Abert and O Challéat, 10–13 March 1974

*The first ascent of this elegant and beautiful face, overlooking the Mer de Glace, was a long and sustained epic in atrocious weather. In the upper section the party traversed across the the foot of the long narrow ice couloir issuing from a point slightly L of the summit and climbed the pillar to the L, making an exit onto the upper part of the NE ridge (IV, mixed).*

*Nowadays parties follow the direct finish up the steep ice couloir taken on the second ascent. Due to the low altitude very icy conditions are required and the face is frequently attempted in winter when the lower section gives magnificent ice climbing up a series of runnels free from the stonefall that often threatens during the summer months. Good bivouac sites can be found in the boulders below the Thendia glacier or at the foot of the large spur (2395m) forming the Rhand boundary of the face.*

From Montenvers follow the path S but instead of descending the ladders to the Mer de Glace, continue traversing on a faint track at more or less the same level (the recent land slip may have altered this significantly) until it is possible to go directly up steep grass and scree to the E branch of the Thendia glacier. Cross this, ascending slightly, to the foot of the face (2½hr).

Cross the rimaye and climb a huge cracked groove that cuts the L side of the initial rock wall (IV). After 2 pitches climb diagonally L towards the Aig de la République, getting further away from the groove, until a series of ledges is reached ⅔ of the way up the lower section of the face where the angle eases. Slant up cracks and ledges on the R to the foot of the large ice slope (3–4hr).

Climb straight up the 50° icefield to the foot of the steep ice couloir splitting the top section of the face. Climb this directly taking the main L branch where it splits and exit on the NE ridge (65°, Scottish 4). Follow the ridge, turning 2 pinnacles on the S side, to the summit. 900m, 10hr from the foot of the face.

**177**    **BOUCHARD ROUTE**
ED2    J Bouchard and S Zajchowski, 7 Aug 1975

**76**

*This modern route on the L side of the N face involves difficult rock climbing to start and finishes via a very narrow ice gully that is harder than anything on the Dru Couloir. It is not that often fully iced and very cold conditions are required to avoid stonefall. There have been several winter ascents.*

Start directly below the couloir that descends from the brèche immediately R of the Cornes de Chamois on the NE ridge. Climb up R to reach the main system of cracks and chimneys. The first 20m are VI after which 3 more pitches of V lead to the snowy section of the couloir. Go up this for 200m (50°) and near the top break out R on ledges and climb a short corner that is 20m to the R of a huge dièdre. Climb a flake and chimney above (V) to a couloir that leads to the central icefield. Go up its L side (50°) to the exit couloir. 4 steep pitches (Scottish 4) lead to the crux, a 60m section of goodScottish 5. A mixed pitch, then 2 more on rock (V) lead to the NE ridge from where the summit can be reached in 1hr. 900m, 12–15hr

**178**     **NORTH-EAST RIDGE INTEGRAL**

TD–     P Allain and Y Feutren, 3 Aug 1937

**45**

*A long and classic mountaineering route which despite some excellent climbing on generally sound rock has been somewhat neglected in recent years. A number of variations are possible in both the lower and upper sections, which reduce the difficulty. See also Photo 66*

From the Envers Hut traverse under the Trélaporte glacier to reach the Fenêtre de Trélaporte (2523m) in ¾hr. Contour round the N side of the Doigt de Trélaporte (c2548m) and climb a loose chimney-couloir (30m. III). Continue up easy ground for 400m (steps of III) to the base of Pt 3038m. Climb a couloir on the L, then the chimney-cracks that follow (IV+), finally passing under a large block to reach Pt 3038m. Make a short descent on the S side then turn the next gendarme to a gap. Follow the ridge until 50m below the Cornes de Chamois then turn these on the L by a good ledge line to reach the couloir coming down from the brèche between the Cornes and the Aig de la République. Slant up L to a secondary E ridge of the Aig (III, 3½hr).

    Go up this, passing over 2 or 3 small steps then slant L up a wall finishing via a short thin crack (15m, V). Step L and climb straight up (V, exposed) to a second buttress 15m high, which is climbed at first on the ridge (IV+) then by a short crack on the L (IV) followed by a dièdre (IV). In a further 15m there is a shoulder on the ridge below the steep walls of the Aig. Go L to a good platform between the wall and a huge block. Climb a large dièdre with a move R onto the ridge at one point to avoid a steep step. Return to the dièdre and climb it to a difficult exit on the L (V+). 2 short walls (V) lead to a block below some roofs. Make an exposed descending movement to the L using a crack (IV+) then traverse L and climb 3 short steps (the dièdre on the second is V) to reach the couloir descending from the Brèche de la République on the L. Climb it for 30m to the gap (4hr).

From here it is possible to reach the summit of the Aig de la République by Route 180 returning to the brèche (3–4hr). Now climb the first step on the NE ridge of the Grands Charmoz , keeping to the L of the crest for several pitches up a series of cracks (IV). Regain the ridge above the step and continue on the crest over several buttresses and gendarmes (pitches of IV) to join the main ridge between the 'Baton Wicks' and the summit. c900m, 10hr from the hut, not including the République.

| 179 | **EAST PILLAR** |
|---|---|
| D– | G Mallory and H Porter, 2 Aug 1919 |

**64**

*This little-known route gives a safe and interesting climb to the NE ridge, a little below the summit. See also Photo 45*

Follow Route 149 to the large scree terraces on a level with the col behind the Tour Rouge. Climb up to gain a secondary ridge that forms the R side of the couloir coming down from the Charmoz-Grépon gap. Turn the first step on the R and the second on the L then continue more or less on the crest, avoiding any serious difficulties by using chimney lines on either side. The ridge bends R towards the top and becomes more sustained at IV. Exit near the top of the NE ridge. 8hr from the Envers Hut.

| 180 | **AIGUILLE DE LA REPUBLIQUE 3305m** |
|---|---|
| D– | H Beaujard, J Simond, L Simond and A Tournier, 29 July 1904 |

**45**

*The summit block of this spectacular spire has not been climbed free and it was usual to perform difficult rope-throwing manoeuvres in order to effect an ascent. However in 1971 the S side was unfortunately equipped with expansion bolts which only real purists will scorn for the romantic novelty of a traditional ascent. See also Photo 64*

From the Envers Hut follow Route 149 to the large scree terraces on a level with the col behind the Tour Rouge. Go up R into a large secondary couloir and climb the slabs on the R, then the L side to where a series of ledges zig-zags up Rwards. Follow these to a point about 30m below the level of the Brèche de la République and traverse across to the couloir coming down from the brèche. Continue on the SE face passing behind a small pinnacle, and by a slightly descending traverse reach the E ridge of the République. Climb up onto the crest (IV) and follow it, climbing a crack on the

R flank, to a good platform. Climb the vertical buttress above by a thincrack and small pinnacle, then turn several blocks and climb a vertical wall by a thin crack on the R (4m, IV+). Continue up the ridge and climb the final block by a 12-bolt ladder (A1) to the summit (6½hr).

It is now possible to descend from the summit in 3 long rappels and gain the couloir below the brèche. Continue to the top of the Grands Charmoz via Route 178. 9–10hr from the Envers Hut.

# Pointe 3082m

This small pinnacle on the lower NE ridge of the Charmoz throws down an impressive pillar on the N side. The granite is not that good in places, slow to dry after bad weather and due to its orientation can often be grassy or lichenous. There is a comfortable bivouac site about 5mins from the foot of the climbs. The easiest descent goes down the NE ridge (sections of III with 2 rappels near the end) to reach the Fenêtre de Trélaporte. Continue down the couloir on the N side to reach the Thendia glacier and so regain the bivouac site.

**181**   **PETITE FUGUE**
V+/VI   C Carli and J Chassagne, 11–12 Aug 1982

**27**

This is a superb line marred by several loose sections. It starts in the small bay on the L side of the pillar. Slant up R to the crest of the pillar in the prominent red dièdre (8 pitches) then follow the crest for a further 13 pitches to the top (mainly IV/IV+ with 3 sections of V+/VI). c500m. See Photo 66

**182**   **ORIGINAL ROUTE**
VI+   P Brashaw and A Parkin, 15–16 July 1976

**27**

*This follows strenuous cracks on the L of the pillar, finishing at the brèche to the L of the Pt. Good climbing on mostly sound granite.*

Start in the small bay immediately R of the obvious rock scarand climb directly up a groove for 90m (VI/VI+ then V). Take a groove on the R to a ledge then go L past a flake to another groove/crackline and follow it to a flake ledge (VI+, 110m). Descend L to a small rib and climb it, followed by the chimney system above to a snow patch (160m, V/V+). Go up the cracks and the obvious corner above on the L to a zone of ledges (180m. IV and V). On the R take a crack system to a large bay (60m, V+) then slant R for 150m to an obvious pinnacle on the ridge (III with a little V). 16hr

## Pointe 3038m

The N face of this Pt is unfortunately split by 2 large ledge systems but has been climbed by several lines. Most of the rock is reasonably good.

**183**    **DALE-YATES ROUTE**
VII    C Dale and S Yates, 24 Aug 1985
27

This starts at the foot of the buttress halfway between an obvious monolithic corner and a sickle-shaped groove. Although obviously disjointed, there are some excellent and sustained pitches especially in the white corner. c500m, 9hr

The next few routes lie in close proximity above the Nantillons glacier and several can be climbed on the same day.

## Gendarme 2959m

This lies on the lower NW ridge of the Grands Charmoz about 150m S of the Doigt de l'Etala.

**184**    **SOUTH-WEST PILLAR**
V    F Audibert and Y Masino, 6 Oct 1966

*A short non-serious rock climb on excellent granite. It clears quickly after bad weather and is quite popular.*

From the Plan de l'Aiguille follow Route 133 to the Nantillons glacier and cross it to the foot of the face (1¼hr). Begin by climbing 1 pitch up the snow slopes on the L then slant up to a shoulder at the foot of the steep section of the pillar. Starting on the R side, via 2 pitches in a chimney (III), climb directly to the summit keeping fairly close to the crest at all times (IV and V with several aid moves near the top). 4hr from the Plan de l'Aiguille.

Descent: Rappel from the summit and go down the ridge to the Col de l'Etala.

**185** **ARETE DE L'ETALA WEST FACE**
V  E Masserey, T Jadod and J Savioz, 14 Aug 1974

*Another short rock route leading up to a Pt on the ridge about 80m R of the Doigt.*

Start up the couloir leading to the Col de l'Etala then traverse R on easy ground to a dièdre on the L of some smooth walls. Climb it and the system of chimney-dièdres that follow to the ridge (IV and V). 200m, 3hr from the Plan de l'Aiguille.

## Doigt de l'Etala 2850m

This small spike, just above the Col de l'Etala, can be climbed by a short artificial pitch from a good platform on the N side. Gain this platform by more or less following the ridge from the col (IV).

## Aiguille des Petits Charmoz 2867m

J Hutchinson, 18 Aug 1880

A very popular little peak and a good first route for novices. It can easily be combined with an ascent of the Aig de l'M from the Col de la Bûche.

**186** **TRAVERSE VIA AN ASCENT OF SOUTH-EAST RIDGE**
IV  M Pasteur, J Wicks and C Wilson, 5 July 1898

**67**

*A highly recommended little route which is extremely popular. The granite, though sound, is often very polished and the ascent to the Col de l'Etala provides a classic initiation into the delights of the typical 'Chamonix' chimney!*

From the Plan de l'Aiguille follow Route 133 to the Nantillons glacier and cross it to the couloir coming down from the Col de l'Etala on the R of the peak. Go up the couloir until it narrows and steepens to a rock wall split by chimneys. Climb the L hand set of chimneys (IV) then continue up a second (III+) and a third (III) to the Col 2786m (2¼hr).

Starting on the L go up the ridge (bits of III) to the foot of a buttress and climb it by a superb dièdre on the L (IV). Rejoin the ridge and follow the jagged, nearly level, crest on the Thendia side for a short distance until a little steep buttress leads up to the gap below the summit tower. Climb this just R of the crest (III) to the top. 3½hr from the Plan de l'Aiguille.

From the summit, descend a chimney on the W side for 15m (III) then working to the N descend more chimneys and traverse across the W face to the ridge. Follow it down to the Col de la Bûche from where it is possible to reach the summit of L'M easily in 15min. Descend the snow and scree couloir (keeping close to one side or the other to avoid stonefall in the bed) and near the bottom go onto the L side and climb down a series of ladders to reach the Nantillons glacier (1hr).

**187**    **SOUTH-WEST PILLAR**
V

E Cadet, B Delafosse, P Gillet and J Mansart, 31 Aug 1975. Winter: G Coutex, B Delafosse, J Mansart and D Potard, Jan 1976

67

*A short modern classic of medium difficulty which due to ease of access and orientation is possible with a lunch-time start.*

Start on the white-coloured rock to the L of the pillar by climbing blocks to a terrace. Move R and follow chimneys and dièdres to a huge grassy terrace (IV and V). More chimneys follow, again L of the crest (IV and V) until grooves and slabs on the R lead up to the crest. Follow it, slightly on the R side, to the SE ridge (III+) and continue along this to the summit. 200m, 5½hr from the Plan de l'Aiguille.

# La Brioche 2779m

E Fontaine, 1910

This little peak, almost a subsidiary of the Aig de l'M, lies in a surprisingly remote but very easily accessible spot E of the Col Blanc.

**188**    **SOUTH-EAST FACE**
IV/IV+

A McKeith and I Rowe, 13 July 1966

From Montenvers follow Route 176 towards the Thendia glacier then slant up steep grass and scree slopes, finally crossing snow, to the foot of the E ridge (1½hr). Go L round the ridge to the centre of the face below a large amphitheatre. Climb the prominent fault leading up to it (IV+). Traverse R below a narrow chimney then climb a steep slab (IV) and regain the fault. Continue easily until it bends L and splits into 4 cracks. Take the one on the L then slant up the steep slabs above (IV) to the ridge on the L of the amphitheatre. Follow this via an awkward crack to the main ridge and so reach the summit block. climb it on the W side. 3½hr from Montenvers.

**189**    **EAST RIDGE**
V/V+    E Ischwall and R Merle with A Contamine, 5 July 1953

66

*A classic little route which can easily be combined with an ascent of the Aig de l'M by the NNE ridge. It is however a harder proposition than the latter.*

Follow the previous route to the foot of the E ridge then starting 20m up on the R side climb onto the crest via a flake (III+). Above the point where the flake ends, climb a wall (V−) and the R hand of 2 wide cracks (IV) until it is possible to traverse L into a chimney-couloir leading up to an area of green walls split by some cracks. Take the vertical central crack (IV) avoiding the overhang by short steep walls on the R (V−) to a terrace below the central buttress. On the extreme R climb a flake (IV) and the crack above (IV+) before working L round overhanging blocks (IV+) to the upper terraces. Climb a huge couloir easily, then IV, to an obvious shoulder below the final step. There are several ways to finish but the best climbs a short dièdre then grooves on the R (V+) to the summit block. 350m, 6−7hr from Montenvers.

**190**    **NORTH-EAST SPUR**
IV/V    G Gesgeorges and B Germain, 1981

66

*An easier climb up the face to the R of the previous route. It is not very sustained.*

100m to the R of the E ridge, climb a short dièdre (IV) into an easy couloir. Follow it, then cross a secondary ridge on the L (IV) to reach the crest of the spur falling directly from the summit. Follow it (IV and V) to the top. c330m, 3hr

The spur to the R again was climbed by B Germain, Y Grenetier and X Neuville in 1984. c300m, III/IV

# Aiguille de l'M 2844m

Perhaps this is still the most popular peak in the Aiguilles. So called because of its shape when viewed from Chamonix, the L point of the M is the true summit and the R is named Pt Albert. There are now many routes, all well-equipped, which provide suitable venues for a short day or when bad weather puts many of the higher peaks out of condition.

**191**    **NORTH-NORTH-EAST RIDGE**
IV+/V–    F Batier, M and M Damesme and J Morin, 25 Aug 1945, though the
**68**    route followed today was first climbed by Contamine's party, 24
**28**    Aug 1948

*An interesting and extremely popular climb with a magnificently polished chimney pitch. It is an established classic of its genre.*

The route can be reached in equal time from both Montenvers and the Plan de l'Aiguille. Follow Route 133 from the Plan de l'Aiguille to the Nantillons glacier. Cross it, descending slightly to a couloir leading up to a col just R of Pt 2503m on the moraine ridge NW of Pt Albert. Cross the col and slant up scree and snow to the base of the NNE ridge (2hr).
    From Montenvers follow the path to the Plan de l'Aiguille and once round the Frêtes des Charmoz crest take a smaller track on the L then go straight up the cwm on scree and snow to the NNE ridge . 200m, 2hr

There are comfortable bivouac sites on the moraine below Pt 2503m.

**67**    Descent: Climb or rappel down the summit block (III) then go down the NE ridge for a little distance before slanting down R towards the Col de la Bûche. About ⅔ of the way down, go through a letter box and slant down under the S face of the col to the couloir. Follow Route 186 to the Nantillons glacier (30min).

Use the same approach as for the NNE Ridge. There are many short routes on this face which give generally strenuous crack climbing on excellent granite.

**192**    **MENEGAUX ROUTE**
VI+    J and S Ménégaux and J Poullain, Aug 1948

`68`
`30`

The most direct route to the summit taking the large dièdre on the L of a conspicuous pillar about 50m high. The difficult pitches were originally done on aid which remains in situ. 200m, 4hr

**193**    **COUZY ROUTE**
V    J Couzy and M Proust, 25 July 1952

`68`
`30`

This equally fine climb takes the dièdre line to the R finishing on the ridge to the R of the summit tower. As with the previous route the rock on the lower section can be slow to dry. There is one move of V+/VI−. 200m, 3hr

**194**    **GALBRAITH-MCKEITH ROUTE**
VI    M Galbraith and A McKeith, 16 July 1966

`68`
`30`

The slanting crack line to the R of the previous route. There is one short aid section. 180m, 6hr

## Pointe Albert 2816m

The Rhand of the two summits of the Aig de l'M.

**195**    **GHILINI-RATHEAUX ROUTE**
VI    R Ghilini and O Ratheaux, 26 Aug 1982

`68`

50m L of Route 196 is another line of dièdres. This gives some excellent crack climbing that is mainly V with 2 pitches of VI, the crux being a 30m layback. 220m, 5½hr

**196**    **WEST FACE**
V/VI    J and R Leininger in several instalments, Sept 1945

`68`
`30`

Several aid points allow this route to be completed at a fairly sustained level of V/V+. Some of the rock is a little suspect but the situations are tremendous and there is plenty of in situ gear, as traditionally this was the classic stamping ground of aspiring artificial climbers.

The climb starts almost directly below the summit in a 40m dièdre capped by a roof. c220m, 5hr. See also Photo 67

Descent: Rappel to the Brèche de l'M then slant down (or rappel) on relatively easy ground to the Col de la Bûche.

# Traverse of the Aiguilles

This is without a doubt one of the most magnificent undertakings in the Aiguilles with varied and enjoyable climbing on all sorts of terrain. The most aesthetic traverse which also offers the best climbing begins with the Grands Charmoz and finishes on the highest summit – the Aig du Midi. It is however a good two days' expedition whereas a very fast party can reach the Charmoz from the Aig du Midi in one day (though most parties bivouac). Many combinations and variations have been recorded including a complete traverse from the Aig de l'M to Mont Blanc.

**197    NORTH-SOUTH TRAVERSE**
TD/TD+  First traverse: S d'Albertas with A Ottoz, 14–16 Aug 1939
(Charmoz to Plan)

First reach the summit of the Grands Charmoz via the normal route, or, harder, the NW or NE ridges. Traverse this and the Grépon (Routes 168 and 146). Climb the Blaitière by Routes 112 or 113 and continue to the summit of the Fou via Route 105. Descend the SW ridge to the Col du Fou then reach the Col du Caiman either by climbing the Pts Lépiney and Chevalier or avoiding them on the Chamonix side. Rappel 50m on the Envers side and climb Route 95 to the summit of the Caiman. Continue via Routes 94 and 92 to the summit of the Crocodile. Traverse the Plan (Route 91) then reverse Route 18 to the summit of the Midi. Over 4km of ridge, 2–3 days

**198    SOUTH-NORTH TRAVERSE**
TD      First traverse: P Allain and G Poulet, 4–5 Aug 1945 (Plan to Grands Charmoz). Winter: no complete expedition but first

traversed from the Midi to the Blaitière by C Mollier and G Payot, 24–27 Jan 1964

*Less difficult, quicker and certainly more popular in this direction, though still not generally achieved more than two or three times a year. It involves a spectacular piece of rappeling on the Caiman.*

From the Aig du Midi follow Route 18 to the Plan then traverse the Crocodile and Caiman by Routes 91, 92, 94 and 96 to the Col du Caiman. Either climb the Pts Chevalier and Lépiney or turn them on the Chamonix side. Climb the SW ridge of the Fou (Route 106) and reverse Route 105 to the Blaitière. Descend Route 114 and reverse the Charmoz-Grépon traverse as far as the Grands Charmoz descending the normal route to the Plan de l'Aiguille. 1–2 days

# Aiguilles Rouges

Although not part of the Mont Blanc chain, this rocky crest lying between the valleys of La Diosaz and Chamonix is extremely popular with parties based in the latter. Access is easy via the Brévent or Flégère téléphériques and the views across to the N side of the Mont Blanc range are superb. The climbs are generally short, not serious and apart from early in the season do not usually involve crossing any snow. The S facing routes get a lot of warm sunshine and being low, clear quickly after bad weather. The rock here takes on a different form, and the climbing is more akin to limestone than rough granite. Although generally sound it can be rather friable at times. By taking an early téléphérique several routes can often be climbed the same day. Routes are often possible here when dubious weather or conditions put climbing on the Chamonix Aiguilles, for example, in question.

**1** **CLOCHER AND CLOCHETONS DE PLAN PRAZ 2428m**

IV  *A delightful little traverse giving good practice in a variety of chimney techniques and taking only a few hours.*

From the Plan Praz Téléphérique Station take the path in a NW direction and reach the col to the W of the Clocher in 1hr. One can climb this by the W face until it becomes vertical then traverse R onto the S face and climb a crack to the summit (III). It is also possible to continue directly up the W face via a strenuous layback on a detached flake (V). The N ridge gives an exposed, delicate pitch (IV+) and is also very worthwhile.

Rappel from a huge ring peg and climb over the Petit Clocher (III) to reach the first Clocheton. Climb it via the S face (20m, III+) and rappel to the foot of the second Clocheton. Climb it on the NW side (IV) and make a free rappel down the SE flank. The third Clocheton has a typically strenuous 'Chamonix' chimney on the W side (IV). Finish via the E face. Rappel down the W face and return via the foot of the N ridge of Le Clocher to the starting point.

# L'Index 2595m

An exceptionally popular little peak of sound but over-polished rock. It can be reached in a quick 10min sprint from the upper terminus of the Index télésiège.

**2** **SOUTH-EAST RIDGE**

IV  Agussol, H Benim, M Demesme, J and T de Lépiney, 16 Aug 1913

This is gained by following a grassy ledge across the E face to a detached flake and reaching the crest by a dièdre-chimney (IV). Unclimbable steps on the ridge above are turned on the R (III, sustained). 100m, 1½hr

Descent: Go down a ledge on the Brévent side then come back R to a small shoulder from where a long rappel leads to the Col de l'Index. Descend the tiresome rocky couloir or better the ridge on the L side.

# Chapelle de la Glière 2663m

**3**
**IV+**

**SOUTH RIDGE**

G Belin, G Bourasset, A Comte, J Engelmann, R Ratty and F de Sieyes, 20 Aug 1964

*This is one of the best routes of its class in the Aigs Rouges and affords delicate rather than strenuous climbing. It is continuously interesting and well sustained.*

Reach the couloir on the R of the ridge in ½hr from the upper terminus of the Index télésiège. Go up this for 20m then climb a dièdre on the L that leads to the top of the first step on the ridge (IV+). Go up for a pitch, climb a big dièdre (IV+) and continue up the ridge to the L side of a large smooth slab. Traverse horizontally across it (IV/IV+) and follow easy ground up R, cut by a short dièdre (IV) to reach the gap between the huge shoulder on the L and the Chapelle. Climb the latter, starting on the L side of the ridge (IV) and finish up the crest via a slab (IV+). 400m, 3–4hr

Rappel 20m on the far side, reach the Col de l'Index by a gentle scramble, and descend as for the Index.

# Aiguille du Pouce 2874m

This lies on the wilder N side of the main ridge line and is reached from the Index terminus by crossing the col to the N of the Aig de la Glière in 1hr.

The S face of this peak is one of the most impressive faces in the Aigs Rouges with many hard and attractive lines. The rock tends to be sound on the whole but becomes a bit broken on the easy ground just below the summit. Allow 6–8hr for most routes.

**4**
**VI/VI+**
**43**

**FRENCH ROUTE**

P Kohlmann, P Mazeaud and P Saint-Armand, 25–26 July 1960

This takes a direct line via the huge dièdre, well visible in the centre of the face. It gives a sustained succession of cracks and corners which have become very popular in their free form. 400m

**5** **POUCE CAFE**

VII R Ghilini, O Ratheaux and T Renault, 10 July and 4–6 Aug 1986

43

Some very fine climbing on the walls immediately to the R of the last route with an impressive Rwards traverse through the upper overhangs. 400m

**6** **VOIE DES DALLES**

VI– B Kintzele, R Mallon and J Marutzi, 2 Sept 1967

43

The best of the traditional routes on the wall, offering some extremely enjoyable slab climbing and an easy finish. 400m

## Aiguilles Crochues 2840m

**7** **TRAVERSE**

The traverse from S to N is a very pleasant scramble that can be started at the Col des Aigs Crochues. It is more interesting to climb the E face of Pt 2840m via a chimney system and Lwards slanting ramp (IV). Start by traversing R along a huge ledge situated about ⅓ of the way up the couloir leading to the col (1hr from the Index terminus). Reach the main ridge at a point to the S of the summit. At the end of the traverse descend the stony slopes to Lac Blanc.

## Aiguille de la Persévérance 2901m

Many consider this to be the finest summit in the Aigs Rouges. It is undoubtedly an impressive spire set in an isolated part of the chain and a fine viewpoint for gazing into the Argentière basin.

**8** **SOUTH RIDGE**

IV+ G Bicquelle, J Menegaux and J Poullain, July 1948

*The ridge rises in a series of 4 steps and can be joined (or left) below each.*

Reach the foot of the ridge in 2hr from the Index terminus, although it can also be reached via a steep walk from the Col des Montets. Avoid the first step on the L and slant up a terrace below the second. Climb to the L of the crest for 2 pitches via a chimney system (IV and IV+) then slant R up the second terrace and climb the third step just L of the crest (III). 3 pitches up the fourth step, starting with a chimney (III+), lead more easily to the summit. c300m, 3hr

**9**
IV+

**NORTH-EAST RIDGE**

A and G Charlet, 7 June 1925

*The final ridge, though short, has great character and is well* [...]
*between sunlight and shadow.*

Ascend the wide and generally snowy couloir on the R of the Aig Martin for 150m. Slant up L towards the couloir coming down from the Brèche de la Persévérance at the base of the NE ridge. Before reaching the couloir climb up short chimneys and pillars (III) to reach a platform on the SW shoulder of the Aig Martin and 10m above the brèche. Rappel to an imposing stance in the brèche then traverse L for 15m and climb a secondary ridge that leads back above the bulging walls overlooking the brèche (IV). Follow the broad ridge via a series of cracks and dièdres (IV+ then IV) to the summit. c300m, 3–4hr

Descent: Go down the W ridge (1 short rappel) to the Col de la Persévérance. One can now descend the couloir to the S but it is far better to continue over the Aig des Chamois (2902m) and go down to the Chamois cwm above the upper lake.

## Dalles de la Remuaz

There are a number of worthwhile and very well equipped climbs between grades IV and VI on this 120m high wall, reached in 1hr from Tré-le-champ via the Tour de Mont Blanc path. It passes the foot of the crag after a series of steep zig-zags.

## Aiguille Nord-Est de Praz Torrent 2473m

Reached from Le Buet by a delightful walk of 1½–2hr. The climbs described are on the SE face.

**10**
VI–
**44**

**PARAT-SEIGNEUR ROUTE**

J Parat and Y Seigneur, 1969

This climbs a rampline on the red rock of the L side of the face. Most of the necessary gear is in situ and the climb is not sustained at the grade. 250m

**CENTRAL PILLAR DIRECT**

11

44

M Piola and J Wintenberger, 1986 (start). Arrizzi and D Monaci, 1975

Basically a hard direct start to an older route. Good climbing but not homogeneous in difficulty. 250m

12

VI−

44

**VOIE DES DALLES**

A Loigeot and R Ravanel, 3 Sept 1973

Quite interesting climbing on the first section though not sustained. A direct start has been created at VII. 250m

Descent: easily along the ridge then down a couloir on the W side.

## Vallorcine Slabs

Marked Rochers d'Escalade on IGN. They lie midway between Vallorcine and Le Buet, and are reached in 20min from the latter. These give many 3 or 4 pitch routes of high quality in all grades. Rappel descent.

# Col de Talère to Swiss Val Ferret

## Col de Talèfre 3544m

First traverse: E Whymper with C Almer and F Biner, 3 July 1865

This is the easiest pass between the Triolet and Talèfre glacier basins. For a full description see Volume 1.

**1**
PD+

**1**

**FRENCH SIDE**

From the Couvercle Hut cross the glacier to the Jardin. Follow the moraine on the R side then cross the glacier to the base of the couloir coming down from the col. This is exposed to stonefall when not frozen and leads in 250m (45° snow/ice) to the col. 4½hr from the hut.

## Pointe des Papillons

Twin summits, N of the Aiguille Savoie, that are strictly reserved for lovers of solitude. The N summit 3644m can be reached easily by following the ridge from the S summit 3633m. Exposed scrambling on shattered rock. 30min

## Pointe des Papillons: South Summit

**2**
PD+

**SOUTH-EAST RIDGE**

A Brun with A and J Ravanel, 11 July 1903

*The easiest and quickest means of ascent from the Couvercle Hut.*

Follow Route 1 to the Col de Talèfre and continue easily up the shattered rock ridge to the summit. 5hr

**3**
AD

**70**

**WEST RIDGE**

E Davidson and J Hartley with L Lanier; C Dent and J Maund with A Maurer, 1878

*Probably the most interesting ascent of this peak.*

Follow Route 1 to the upper glacial plateau below the Col de Talèfre. Slant L and take a short couloir leading to the snow crest on the W ridge. Follow this to the foot of the W peak and either climb over it or turn it on the N side. Continue along the ridge to the summit. 5hr

## Pointe des Papillons: North-West Face of North Summit

The foot of this steep icy face can be reached in about 3hr–3½hr from the Couvercle Hut by following Route 1 across the Talèfre glacier before slanting L under Pt 3118m.

**4**    **ORIGINAL ROUTE**
D–    R Gréloz, R Jonquière, C Rondet and L Valluet, July 1936

A central buttress falls directly from the summit. On the R side, 2 vague couloir lines separated by a rocky spur converge at mid-height. The line follows the Lhand couloir and continues to the summit ridge via steep but easy rock. 300m

**5**    **NORTH-WEST COULOIR**
TD–/TD    G Perroux and B Sanchez, 25 Sept 1980

**70**

*The very steep couloir on the NW face that lies between the rocky pillars.*

Climb the couloir for 4 pitches (55°) until it narrows. A steep pitch (80°) leads to a 40m vertical section. Above, 3 mixed pitches lead to the summit. 300m, 4½hr from the rimaye.

The first ascent party followed the ridge towards the Col du Piolet then made 8 rappels (pegs and slings in place) down to the Talèfre glacier. 2hr

## Pointe Isabella 3761m

I Stratton with J and P Charlet, 1875

A delightful glacial expedition and a popular outing from the Couvercle Hut. It can easily be combined with an ascent of the Aig de Triolet.

**6**    **NORMAL ROUTE VIA NORTH-EAST RIDGE**
PD    First ascent party

**70**

Follow Route 9 to the Col de Triolet then continue up the snowy NE ridge. A short and steep rocky scramble leads to the summit. It is also possible to climb directly up the rocks of the little N face. 4½–5½hr from the Couvercle Hut.

## Petit Triolet 3719m

An undistinguished summit that is easily reached by a short diversion from the Normal Route to the Aig de Triolet.

**7**
TD−

**NORTH COULOIR**
P Couval, Y Gilles and A Nicollet, 26–27 July 1975

*This superb ice route gives continuously interesting climbing and in good conditions, objective danger is negligible. It provides a fine alternative to the N face of the Triolet if the seracs on the latter are found to be in a dangerous state.*

The crux is the central section of the main couloir which gives 3 pitches of delicate mixed climbing up to 75°. Finish up a narrow couloir on the L of the N spur. 700m

**8**
D
**NORTH SPUR**
C Dufourmantelle, C Jaccoux and M Lenoir, 6 Aug 1958

The crest of the spur to the L of the previous route gives mixed climbing on inferior granite. Rock pitches up to V−. 700m

## Aiguille de Triolet 3870m

J Marshall with U Almer and J Fischer, 26 Aug 1874. Winter: R Lambert and W Marquart, 25 Feb 1934

A fairly remote summit which is rarely ascended for its own sake. Its N face, overlooking the Argentière glacier, is one of the most famous in the Alps.

**9**
PD+
**NORMAL ROUTE FRENCH SIDE**
T Maischberger, H Pfannl and F Zimmer, 27 July 1900

*Although most often used in descent, this is a highly recommended expedition with a long but interesting glacier approach and a very fine finish. In less than perfect conditions it will be hard for the grade.*

From the Couvercle Hut, cross the glacier to the Jardin and follow the moraine on the E side to the top. Head for the base of the spur (3063m) coming down from the Aig Chenavier, turning a crevassed section on the L. Swing round to the R and by a short snow slope reach the crest of the snow ridge that descends from Pt Isabella. This marks the S edge of the Courtes glacier above Pt 3401m.

Follow the crest to the plateau and move L to gain the Col de Triolet (3703m, 4–5hr). In descent and during poor visibility, the top of this ridge can be hard to locate and a common mistake is to drop too low on the plateau before reaching it.

When the glacier below the Courtes is badly crevassed, it is possible to climb the broken rockwall R of Pt 3401m. Reach the snow ridge at the first group of rocks above its base.

From the Col de Triolet, traverse the R (S) flank of the Petites Aigs de Triolet to reach the Col Sup de Triolet (3767m). Cross a snow slope on the N face until a steep chimney (III) leads to easy rocks and the summit. 6hr from the hut, 4hr in descent.

**10**  **NORMAL ROUTE ITALIAN SIDE**
PD+  First ascent unknown. The Col de Triolet was reached from the Italian side by A Reilly, E Whymper with M Croz, M Payot and H Charlet, 8 July 1864 during the first traverse

*The safest route from the Italian side but very rarely climbed.*

From the Triolet Hut, follow the path to the lateral moraine and continue along this to the flat plateau of the Triolet glacier. Work up the Triolet glacier keeping near the rocky flanks of Mts Rouges de Triolet. Ascend the snow slopes and easy rocks directly below the col. Join the previous route and follow it to the summit. 5hr from the hut.

*Aiguille de Triolet continued on page 125*

# Aiguille de Triolet: North Face

This magnificent and imposing ice wall has an average angle of 53° and is easily reached in 1½hr from the Argentière Hut by a straightforward walk up the flat and generally uncrevassed glacier.

**11**  **ORIGINAL ROUTE**
TD–  R Gréloz and A Roch, 20 Sept 1931
**69**

*One of the most famous ice climbs in the Alps and an established classic. It gives sustained, interesting, though rarely very steep, front pointing and over the years has become quite a popular undertaking. It has also become something of a yardstick for comparing standards of lesser known faces throughout the Alps. The overall difficulty can vary from year to year and is determined by the state of the seracs. At the time of writing these are rather dangerous and make the ascent a very serious proposition.*

Starting well to the L, slant R on the lower slopes (50°–55°) and pass between the 2 rock buttresses. Work R up a series of crests and gain the L edge of the hanging glacier either by a steep ice pitch on the L of the serac barrier, or a mixed traverse across the rock that lies above and to the L of this pitch (Scottish 3). Follow the shelf R for 250m (30°–35°) and either climb directly to the gap between the Petites Aigs de Triolet (50°–55°), or cross back above the upper serac barrier and climb the ice slope to the Col Sup de Triolet. Follow the Normal Route to the summit. 6–9hr

| | |
|---|---|
| **12** | **DIRECT FINISH** |
| TD | A Contamine and L Lachenal, 13 Sept 1947. Winter : first ascent of |
| **69** | the N face was completed via this route, by P Desailloud, 8–9 March 1972 |

The takes the most aesthetic line on the face, following the steep couloir between the second serac barrier and the rocks to the L. It is 200m high with an average angle of 57° and gives 4–5 pitches of Scottish 3 and 4. On the final rock wall a small mixed couloir to the L of the Normal Route can be followed to the summit ridge. Serious, 750m, 7–10hr

| | |
|---|---|
| **13** | **NORTH SPUR** |
| TD+ | H Bachli, H Horisberger, C Jager and M Marchal, 7 Aug 1967 (after |
| **69** | fixing ropes on the ice field). Winter: C Bonington and D Haston, 11–14 Jan 1975 |

*A serious mixed route which has received few ascents. There are sections of poor rock and the lower half of the face is exposed to stonefall. Despite this drawback, the line is elegant and the difficult pitches occur on relatively sound granite making this route an obvious target for winter alpinists.*

Climb the ice slope to the foot of the spur (55°). Climb the first mixed section on the R (IV) then return to the crest and follow it for several pitches (III) to the foot of the 200m high pillar of red granite. Turn the first step on the L side (IV) then climb a crack (V) before moving L on icy slabs to easier ground (III). Climb a shallow groove on the R to a small shoulder (III) then follow a short chimney (III), crossing over the crest to reach a small terrace and the only good bivouac site on the route. Follow the R side of the crest for 1 pitch (IV) then move L and climb a loose overhang (A1) to regain the crest. Follow it for another pitch (V) then slant R (A1) to some slabs. Cross these (V) to reach an icy couloir. Slant up R on icy rock (III and IV) to gain a notch in the summit ridge. Follow the crest easily (II) for 100m to the highest point. 15–18hr

**14**  **VIA NORTH FACE OF BRECHE DE TRIOLET**

D+  R Desmaison and Y Pollet-Villard, 19 June 1960. Winter: T Leroy and D Marquis, 27–28 Dec 1975

**69**

*A very fine ice couloir with few ascents to date. It is a serious proposition as the easiest way off is to follow the NE ridge over the summit of the Triolet – a long climb on rock that is often of poor quality. Only when the face is well-frozen, will the stonefall danger, normally occuring later in the day, be negligible. See also Photo 74*

The couloir has an average angle of 54° with the steepest and narrowest section near the base (70°). The brèche can be reached in c4hr. Follow the crest of the NE ridge towards a large red buttress. Turn this, using a ledge on the S side, to an icy couloir and climb this for 60m to the top. Follow a rocky ridge which forms the R side of the large couloir descending to the Pré de Bar glacier and rejoin the NE ridge. Continue up this ridge over 4 gendarmes, to the summit. 450m for the couloir, 750m to the summit, 8hr

*Aiguille de Triolet continued*

**15**  **SOUTH-EAST (MONTS ROUGES) RIDGE INTEGRAL**

AD+  M de Benedetti with A Ottoz, 5 Aug 1933

**74**

*Were this route in less isolated surroundings, it would by now be a classic of its grade. It gives a long, splendid rock climb on excellent granite and has received few ascents.*

Follow Route 10 to the upper plateau of the Triolet glacier below the Brèche des Mts Rouges. This lies just N of Pte 3432m on the Mts Rouges ridge. Climb the couloir, or the easy rocks on the R side, to the brèche (2½hr). This point can also be gained from the Pré de Bar glacier via a short ascent of an atrocious piece of rock!
    Follow the ridge directly along the crest. The first gendarme is climbed by a long crack (III). The second has a dièdre, capped by an overhang, which is entered via a smooth slab (IV). The third, a huge buttress, presents 3 pitches of III, starting up a slanting crack. Continue up the ridge easily for about ½hr then follow a ledge onto the R flank. Climb through a magnificent letterbox and head directly to the summit. c500m, 7½ hr from the hut.

# Monts Rouges de Triolet

This rocky crest, over 2km long, has many middle grade rock climbs of between 20–25m on its SW flank.

# Aiguille Rouge de Triolet 3279m

This is the distinctive summit above the Triolet Hut and lies at the S end of the Mts Rouges ridge. The traverse, which begins just behind the hut, is a delightful excursion. The correct route is none too obvious.

**16**    **SOUTH-WEST RIDGE**
AD–/AD   Miss Jones and H Jones with H Brocherel, 24 Aug 1910

*An enjoyable rock climb on good granite.*

From the Triolet Hut follow the track towards the glacier for 200m then work up R to a snow patch below shiny slabs. Slant up a ledge on the R to some terraces. Now work up L on smooth slabs to reach the bed of the couloir which comes down from the gap between the main summit and the SE peak (3228m). The bounding ridge of this couloir on the L side forms the SW ridge of the main summit. Reach a brèche below this ridge via smooth slabs and traverse L to the ridge. Follow the R flank and reach a wide couloir of excellent granite which is followed to a shoulder on the main ridge, just S of the summit. 4–5hr from the hut.

**17**    **DESCENT BY NORTH-WEST RIDGE AND WEST FACE**
PD   Descended by the same party (Route 16) after the first ascent of the main summit

*Quick, but the correct route is difficult to follow.*

From the summit go down the NW ridge to the gap between the Aig Rouge and Pt 3261m on the Mts Rouges ridge. Descend a huge couloir on the SW side, climbing down smooth rocks and ledges to a narrow section. Go down this and as soon as possible break out R on some fine slabs to reach, lower down, a sandy area. Cross a spur on the R and reach a snow patch (cairn) below a smooth rock buttress. Follow a series of sandy ledges Rwards to a spur that leads easily down to the Triolet glacier. Descend the moraine to the hut. 2hr

**18**   **SOUTH SPUR OF POINTE 3228m**
V    P Ferraris and G Glarey with U Rey, 30 Aug 1958

*Pleasant climbing, though not sustained at the grade.*

From the Triolet Hut follow the track for 50m towards the glacier then work up the slabs that form the base of the S spur. There are a few interesting pitches broken by grassy sections. In the upper half and to the R of the large couloir descending from the gap between the 2 summits, the crest becomes steeper. 3 pitches of IV lead to a terrace and although it is possible to escape L from there, it is better to move R where a section of excellent climbing, with some aid moves, leads to easier ground.
    From the top of Pt 3228m reach the main summit by following the R side of the rocky crest, avoiding several small gendarmes. c600m, 4hr from the hut.

## Brèche du Domino 3575m

**19**   **SOUTH SIDE**
AD    E Fontaine with J Ravanel and L Tournier, 24 June 1904

**74**   Follow the track from the Fiorio Bivouac Hut Nwards onto the Pré de Bar glacier. Go up this, passing just L of the rocky island 3188m. Cross the flat plateau and go up the steep snow slopes, on the L of the S ridge of the Pt du Domino. Reach the rocky barrier and climb it easily on broken rock for about 100m to the brèche. 3–3½hr from the hut.

**20**   **NORTH SIDE**
TD    J Charlet and D Ducroz, 6 July 1979

**69**   A steep ice climb (75°) with a difficult mixed finish on poor rock (V/V+). Very snowy and well frozen conditions, that would generally be found in the spring, are recommended to render this climb in condition and free from stonefall. 500m

## Pointe du Domino 3648m

E Fontaine with J Ravanel and L Tournier, 24 June 1904

The most important summit on the frontier ridge between the Triolet and Dolent. The N side, above the Argentière glacier, offers some excellent ice/mixed climbing. Due to its ease of access from the Argentière Hut it is probably climbed as much in winter as in summer.

**21** **SOUTH-WEST RIDGE VIA BRECHE DU DOMINO**

AD First ascent party

**74**

*This is the only easy route to the summit but is climbed less often than those on the N side. See also Photo 73*

Follow Route 19 to the Brèche du Domino then continue up the frontier ridge, climbing a gendarme to reach the summit. 4–4½hr from the Fiorio Hut.

**22** **PETIT VIKING**

TD– B Cormier, D Radigue and S Tavernier, 12 April 1984. Winter: B Balmat and V Banderet, 14 Feb 1985

**73**

The NW couloir, steep at the bottom but easing towards the summit, has quickly gained a certain popularity. It gives an enjoyable 10-pitch climb with ice up to 80°. 500m, 5–6hr

**23** **NORTH-NORTH-WEST SPUR**

D+ J Charlet and G Rébuffat, 12 June 1945. Winter: M Geddes and B Hall, 23–24 Dec 1975

**73**

*An elegant and appealing line giving interesting mixed climbing.*

Climb the snow slopes in the centre of the lower buttress. Higher, these narrow to a steep couloir which is followed directly to the ridge on the L. Continue over a gendarme to a col and follow the mixed ridge less steeply to a second col below the steep upper spur. Climb some cracked slabs and slant R up a snowfield to the base of a couloir 200m high leading up to the summit. First climb the L side for 30m then cross to the Rhand ridge which is followed throughout. Turn a final buttress on the R side to reach the top. 600m, 6hr

**24** **DESCENT ON NORTH SIDE**

**73**

The most commonly used descent from the summit is to make 7 or 8 rappels down to the first col on the NNW spur. From this point a couloir on the W side can be down-climbed to the Argentière glacier. 3hr

**25** **NORTH COULOIR**

TD– M Marchal and R Messner, 27 July 1969. Winter: A Burgess, C

**73** Hubler and A Rouse 27–28 Feb 1979

The wide and steep ice couloir on the L of the NNW spur is almost 400m high with an average angle of 57°. A direct start over the rimaye wall, close to the rocks of the spur, is more difficult than an ascending traverse from the foot of the Col du Dolent. There is some risk of stonefall, though in well frozen conditions this should be minimal if the L side of the couloir is followed. At the top traverse R and climb steep mixed ground to the summit. c500m to the summit, 5hr

**26**    **NORTH-EAST RIDGE**
D    R Jonquière with M Bozon and F Ravanel, 27 Aug 1929

**73**

*A short rock route in a magnificent position that is seldom climbed.*

From the Col du Dolent, follow the ridge to the base of the summit block of a huge gendarme. Either turn it by a rising traverse on the L side, or climb it starting by a slanting crack and exposed slab on the L flank (V). A short rappel leads down to the gap beyond. Continue up the ridge to an overhanging section and turn it on the R to reach a large chimney (IV). This leads back to the ridge a little below the summit. 2–3hr

# Col du Dolent 3490m

First traverse: E Whymper with C Almer, F Biner and M Croz, 26 June 1865

Situated between the Pts du Domino and Pré de Bar. The first traverse from S–N was an historic occasion.

**27**    **NORTH-NORTH-WEST (FRENCH) SIDE**
D    W Davidson and J Hartley with J Jaun and L Lanier, 2 Sept 1878

**73**    using the rocks on the L side (which can be used for rappel anchors in descent). Winter: O Challeat and B Germain, 7 March 1973

A steep ice couloir which, though of classic status, is seldom climbed. Average angle 55°, 300m, 3hr

**28**    **SOUTH-EAST (ITALIAN) SIDE**
PD–    First ascent party

**74**

*Short and straightforward with some stonefall danger.*

129

From the Fiorio Bivouac follow Route 19 across the Pré de Bar glacier and climb the snowy couloir and rocks on the R side to the col. 4hr from the hut.

It is also possible to climb the rocks on the L, below a small col just E of the Pt de Domino. Traverse R near the top to reach the Col du Dolent. This is more difficult but sheltered from stonefall.

## Brèche de Pré de Bar

**29**    **NORTH SIDE**
D

J Batkin and Y Kollop, 14 July 1960

**71**

Similar to the Col du Dolent but with several steeper pitches (60°) in the upper section. The most practical descent is by rappel, although the S side is relatively easy. 350m, 4hr

## Pointes Supérieur de Pré de Bar 3658m

E Fontaine with J Ravanel and L Tournier, 23 June 1904

This is an almost horizontal ridge with 4 spikey summits. The N side is seamed with buttresses and couloirs. Most of the obvious lines have now been ascended.

**30**    **NORTH-WEST COULOIR**
ED1

J Charlet and R Ghilini, 10 May 1979. Winter: V Banderet, J Bovard and X Bongard, 10 March 1985

**71**

*This exceptionally steep and narrow couloir falls from a tiny brèche just E of the main summit. As with most of the routes on this side, the accepted and most practical means of descent is to rappel back down the line of ascent. See also Photo 73*

Climb 150m up the couloir of Route 29 then climb the thin couloir line in 10 pitches. It is generally 60°–70° with a difficult mixed pitch low down and several vertical sections above (Scottish 5). Rock protection is not that easy to arranged. c550m, 10hr

**31**    **MADNESS TRES MINCE**
ED2

E Carquillat, J Delettre and G Perroux, 8 May 1980

**71**

This is technically the most difficult route on the wall, taking the thin couloir L of the previous climb. It is reached, after climbing a few pitches at the start of the steep upper section of Route 30, by a rising snow ramp. It is rarely in condition and gives sustained vertical ice pitches (Scottish 5/6). c550m, 10hr

## Mont Dolent 3823m

A Reilly and E Whymper with M Croz, H Charlet and M Payot, 9 July 1864. Winter: G Couchepin, O Dehms, J Sautier and R Schanze with M Crettez, 12 March 1911

An important geographical summit lying just SE of the junction of the 3 frontier ridges of France, Switzerland and Italy. The mountain has 4 irregular faces which provide high quality snow and ice climbs of all standards, and the view from the summit is both superb and extensive. The long and complicated frontier ridge from the Aig du Triolet was first traversed by P Merlin and P Desveaux, 26–27 Aug 1976.

**32**
PD
**74**

### SOUTH FLANK AND SOUTH-EAST RIDGE (NORMAL ROUTE)

First ascent party

*The only straightforward way to the summit and a very fine ski ascent early in the year. The slopes can be dangerous after heavy snowfall.*

From the Fiorio Bivouac Hut, walk up to the Pré de Bar glacier. Work up the steeper slopes passing well R of Rognon 3188m towards a large snow saddle situated on the SE ridge. If the rimaye proves too difficult, it is possible to climb the rocks of the minor rock peak L of gap 3552m and traverse the peak to the saddle. Otherwise, reach it directly. Follow the ridge, keeping slightly below and L of the crest, to a loose easy couloir which leads up to Pt 3774m on the ridge. It is also possible to traverse round to the L below the buttress forming the true R side of the couloir into a snow/ice couloir which leads to the summit crest. Continue along the crest, in a fine position, to the summit. 4hr

**33**
TD–
**71**

### NORTH-WEST FACE

M Couturier with A Charlet and A Simond, 10 June 1934. Winter(and second ascent): J Belleville and G Glarner, 17–18 March 1973

*A very interesting but neglected climb up a series of icy grooves and runnels. Belays are good but cold and snowy conditions are essential to produce good climbing.*

Reach the foot of the wide couloir in 2hr from the Argentière Hut. Climb the initial couloir on the R to about ⅓ height and traverse L to a series of grooves that lead to an exit on the summit ice slope where the N ridge comes in from the L. Follow this on broken rock and snow to the summit. 8–10hr from the hut.

**34    POINTE 3534m WEST COULOIR**

ED1/2    J Delettre and G Perroux, 12 April 1980

**71**

This 9-pitch climb takes the line of the narrow couloir, well visible from the Argentière Hut, to an exit on the N ridge. There are many steep sections (Scottish 4 and 5) and a difficult pitch of icy rock (V/VI). Descent was made by rappel. The climb is seldom in condition. 400m, 8hr

**35    NORTH RIDGE**

D    G Bolaffio and J Kugy with J Croux and C Savoye, 25 July 1904

**72**

*The finest ridge on Mont Dolent and a classic expedition from the Argentière basin. It is a long and interesting mixed route with sound rock on the difficult pitches. The granite can be very shattered from time to time but the superb situation, high on the sharp crest dividing France and Switzerland, more than compensates. Serious. See also Photo 71*

Reach the foot of the couloir descending from the Brèche de l'Amône in 2hr from the Argentière Hut. The rimaye is often difficult but can be turned on the L. Climb the couloir to where it steepens into a huge dièdre, then exit R along a ledge. Climb a smooth slab (IV) followed by 50m of broken rock to rejoin the couloir. Above, the headwall is climbed by cracks on the R – a fine pitch of 25m (IV). (3hr)

Follow the ridge, at first on snow and ice then higher up some mixed climbing, to the summit. c600m, 8hr from the hut.

The first ascent party reached the brèche from the Swiss side. This is easier but far longer and more complex. Follow Route 36 to the base of the rocky spur, then climb it directly (II) to reach the N ridge about 200m above the brèche. 6hr from the A Neuve Hut.

**36    NORTH FACE DIRECT**

TD    L Dubost and L Gevril, 16 July 1950. Winter: J Baugey, J Belleville and J Dupraz, 16–17 Jan 1974

**72**

*This beautiful ice face, remotely situated above the A Neuve glacier, has received few ascents. The configuration of the serac barriers varies from year to year and no two parties have taken the same line. The average*

*angle of the face is not great nor the climbing sustained. Some objective danger from falling ice.*

From the A Neuve Hut cross the crevassed glacier to the foot of the spur coming down from the Col d'Argentière (2661m) and continue to the foot of the buttress descending from the Aig de l'Amone (2hr). Go up the glacier to the foot of the face and climb up it towards a rocky spur descending from the vicinity of the Brèche de l'Amone (2hr). In winter the ice wall to the L was climbed direct to the upper plateau (fairly straightforward but dangerous). In summer it is best turned on the R to reach the upper plateau which is crossed to the large serac barrier directly below the summit. Climb this (Scottish 5) and continue to the rimaye below the final 150m ice slope. Crossing the rimaye gives a steep and difficult pitch but thereafter straightforward front pointing (50°) leads to the summit. c550m, 9hr from the hut.

**37**  **NORTH FACE AND NORTH-EAST RIDGE**
D    J Belleville and R Devouassoux, 4 June 1974

**72**

An easier and often safer route which climbs a thin slanting couloir well to the R of the lowest point on the NE ridge (2665m). Gain the hanging glacier above and L. Climb this directly over the serac barriers to the easier-angled NE ridge and follow it to the summit. Ice pitches of 55°, c950m, 8hr from the hut.

**38**  **EAST RIDGE**
AD   By the route described: A Jacquerod and M Kurz with J Gabiou, 2 Aug 1907. The upper section, reached from the A Neuve side, had

**72**  been first climbed by J Gallet with J Balleys and A Muller in 1901. Winter: J Sanseverino, 4 Feb 1959

*A delightful, interesting and varied expedition, mostly on snow. Although considered of classic status, the climb has been somewhat neglected.*

From the Dolent (Maye) Bivouac Hut, ascend the Dolent glacier keeping close to the ridge. Either reach the ridge at a steep gap in the vicinity of Pt 3188m, or higher, at a prominent shoulder, below the upper section of the ridge (1½hr).
  Follow the ridge, on the broad glacier shelf to the R of the crest and climb directly up the final steep section (45°–50°) to the summit. 4½hr from the hut.

## Mont and Petit Grépillon 3534m and 3358m

Both summits, situated on the SE ridge of Mont Dolent, can be reached via easy snow slopes in 2hr from the Fiorio Bivouac Hut. The NE faces offer a number of 600m routes which, though highly praised by their originators, will only appeal to connoisseurs of decomposing rock.

## Aiguille de l'Amône 3584m

E Fontaine with J Ravanel, 28 June 1902

Situated at the end of the SE ridge of the Aigs Rouges du Dolent. It offers some fine little rock routes and a delightful N face, all rarely climbed.

**39**    **WEST FLANK AND NORTH RIDGE**
PD    First ascent party

**71**

*The normal route from France and the easiest means of descent. There is some stonefall danger in the couloir.*

Reach the foot of the couloir coming down from the col N of the Aig de l'Amone in 1½hr from the Argentière Hut. Climb the snow slopes and loose rock above to the col, then follow the N ridge on snow and rock, narrow at first, to the summit. 400m, 3¾hr from the hut.

**40**    **SOUTH FACE**
V/V+    G Bettembourg and J Charlet, 8 July 1973

**71**

*A lovely little rock climb of 250m*

Follow Route 39 and after climbing a short distance up the couloir, take to the rocks on the R side and reach a narrow icycouloir that comes down from a small gap in the ridge just S of the Aig. Climb it only a little way then come back L on easy ledges to the foot of a buttress. Climb this in 3 pitches (V and V+) then head directly to the summit over 2 buttresses (5 pitches; IV and V). 5–6hr from the hut.

**41**    **SOUTH RIDGE**
III    P Chevalier and G Labour, 1 Sept 1927

Another nice little rock climb following the ridge directly from the Brèche de l'Amône. There is 1 pitch of IV. 3½hr from the Brèche.

| **42** | **EAST PILLAR** |
|---|---|
| IV | I Drouot, T Girard and R Gréloz, 20 Sept 1942 |

**72**

The SE side of the Aig, directly opposite the N face of Mt Dolent, is reached in 4hr from the A Neuve Hut. This reputedly excellent little route takes the pillar immediately R of the central couloir splitting the face. 2½hr

| **43** | **NORTH-NORTH-EAST FACE** |
|---|---|
| D | R Gréloz and A Roch, 24 June 1935. Winter: J Belleville, J Dupraz and J Maruzzi, 13–14 Jan 1973 |

A very fine, rarely climbed and somewhat unusual ice face (average angle 50°) which takes the form of a huge L-ward slanting ramp. The central section is quite steep. c500m, 6–8hr from the hut.

## Aiguilles Rouges du Dolent

First complete traverse of both sections: M Blanc and W Widmer, 1935 (17½hr). Winter: G Formaz, R Mayer and J Troillet, 9–13 Feb 1975

This long ridge of imposing towers and pinnacles extends from the Brèche de l'Amone to the Col d'Argentière. It is usually considered in 2 parts. Pt Kurz (3680m) is the highest peak of the Grandes Aigs to the S, while Pt Morin (3592m) is the culminating point of the Northern or Petites Aigs. The traverse of the Grandes Aigs is a long expedition (AD, IV, 14hr round trip from the Argentière Hut). The traverse of the Petites Aigs is nowadays considered classic though very rarely done.

The faces and spurs rising from the Argentière glacier to the various summits of the Petites Aigs sport numerous short rock routes on good granite.

| **44** | **POINTE KURZ SOUTH-WEST FLANK NORMAL ROUTE** |
|---|---|
| PD+ | A Barbey, L Kurz with J Bessard and J Simond, 12 Aug 1888 |

*A distinctive summit and excellent viewpoint.*

Go up the glacier from the Argentière Hut and, passing either above or below Rognon 3041m, reach the foot of a couloir (1½hr). This couloir is situated to the L of a much larger couloir that begins some way up the face and leads to the S ridge quite close to the summit. Climb the L couloir to a chimney which can be hard if icy but is often a straightforward snow gully. Make an overhanging exit onto a snowy shoulder at the lower extremity of the much larger couloir mentioned above. Climb this and the narrow S ridge to the summit. 350m, 5hr from the hut.

**45**  **WEST RIDGE**

IV+  Probably: R Gréloz, J Grobet and F Marullaz, 19 July 1931

This climbs the ridge above Rognon 3041m, turning difficult buttresses and gendarmes on the crest, by their R flank. Not sustained. 500m, 5hr from the hut.

# Petites Aiguilles Rouges du Dolent

**46**  **TRAVERSE**

D–/D  First traverse: A Charlet and C Devouassoux, 4 July 1926

*An interesting expedition which perhaps due to its length does not appear to have gained the popularity it deserves. Although similar to the Grépon Traverse, it is not quite of the same quality nor as exposed.*

Follow Route 173 to the Col d'Argentière and continue up the NE ridge of Pt Morin to a short chimney. Climb it then follow cracks and a chimney on the L side (III) to the foot of the N pinnacle. Turn it on the L, cross a jammed block in the gap beyond and climb the ridge, using a long groove set between slabs, to the top (4hr).

Go down the L side of the SSW ridge to a gap, then make a short descent to another gap on the E side of Pt Dalloz. Reach the top by a series of steps (3575m, 10min). Go down broken rock on the S side to the Brèche de la Mouche then climb a chimney on the R flank to the Brèche de la Guêpe (¼hr). The small pinnacle of La Guêpe on the R can be climbed by a pitch of VI.

Rappel onto the A Neuve side then traverse 10m (III) to gain a large chimney leading to a gap (30m, IV). Climb the crack on the L to a platform (10m, IV) and continue up the steep but easy ridge to the summit of La Mouche (3567m, 1½hr). Rappel down the S side and continue to the next brèche (3509m, ½hr). Climb the crack on the far side (IV) then continue more easily, turning a tower on the L, to a broken ridge. Follow this and climb the steep rocks above by a chimney to the R of the highest (E) tower of Pt Lagarde, which leads to a gap bridged by a jammed block. Descend a little on the far side and traverse R to a narrow crack leading up to the NE ridge of the Pt. Climb the 6m crack (IV with some aid to start) and continue in an exposed position to the summit (3572m, c7hr from the Argentière hut).

Rappel back down the crack and continue down the SW side of the Pt to the Brèche Lagarde (c3540m). Descend the couloir on the R and continue down the Rouges du Dolent glacier. 10hr round trip from the hut.

## Col des Courtes

First traverse: G Moore with A Simond and E Payot, 26 July 1900

The lowest depression in the Arête des Rochassiers to the N of the Petite Triolet. The Talèfre side is an unpleasant couloir with much stonefall danger (AD). The Argentière side is a narrow ice couloir (400m, D) with a little stonefall danger. However it would be easier and simpler to climb the objectively safe open slopes on the L, to reach the ridge in the vicinity of Pt 3612m.

## Pointe 3608m

**47**
TD−
**70**

### SOUTH-WEST RIDGE
J Charlet and J Payot, 31 July 1946

*This is the well-defined crest to the R of the couloir descending from the Col des Courtes. The upper half gives great climbing with tremendous exposure.*

From the Couvercle Hut follow Route 9 to the foot of the ridge (2hr). Climb up to the L for 100m in a couloir of broken rock until it overhangs. Traverse R (V) then climb straight up for 80m to the crest. Follow this throughout in a superb position (pitches of V+). c300m, 7hr from the hut.

Descent: Follow the rocky ridge to the SE with no particular difficulty and join the Normal Route to the Aig du Triolet in ½hr.

## Col des Cristeaux 3601m

First traverse: J Withers with A Anthamatton and A Andenmatten, 25 Aug 1908

137

Between the Courtes and the Aig Ravanel. This offers the only recommended and relatively straightforward passage between the E and W sides of the chain.

**48**    **NORTH-EAST SIDE**

PD+    Descended by E Fontaine with J Ravanel and L Tournier, 11 July

**73**    1904

*In ascent, when the ground is well frozen, the route takes the straightforward 45° snow slope to the col. However a popular descent, for parties completing a route on Les Courtes and wishing to return to the Argentière Hut, is to take the broken rock ridge on the W side.*

The top of the rocky ridge lies just N of a small gendarme situated a few minutes along the ridge to the NW of the col. Descend the ridge, at first on rock then largely snow. Where it divides in the lower section, take the R fork and lower down move L onto the snow slope between the 2 ridges and descendit to the glacier. 400m, 2½hr

**49**    **SOUTH-WEST SIDE**

F+    Almost certainly early crystal hunters

**70**    *An easy but tedious ascent on loose broken rock.*

Follow Route 9 from the Couvercle Hut to Pt 3063m at the foot of the spur coming down from the Aig Chenavier. Climb a little way up the couloir on the R. Move R again onto the rocks just before they steepen into a wall flanked by a large rock pinnacle. Slant up R beneath the wall and continue in the same line up a snow slope, dotted with rock islands, to the col. 3hr, 2hr in descent.

# Aiguilles Ravanel 3696m and Mummery 3700m

2 beautiful spires, just S of the Col des Cristaux, which are generally combined in a traverse. They can be conveniently climbed after a traverse of Les Courtes, giving a splendid expedition at high altitude. Although traditionally classic and very popular outings, they have seen much less traffic in recent years due to the innovation of other short climbs, with easier access, elsewhere in the range.

**50**    **AIGUILLE MUMMERY EAST FACE**

IV+    E Fontaine with J Ravanel and L Tournier, 16 July 1903

*The normal route, via the gap between the 2 spires, gives a very fine
climb on excellent granite. There are some delicate moves in an exposed
position and the route is quite intricate.*

From the Col des Cristaux go up the main ridge to the foot of a
triple gendarme below the Aig Ravanel. Descend a loose chimney
on the R and the couloir below for 10m, before climbing some
cracked slabs up the W face of the Ravanel for 30m to an
overhanging block. Climb the 'Ravanel Slabs' above (IV), to a
chimney system which leads to a terrace (IV+). Reach the ridge on
the R and climb up and over a huge block (IV). A few m. above
traverse horizontally R to reach the gap between the Aigs Ravanel
and Mummery (IV. 1¼hr).

Reach the lower terrace below the NE ridge of the Mummery
by the N side of the ridge or a crack on the E face (IV). Climb a
short chimney on the L (IV) then cross L onto the E face. Follow a
ledge L to a flake then climb a vertical crack on the R (6m, IV).
Move L onto a narrow ledge which leads to the upper terrace. A
twisting crack leads to a steep slab and the final open chimney (IV.
¾hr). c100m, 2hr

Descend by making 2 rappels of 25m down the NE ridge to the gap.

**51**  **AIGUILLE MUMMERY SOUTH-WEST FACE**
V/V+  C Authenac and J Vitrier with F Tournier, 17 Aug 1942

**70**

*A strenuous, sustained and exposed climb of superb quality.*

From the Couvercle Hut follow Route 9 across the Talèfre glacier
and climb the R side of the couloir coming down from the SW face
of the Aig Mummery (2½hr). From the Col des Cristaux descend
the couloir mentioned near the start of Route 50 all the way to the
foot of the face (½hr). About 20m above and R of the lowest point,
climb a steep wall on poor rock (III, numerous crystals) and
traverse L to the top of a big crack. Climb the wall above for 1 pitch
(V) until it overhangs. Start this on the L, then slant up R of some
overhanging flakes (V) and climb a slanting crack in the slab on the
R to an easy ledge (IV). Follow this L and climb a 10m chimney.

Either cross a spur on the L and slant up a crack and the walls
above (III to IV+) to a platform, or move R and climb a big
chimney to the platform (V+).

Move up R onto the huge face and follow a long vertical crack
(V) and chimney above (IV+) for several pitches to a platform.
Climb up L on the wall facing the Ravanel for 1 pitch (III and IV)
then, either continue up the chimney line to the gap between a

gendarme and the summit (IV, but likely to be icy), or take the direct finish which climbs diagonally up R to a ledge (IV+) then directly up the front face to the gendarme (V+) starting with a crack on the L. Turn the gendarme on the R to the gap.

Traverse the L side of the summit block and climb it from the N. 200m, 5hr from the foot of the face.

| | |
|---|---|
| **52** | **AIGUILLE RAVANEL SOUTH FACE AND EAST-SOUTH-** |
| IV+ | **EAST FACET** |

E Fontaine with J Ravanel and L Tournier, 22 Aug 1902

*The normal route via the gap between the 2 Aigs and normally climbed after an ascent of the Mummery. See Photo 70*

Reach the gap via Route 50 (IV+). Above this the ascent is straightforward. Climb easy rock steps on the ESE face and turn an enormous cube of rock on the R to gain the summit. 100m; ¼hr.

**53**  **AIGUILLE RAVANEL NORTH-WEST RIDGE**
First descended by Miss Schoetlander, R O'Gorman and A Vitipon with J Burnet and J Ravanel, 2 Aug 1904

This is normally followed in descent, giving 4 spectacular rappels of 25m from the summit to the base of the triple gendarme. Traverse the latter and make a short rappel to the ridge leading to the Col des Cristaux. In ascent, the ridge has several good pitches of V on perfect granite.

# Les Courtes 3856m

First recorded ascent: H Cordier, T Middlemore and J Oakley Maund with J Anderegg, J Jaun and A Maurer, 4 Aug 1876. It is more than likely however that the summit had previously been reached by crystal hunters.

A beautiful and symmetrical mountain that is frequently ascended and generally traversed. The Argentière wall offers big ice routes of classic status which are now quite popular. Many consider the scenic panorama from the summit to be amongst the finest in the range.

**54** **TRAVERSE OF MAIN RIDGE**
PD+ WNW ridge: O Schuster and A Swaine, 17 Aug 1897. First descent
**77** of SE ridge: E Fontaine with J Ravanel and L Tournier, 11 July 1904

*The normal route and a classic expedition from the Couvercle Hut,*
*ascending the WNW ridge from the Col de la Tour des Courtes. The*
*standard is the same in the reverse direction but the slopes below the Tour*
*des Courtes can be dangerous in soft snow conditions and prone to*
*avalanche. Turning the Aig Qui Remue on the Argentière side is steep*
*and exposed. In anything less than good snow conditions it is hard for the*
*grade. See also Photo 76*

Follow Route 49 towards the Col des Cristaux and when well past
the Jardin, head towards the snow slopes below the Tour des
Courtes. Start well L on the slope descending from the Col des
Droites (3733m). Ascend this, working R towards the top under the
Tour des Courtes, to reach the upper part of the couloir below the
Col de la Tour des Courtes. Climb steeply up to the col (3720m,
4hr) and follow the fine snow ridge to the summit in 1hr. If the
ridge is corniced it is possible to use the rocky lip a few m down on
the Talèfre side.
    If this route is used for descent in the afternoon beware of
rockfall from the S side of Les Droites, some of which can be of
major proportions.
    Continue along the crest over the Aig Chenavier (3799m) then
descend a long chimney on the Talèfre side to the gap below the Aig
Croulante. Turn this on the R and the next gendarme, the Aig Qui
Remue (3724m) on the L (or climb them by their S faces, III and
IV). Then descend the broken rocky ridge, passing a small
gendarme, to the Col des Cristaux (2hr). Reverse Route 49 to the
Couvercle Hut (2hr). (It is possible to descend directly to Route 49
from the small gendarme). Allow 9hr for the round trip from the
hut. If an early start is made it is possible to include a traverse of the
Aigs Ravanel and Mummery which adds another 3–4hr to the day.

**55** **SOUTH-SOUTH-WEST BUTTRESS**
PD T Graham Brown and F Smythe, 10 Sept 1927

This is probably the most solid buttress on the Talèfre side, though
there is still a fair amount of broken rock. It gives a longer and more
difficult means of descent. However it might be worth considering
if an urgent escape is considered necessary from the ridge, in the
vicinity of the summit. 700m. See Photo 77

**56**

AD

73

**NORTH-EAST SLOPE**

P Chevalier and G Labour, 12 Aug 1930

*One of the most popular routes on the Argentière side and an excellent introduction to the bigger snow climbs in the area. It is essential to make a very early start as the sun hits the face at dawn.*

From the Argentière Hut, cross the glacier to the foot of the ENE spur (2940m) that comes down from the Aig Chenavier, in a little over 1hr. The slope is 48°, but eases in the middle 200m before steepening again below the summit ridge. From time to time the initial slope has developed difficult serac barriers and it has then been necessary to climb the ENE buttress on the L. 800m, 5–6hr from the hut.

**57**

AD

73

**CORDIER ROUTE**

First ascent party. Winter: J Georges and J Midière, 8–11 March 1974

*The original route of ascent to the summit but not nearly so fine as the NE slope. Although a safe proposition, it can, in dry conditions, develop into a long and tedious climb on very broken rock.*

Reach the foot of the broad buttress in 1hr from the Argentière Hut. Cross the rimaye below the snowy couloir that splits the L side of the buttress and climb up the rocks on the R side of this couloir for 10–15m. Cross the couloir and climb up alongside it until it is possible to gain the crest on the L (II). Now generally follow the crest, turning a prominent yellow tower on the L. Higher, it becomes less distinct and finally merges into snow. Climb up broken rock on the R and follow the final 50° ice slope to the summit. 850m, 6–8hr from the hut.

**58**

D

73

**NORTH-NORTH-EAST (CENTRAL) SPUR**

J Jonquière, A Maillol, M Villarem with E Frendo and A Tournier, 12 July 1939. Second ascent (via the red tower): R Guillard and G Rébuffat, 24 June 1943. Winter: A Fyffe and I Rowe, Feb 1972 (2 days)

*This is an elegant mixed climb that has gained increasing popularity in recent years. The inclusion of the red tower adds rock climbing appeal and a certain directness but it is arguably somewhat out of character and a little more difficult (D+/TD−).*

Reach the foot of the spur (2876m) in 1hr from the Argentière Hut. Climb directly up the crest from its foot or follow snow slopes on the L or R to reach the crest after about 100m. Continue up easy broken rock and mixed ground until level with the red tower in the middle of the face (3467m).

Either climb diagonally Rwards across a 55° snow slope studded with rocks, to gain a secondary snow ridge and follow this back to the main crest above the tower, or climb the L side of the tower at first by a system of cracks leading to a horizontal shoulder and then working L, using more cracks where the wall steepens, to the summit (V).

Follow the snow ridge and the final 50° ice slope to the summit. 1000m, 8hr from the hut (10hr with the red tower).

## 59    NORTH FACE – AUSTRIAN ROUTE

D+/TD–    H Drachsler and W Gstrein, Aug 1961. Winter: P Brient and J Gaboyer, 28 Feb–2 March 1968

**73**

*This is an interesting and sustained ice climb of classic status on the L (and slightly less steep) side of the face. The route is objectively safe and is considered by some to be of better quality than its more popular neighbour, though less difficult.*

Reach the foot of the face in 1hr from the Argentière Hut. Cross the rimaye to the R of the central spur and climb the ice slope above to a vague gully line in the first band of rocks. 3 steep pitches (Scottish 3) lead to another icefield. Slant R up this to a snow crest that is followed steeply into a wide couloir. Move R near the top of the couloir, breaking through another rock band (Scottish 2/3) to the summit ice slopes and join Route 58. 800m, 7–9hr from the hut.

## 60    NORTH FACE – SWISS ROUTE

TD–    C Cornaz and R Mathey, 31 July 1938. Winter: U Gantenbein and P Kung, 7–9 Feb 1965

**73**

*One of the most famous ice routes in the Alps and consequently a highly desirable prize. It is now possibly the most frequented climb on the whole Argentière wall. In good conditions (which are quite common) the objective danger is negligible and it is possible to use good rock belays for much of the time. Although the route as a whole is sustained at a fairly reasonable standard, the crux should not be underestimated. Average angle is 54°*

Reach the foot of the face in 1hr from the Argentière Hut and climb the 50° snow couloir on the R side of the face to the narrows at ⅓ height. 3 long pitches here form the crux and lead to a steep exit (Scottish 3 and 4, 65°–70°) onto the broad ice face above. This is

50° and is followed to the top where a Lwards traverse (60°) leads onto the vast upper slopes. Climb these direct (55°) to the summit or, if deteriorating conditions of either snow or party prevail, work diagonally R to join the snowy ridge of the upper WNW spur and follow it to the top. 800m, 8–10hr from the hut.

**61** **NORTH-NORTH-WEST SPUR**

D M Lenoir and Y Martenet-Guidet, 11 July 1961

73

The spur to the R of the previous route gives a steep mixed climb. There is some stonefall danger from the broken rock buttress in the upper half of the face. 750m

# Col de la Tour des Courtes 3720m

**62** **TRAVERSE**

TD– First traversed from N to S by climbing largely on the R side of the icefall: P Dilemann with A Charlet and J Simond, 20 July 1933

*A serious undertaking! Average angle 51°*

The S side of this col is taken by Route 54. The N side forms a chaotic jumble of serac barriers. The associated difficulty and danger varies considerably from year to year. 700m

# Col des Droites 3733m

First traverse: E Rochat with J Ducroz and C Ravanel, 9 Aug 1902

The traverse of this col was a fine achievement for its day and gives a worthwhile outing that is still only climbed from time to time.

**63** **NORTH SIDE**

D First ascent party. Winter: M Piola and B Weitlisbacher, 28 Dec

73 1975

There are a number of routes to the col from this side but the one taking the slanting couloir beneath the Tour des Courtes is recommended. The start, reached in 1hr from the Argentière Hut, lies just R of the base of the Col de la Tour des Courtes icefall. The upper slope, taken just R of the spur, is 300m high with an average angle of 48° and a steep exit is made onto the Lhand extremity of

the saddle. In good conditions the route is objectively safe. 700m,
5hr

**64** **SOUTH SIDE**

PD Descend directly, shortly joining the normal route (54) to Les

**76** Courtes. These slopes can be avalanche-prone in conditions of soft
snow. There is also some danger from rock falling from the S side of
Les Droites when the sun is on the face. 2hr to the Couvercle Hut.
See also Photo 77

# Les Droites 4000m

E peak: H Cordier, T Middlemore, J Oakley-Maund with J Jaun
and A Maurer, 7 Aug 1876. W peak: W Coolidge with C Almer and
son, 16 July 1876

A superb and complex mountain with a long crenellated ridge
connecting the 2 summits: W top (3984m) and E top (4000m). An
impressive sight from the Argentière Hut. The W and E peaks are
usually climbed independently and thus each summit and its
associated routes are described separately.

# Les Droites: East Summit

**65** **SOUTH RIDGE**

AD First ascent party. Winter: P Hardegg, H Hoerlin, M Fischer and E

**77** Schneider, 19 March 1928

*The normal route but a relatively serious proposition on interesting
terrain. In good conditions, such as would be found in early morning, or
when the couloir is incompletely filled with snow it is both quicker and
easier to follow Route 54 towards the Col des Droites, then slant up L to
reach the crest of the S ridge. This can often be quite prone to avalanche
and the original route described below is much safer and is especially
recommended for descent. See also Photo 76*

From the Couvercle Hut follow Route 1 onto the Talèfre glacier and
go up it passing to the W of the Jardin to reach crevassed slopes
below Les Droites (2hr). Cross the rimaye on the R at about 3390m
and climb the snowy couloir to reach the crest of the S ridge.
Continue up the ridge on broken rock to a steep wall (the alternative

route comes in here from the snow slopes to the R). Climb the wall on good rock and continue up the ridge to a snow slope. Follow this and the snow crest on the L to finish a little to the R of the summit. 6hr from the hut.

**66**    **DESCENT VIA SOUTH FACE OF BRECHE DES DROITES**
**77**

First descent: R Jonquière with M Bozon, 1928

*This is subject to stonefall and can be a dangerous business in summer. However it is descended quite frequently, and almost universally in winter, by parties completing an ascent of the N face.*

The couloir is 350m high and is rappeled to its base. Slings will be found in situ, generally on the R bank. Cross the rimaye and descend directly to the Jardin and thus to the Couvercle Hut.

**67**    **EAST PILLAR**
TD

**75**    M Kozlowski and J Kurczab, 27–28 July and 3 Aug 1967. Winter: E Belleemans and B Stroobant, Feb 1983

This separates the Lagarde Couloir from the hanging glacier falling from the Col des Droites and it is possible to escape onto the latter from the upper half of the route. The start is threatened by icefall from the hanging glacier. The initial section of the pillar, approached from the R, gives steep climbing (V and A1) on icy rock. The middle section, climbed close to the hanging glacier, is relatively straightforward but the final tower, climbed on the crest, gives 5 consecutive pitches of V. Seldom repeated. 950m

**68**    **LAGARDE COULOIR**
TD

**75**    B Arsandaux and J Lagarde, 31 July 1930. Winter (after fixing ropes on the direct start): W Cecchinel, G Crémion, M Flouret and M Marchal, 6–7 Jan 1973

*The ascent of this magnificent ice climb was a most impressive achievement and well in advance of its time. It established Lagarde as probably the best exponent of steep crampon technique in that era. A serious undertaking exposed to stone and icefall and now most commonly done with the direct start inaugurated during the first winter (fifth overall) ascent. It is rarely in good condition and despite the passage of time has achieved few ascents. Average angle 54°*

Cross the Argentière glacier to the toe of the NE spur (2790m) then go up the glacier bay on the L side to reach the rimaye to the L of the foot of the ENE pillar at c3000m (1½hr). A series of steep icy runnels leads up L for over 200m into the main couloir. These give continuous climbing of Scottish 4 with one 40m section of almost vertical ice.

Above, the R side of the wide couloir is followed to a steep mixed exit on icy rocks and a fine snow crest that leads to the summit. The rock walls in the couloir are smooth and seem most unhelpful in providing main belays. 8–12hr from the hut.

**69    EAST-NORTH-EAST (BERGLAND) PILLAR**
TD–/TD   E Lackner and R Messner, 25 July 1969. Winter: M Bena and J
**75**   Kuhlavy, Feb 1979

*This is the well-defined pillar to the R of the Lagarde Couloir. The route does not follow the crest unfortunately, but takes a line up the depression on its L side. Despite this the rock is good and the climbing completely free with very little snow or ice work in dry conditions. There have been few subsequent ascents but all have confirmed this route to be of very high quality and deserving a greater popularity.*

Reach the foot of the pillar, which is poorly defined at this point, in 1½hr from the Argentière Hut. Climb the couloir immediately R of the pillar for 3 pitches, then cross some difficult smooth slabs to reach a second couloir on the L. Climb this and the walls above the crest. This point can be reached with greater ease but loss of line, by taking the open snow slopes further R.

Climb the large couloir on the L to a vertical step. Move out L along a narrow crest for 2 pitches before returning R to reach the huge dièdre/depression between the main pillar on the R and a subsidiary pillar on the L. Climb cracks in the back for 3 pitches (steep but easier than it looks from below!) to the top of the subsidiary pillar. Now move up and L using some steep cracks to reach a couloir on the L side of the pillar. Climb the couloir, trending slightly L, to reach the start of the final ridge on the NE spur at c3800m. This point is just below the section of pinnacles connected by snow crests from where Route 71 is followed to the summit. 1050m, mainly III to V with one pitch of V+. 12–14hr from the hut.

**70    KOENIG-SUHUBIETTE COULOIR**
ED1    S Koenig and M Suhubiette, winter 1983
**75**

This couloir lies between the ENE pillar and the NE spur. It is exposed to stonefall and is rarely in condition. The cruxes occur on 2 rock steps 60m high and the climbing, in a very deep and austere gully, is direct and inescapable. 600m to the junction with the NE spur; 1050m to the summit.

**71**     **NORTH-EAST SPUR**

TD/TD+    C Authenac with F Tournier, 20–21 July 1937. Winter: M

**75**     Gryczynski, J Michalski, J Stryczinski and J Warteresiewicz, 7–11
March 1963

*A mixed climb of outstanding quality in a magnificent position. It is an
established classic with minimal objective danger and excellent stances/
belays. Although the difficulties are equally sustained on both rock and
ice, they are never very great. Cold conditions will render the upper part
of the route easier and the climb has become relatively popular in winter.
The difficulties increase markedly in this season and the lower section
gives a series of sustained icy runnels (Scottish 4/5) making the route a
lengthy undertaking. The climb is generally achieved with a bivouac
high on the spur though a fast party, finding good conditions, will
complete the route in a day.*

Cross the glacier from the Argentière Hut and enter the bay on the
L side of the spur. Go up to the first series of couloirs L of the spur
(1¼hr). The double rimaye can often be difficult and the initial
pitch in the couloir above (which overhangs at its base and is
climbed on the L or R) can be very hard and icy. Continue up sound
and water-worn rock in the bed of the couloir to the base of a small
gendarme on the L. Broken rock leads to the small gap behind the
gendarme. The crest above is followed for 50m before trending
diagonally R up broken rock and snow to the base of a long deep
couloir. Follow this to a conspicuous gap in the NE spur (Brèche
3384m, 3hr).

Climb the snow crest above to the foot of a bulge barring
access to an icy couloir. Climb this (awkward) and the couloir above
in 2 pitches (80m). Climb diagonally R on snow or ice for 30m to
where a couloir leads back L to the crest. Continue up the crest over
several short steps to the foot of a buttress of smooth slabs. Traverse
onto the N face along icy ledges to the foot of an obvious icy couloir.
Climb this and reach the crest via either a recessed overhang on the
L or steep ice to the R (c3575m).

Slightly on the R of the crest climb a chimney with large
overhanging blocks to a snowy platform. Climb some large broken
blocks for 20m, then traverse horizontally R along ledges and flakes
for 45m to the edge of a steep ice slope. Traverse horizontally across
the slope for 40m to some rocky outcrops then climb up to the foot of
a deep icy chimney. The chimney is very steep and can be
climbed direct or with variations L and R (this can constitute the
crux of the climb, and is at least Scottish 4). After 2 pitches, an

open area of easier snow and ice is reached, and a steeply rising traverse R leads to a gap in the NE spur below the final ridge (c3775m, 5–7hr). Although the climbing now becomes, thankfully, easier, there is still a long way to go.

Continue up the very fine ridge turning any obstacles by ledges on the L. The first group of pinnacles, connected by snow crests, is best avoided by a rising traverse across the N face. After the second group, avoided immediately below on the L side, a final snow crest leads to the summit. 1100m, 12–15hr from the hut.

## 72 NORTH-EAST SPUR DIRECT

TD+/ED1 J Droyer and C Gaby, July 1971, although the direct start had
**75** previously been climbed by C Deck and S Jouty as far as Brèche 3384m where the original route is met. Winter: P Grézat and C Vigier, 18–20 Jan 1976

*The direct start takes the crest of the initial triangular buttress avoided by the original route and gives a brilliant and sustained free climb on excellent granite. It is normally climbed over a period of 2 days with a bivouac in the vicinity of Brèche 3384m. which has the advantage of allowing the upper mixed section of the spur to be negotiated in the frozen conditions of early morning. This combination undoubtedly gives one of the greatest climbs in Europe.*

Reach the very lowest point of the spur (2790m) in 1hr from the Argentière Hut. Slant up R in a chimney couloir (III and IV) that leads to a large ledge and possible bivouac site. Follow the ledge R for 30m then slant back L on a conspicuous slabby ramp which starts as a short chimney (III and IV) and higher has a difficult overhang (V+). Reach some loose blocks on the crest of the spur. Follow the crest, climbing flakes and dièdres for 3 pitches (IV and V), until the ridge becomes smooth. Traverse R for 20m on a ledge then slant back L in a couloir-chimney (IV) to regain the ridge at a gap. Keep close to the crest for a few more pitches (IV and V) to reach a large terrace below a blank overhanging section. Either follow ledges L and climb an obvious dièdre in 2 pitches (IV+ to V+) back onto the ridge above the step, or move round the corner to the R and go up a dièdre (V+) returning L to the crest (V+). Continue along the ridge, crossing another gap and reach an obvious block split by a large smooth crack. Either climb it (V+), or turn it on the R and return to the crest as soon as possible. Carry on turning steps and towers by slabs (often icy) on the R side to reach Brèche 3384m (8–10hr).

Continue by Route 71 to the summit. 1200m, 16–20hr from the hut.

An ascent of this magnificent face was for a long time considered to be the hardest ice and mixed route in the Alps. Today the classic route is climbed quite frequently both in summer and winter, and is considered to be one of the best ice climbs in the world. Few parties try to follow the original line which climbed rock wherever possible, and there are now many routes and variations on the face that can be climbed entirely on ice. Ascents are made in all conditions but it is better and safer when very snowy. In dry summers the entry gullies onto the bottom of the face may almost disappear.

## 73 BARNOUD-MARSIGNY ROUTE

ED2 P Barnoud, B and F Marsigny, 31 Dec 1982 – 1 Jan 1983

**75**

A difficult climb on the far L side of the face that gave some very technical and sustained pitches at around 3500m. The route joins the NE spur about 100m below the summit and was completed in 15hr climbing time. 1000m

## 74 BOIVIN-GABARROU ROUTE

ED2 J Boivin and P Gabarrou, 2–3 Aug 1975. Winter: J Marie, J
**75** Normand, M Parmentier and M Roland, 22–26 Dec 1975

*A superb mixed climb and worthy companion to the classic N face route to its R. Complex route-finding with slightly harder and more sustained technical difficulty makes this a more serious undertaking than the latter. By finishing directly on the E summit, it is probably the most aesthetic line on the face and has been climbed as much in winter as in summer.*

From the Argentière Hut cross the glacier to the foot of the face in 1hr. The start lies c300m to the L of the Classic Route.

The initial slabs composed of smooth grey rock have a single crack line leading up to the icefield above. Climb this in 3 pitches (III, V and V+, A1). In very snowy conditions this has been climbed somewhere on the R where in winter some exciting pitches on poorly consolidated snow at 75° were encountered (bad belays and protection). Slant up the L edge of the main icefield beside a rocky rib to an excellent bivouac site at the foot of a large rounded buttress. Continue to the R of the buttress for 100m until it is possible to slant up a couloir on the L. After 50m work up R following a line of icy grooves for several pitches to a ridge. Follow this on mixed ground for 200m to reach the NE spur about 70m below the summit. All the steep headwall section above the central icefield is sustained at about Scottish 4/5. 1050m, 18–20hr from the hut.

**75**
EDI

## CLASSIC ROUTE

P Cornuau and M Davaille, 8–10 Sept 1955. Lhand (2nd) ascent: W Axt and W Gross, 24–26 July 1962. Winter: H Berger, H and J Muller fixed ropes to within 300m of the top, 23 Dec 1970–3 Jan 1971, reaching the top on 4 Jan 1971. The first continuous ascent was made by J Boulton and D Robinson, 2–5 Jan 1975

*This splendid undertaking of exceptional quality is one of the most desirable routes for high standard Alpine ice climbers, and is frequently ascended in both summer and winter. The line now followed is roughly that inaugurated on the second ascent, a more direct route to the L of that taken by the original pair. For most of its length the climbing is sustained at a reasonable level of difficulty, but the first 6 pitches of the steep upper headwall will always give hard ice climbing irrespective of the route taken. There is only one good bivouac site but good belays can invariably be constructed. In good conditions objective danger is almost negligible and the route can be completed in a day. It is best to climb the icefield at night in order to reach the headwall by dawn. Retreat in the lower section is possible by traversing R to the Couzy Spur and descending alongside this by rappel.*

From the Argentière Hut cross the glacier and reach the foot of the face towards the Rhand side (1hr). Cross the rimaye and climb a short snow slope to the base of a narrow couloir that slants up L through the barrier of rock slabs onto the central ice slope. Climb this in 3 sustained pitches (Scottish 3, 65°). It is also possible to climb the couloir that lies just to the L of the Couzy Spur then slant up L on an icy rampline with equal difficulty. Climb the central ice slope for 300m (50°) to pass just L of the obvious rock rib at the top and so reach the base of the steep headwall where the main difficulties begin. There is a good bivouac site at the base of the rock rib which is often used by winter ascent parties (c6hr).

It is usual to start the headwall c100m L of the rock rib and almost directly below the E summit. Climb steep ice-covered slabs and grooves for 2 or 3 pitches to a snow terrace (Scottish 4/5) then take the shallow couloir above which starts with 2 steep ice pitches (Scottish 4) then eases off to reach the large diagonal snow terrace that cuts across the face (c160–180m in all; good rock belays which can be difficult to uncover). The angle eases here and although there is no definite line of ascent it is best to work up R on mixed ground, then back L towards a fairly prominent buttress. Pass this on the L or R and climb the easier upper slopes to the crest of the NE spur, not far below the summit. It is also possible to traverse diagonally R along the snow terrace until a steep pitch (Scottish 4) leads into the easy gully that falls from the Brèche des Droites. 1050m, 15–20hr from the hut.

**76**    **BRECHE DES DROITES COULOIR**
ED2

J Ginat, G Modica, J Simon and J Troussier, 24 July 1978. Winter: A Long and M Piola, Feb 1980

[75]

*This is sometimes referred to as the Couloir Ginat and more often (incorrectly) as the Shea-Jackson Finish. It is the hardest of any finish on the upper wall but perhaps the most obvious, taking the line of the steep couloir falling from the Brèche des Droites. For over 400m the average angle is 61° but there are 2 manifestly steep sections where belays and protection are difficult to arrange.*

Follow the Classic North Face Route to the base of the rock rib. Climb up L alongside it to the very steep ice runnel in the corner above, that forms the lower continuation of the couloir falling from the Brèche des Droites. The first pitch is probably the crux and in all but perfect conditions gives a sustained lead of hard Scottish 5. Higher up the slope eases to 60° where the original route crosses, having climbed rock on the R. This point can also be gained by a traverse from the first snow terrace on the classic route. The couloir steepens to a second crux which gives another vertical section of hard ice climbing. The slope now eases progressively to the Brèche. 1050m, 15–20hr from the hut.

# Les Droites: West Peak

**77**    **WEST RIDGE**
PD

First descended by E Fontaine with J Ravanel and L Tournier, 15 Aug 1905

[76]

*The normal route and the shortest to the summit. Care is needed with large unstable blocks on the ridge and also in locating the correct route on the upper section.*

From the Couvercle Hut follow Route 81 towards the Col de l'Aiguille Verte. Cross the rimaye on the R and climb the couloir that lies further to the E and comes down from a point on the ridge just L of a slim gendarme below the Signal Vallot. Climb the couloir, passing the gendarme, to reach the Signal Vallot (3848m) and make a gently rising traverse across the Talèfre side passing well below the Tour des Droites. Slant across 2 narrow snow slopes to a rocky spur and after climbing up the latter for 50m, slant up R to reach some ledges just below the crest of the ridge and slightly E of the summit. Climb a chimney to the crest and follow it L to the top. 6hr from the hut, c3hr in descent.

**78**    **TRAVERSE OF MAIN RIDGE**
AD    First traverse: L Distel and H Pfann, 17 Aug 1904 (from W to E)

76

*This marvellous crest, connecting the 2 summits, is a serious undertaking that is rarely completed. Although difficulties are similar in either direction, it is safer to descend from the W summit later in the day than vice versa. Snow covering substantially increases the difficulty. This traverse of the mountain is a lengthy excursion that deserves greater popularity.*

From the E peak go along the main ridge to 2 rock towers. Turn them on the R side and descend the ridge to where it drops into the Brèche des Droites (3944m). Rappel 30m down a chimney on the L side of the ridge and traverse a few m below the breche to a system of steps that lead up to the crest above the gap. Continue along the ridge turning a number of sharp gendarmes on the R but keeping as high as possible. Move onto the L side, passing between the crest and a gendarme on this side before regaining the jagged ridge and following it to the W peak. 4hr

A most aesthetic traverse goes from the Col des Droites to theCol de l'Aig Verte but this requires an 18hr round trip from the Couvercle Hut.

**79**    **NORTH FACE**
ED2    J Boivin, P Martinez, C Profit and D Radigue, 26 July 1980

75

A number of routes have been done on the steep mixed ground to the L of the Couzy Spur. Perhaps the best, a difficult and serious undertaking, climbs directly up the ice slope just L of the spur and continues up intricate mixed ground (Scottish 4/5) to the L end of a conspicuous diagonal rampline. The ramp is followed up R to join the Couzy Spur about 200m below the W summit. 15–20hr

The diagonal ramp had previously been climbed by C Brooks and N Colton in 1977.

**80**  **NORTH (COUZY) SPUR**
TD  J Couzy and R Salson, 14–15 July 1952. Winter: P Aoki, T
**75**  Nakano, H Sekino and M Suzuki, 13–15 Jan 1973

*A slightly shorter but more difficult proposition than the NE spur of the E summit. The rock is generally more shattered and icy. In dry conditions the upper buttress gives sustained rock climbing with a fair degree of stonefall danger. In safer and snowy conditions difficulties on this buttress rise dramatically making this a good candidate for a hard winter ascent. Not having the quality of its famous neighbours, it has seen relatively little traffic. Ice pitches of 60°.*

Reach the foot of the couloir descending from the Col de l'Aig Verte in 1hr from the Argentière Hut. Climb it alongside the spur until it is possible to move L onto the crest. Follow this with increasing steepness (some pitches of IV) to the first buttress. Traverse R for 50m on ledges and mixed ground until the angle above eases and it is possible to climb directly up to the crest (IV and V) above the buttress (6hr).

Continue up the easy snowy crest to the upper buttress (moves of IV near the end) and climb it via a dièdre slanting to the R. A chimney pitch (V) followed by a rather smooth corner (IV+) leads to less steep rock on the R of the buttress. Climb directly up for a pitch then L across a smooth slab (IV) to reach the ridge at the top of the buttress. Follow the crest which soon fades into a steep wall of icy rock. Several difficult pitches lead to a 60m ice slope above which lie the final icy rocks. 1000m, 15hr from the hut.

## Col de l'Aiguille Verte 3796m

First traverse: G and G Gugliermina with J Brocherel, 24–25 July 1901. Winter traverse: J Sangnier, 19 March 1972

Between the Aig du Jardin and Les Droites. The col is divided in two by a large rock tower with 2 prongs, the 'Clochetons' (3857m and 3852m). Routes of ascent from either side normally lead to the eastern depression.

**81**  **SOUTH-WEST (TALEFRE) SIDE**
PD–  First ascent party
**76**  *Generally straightforward with 200m of climbing above the rimaye.*

From the Couvercle Hut head N over slabby rocks to the glacier. Go up in a curve alongside the foot of the Moine-Cardinal chain to below a thin snow/ice couloir coming down from the Rhand (E) gap in the Col de l'Aig Verte. Cross the rimaye (c3600m) and either climb the couloir or rocks on first the L then the R side, to the col. 3½hr from the hut.

**82**
AD+

**79**

## ARGENTIERE SIDE TO EAST GAP
First ascent party

A classic and straightforward snow climb taking the wide couloir that leads to the E gap. Average angle 52°, 800m

**83**
D+

**79**

## ARGENTIERE SIDE TO WEST GAP
In the main by J Sangnier, 1972. First complete ascent was made by J Mangeot with G Bettembourg; J Charlet with J Cuenet and R Ghilini, 20 July 1975

The narrow couloir leading to the W gap has an average angle of 56° with 2 very steep sections. There is stonefall danger throughout its length. See also Photo 78

# Aiguille du Jardin 4035m

E Fontaine with J Ravanel and L Tournier, 1 Aug 1904

An important summit situated at the lower end of the E ridge of the Aig Verte and usually combined with an ascent of the latter. A splendid viewpoint.

**84**
AD

**76**

## SOUTH-EAST RIDGE
First ascent party

*A good, classic excursion and integral part of the Jardin Ridge to the summit of the Aig Verte. Poor rock in the lower section gives way to fine, sound climbing in an excellent position on the summit ridge.*

Follow Route 81 to the rimaye below the Col de l'Aig Verte (2–2½hr) then climb the snow/ice couloir leading to the Lhand (W) gap. At ¾ height move L into a subsidiary couloir and climb it, easily at first, to a narrow chimney. This is steep with rotten rock (IV) and leads to the R (N) side of a gendarme on a secondary ridge separating the couloir from one further L. Climb this ridge on sound granite (III and IV), keeping first to the crest then slightly on the L side, to the main ridge. Continue up the crest over exposed buttresses and narrow snowy ridges until a small buttress leads to the summit. 450m, 6–7½hr from the Couvercle Hut.

*Aiguille du Jardin continued on page 157*

## Aiguille du Jardin: South Face

This face, characterised by 2 granite pillars that converge towards the summit, is reached in 2hrs from the Couvercle Hut.

**85**  **WEST PILLAR**

TD–/TD  J Bernezat, C Jaccoux and P Revilliod, 2 July 1964

*This is the large red triangular pillar with a second pillar above it, that lies on the R side of the couloir leading to the Col Armand Charlet. It is clearly visible from the Couvercle Hut. The climbing is very good and the rock excellent but it appears to be lacking in charisma to have attracted more than a handful of ascents. See Photo 76*

Cross the rimaye below the Col Armand Charlet and climb a snow slope for 100m to a pointed block below a depression in the face above. Climb directly up (III) then traverse R for 50m to reach a crack slanting R. Climb this (IV) to a large block forming a bridge. Take a series of cracks and dièdres (IV to V) on the L to reach the crest of a ridge on the L side of the pillar. Traverse L, climb a short overhang (A1) and slant R up a slab to a dièdre. Climb this (V) and the crack that follows (IV) finishing with a short delicate slab (V+) onto a small shoulder. Climb up snowy rocks to a small col below the upper pillar. Start this by an icy chimney (30m, V and V+) then continue via cracks and slabs (V+ then IV) to the top of the pillar and continue up the ridge (pitches of IV; often snowy) to the summit. 450m, 10hr

**86**  **CENTRAL PILLAR**

TD  E Birch and J Jordan, 2–3 Aug 1967

**76**

*This lies to the R and gives similar, though technically more difficult, climbing before joining the previous route near the top.*

Climb slightly R of the crest in a series of cracks and grooves for 100m or so (III and IV) to reach the base of a huge dièdre that splits the centre of the pillar. 4 pitches in the dièdre (fairly sustained at V and VI) lead to a good ledge on the crest. Continue up grooves and chimneys (V and VI with a little aid) until at about ½ height a traverse is made round the crest of the pillar on the R. After a further 50m (slightly descending) a line of cracks and dièdres slants up L in the wall above (150m, V/V+, sustained) to reach the crest of the ridge. Continue up, joining Route 85, and follow it to the summit. 450m, 18hr

---

*Aiguille du Jardin continued*

---

**87**  **NORTH-EAST SPUR**
TD  A Baud and D Mollaret, 4 Sept 1971

**79**

*This is a splendid route offering equal difficulties on both rock and ice. The climb as described takes the narrow couloir leading to the W gap of the Col de l'Aig Verte. The first ascent party were unable to climb this due to bad conditions and followed the long rocky ridge to the L (pitches of IV) traversing across the couloir for 100m when level with the base of the spur. Unfortunately in dry seasons the couloir is both difficult and dangerous and despite the excellent red granite on the spur the route has seen very few ascents. See also Photo 78*

Reach the base of the W couloir and follow Route 83 for c500m to the foot of the NE Spur slanting down from the summit of the Aig du Jardin. Climb the first buttress on the R side for 1 easy pitch then climb a slanting crack (IV+) and work up L for 2 pitches to the snowy crest. Move L and climb a steep couloir (60°) then take the Lhand of 3 chimneys back onto the crest of the spur (IV, strenuous). Go easily up the ridge for 30m then traverse across slabs on the L (III) to a long dièdre R of an enormous overhang. Climb it for 90m (IV+/V, strenuous). Turn the red tower above by mixed ground on the R (IV+) then traverse L climbing a short wall (A1) and snow to regain the crest. Traverse L for 2 pitches (III and IV) to reach the flank of a very narrow ridge with a prominent hole. Take the dièdre alongside the ridge (IV+), pass through a letterbox and climb an icy chimney, turning an overhang on the R, to reach the summit ridge. Follow this to the top where there are good bivouac sites. 1000m, 12–14hr from the hut.

## Col Armand Charlet 3998m

First complete traverse: P Béghin and T Leroy, 4 July 1973. Winter traverse: E Hanoteau and M Afanassieff, 25–28 Feb 1974

A delicate snow/ice crest between the Aig du Jardin and the Grande Rocheuse.

**88**    **SOUTH SIDE**
AD    E Thomas with J Knubel, 27 July 1927

**76**

*A steep snow couloir, not unlike the Whymper on the Aig Verte.*

It is essential to make an early start from the Couvercle Hut. The lower section is 40° but this steepens to nearly 55° at the top. The couloir is deep and is best climbed close to the R side. c400m, 4–5hr from the hut.

**89**    **NORTH-EAST SIDE**
TD–    P Dillemann with A Charlet and J Simond, 22 July 1932

**78**

An impressive ice climb and worthwhile challenge that has become increasingly difficult over the years. Only cold and snowy conditions will render the ascent safe from stonefall. The lower couloir leading to the W Col de l'Aig Verte averages 56° but contains several steeper sections. The broad upper couloir coming down from the Col Armand Charlet lies at a reasonable angle but gaining access can involve several very steep ice/mixed pitches. 1000m, 9hr from the hut.

## Aiguille Verte 4122m

E Whymper with C Almer and F Biner, 29 June 1865. Winter: G Hasler with C Jossi (by Whymper Couloir), 15 March 1903

Few of the great peaks in the Alps are more difficult or offer such a variety of long and serious mixed routes as the beautiful Aig Verte. Descent is often more difficult than ascent, and in bad weather escape from the clutches of the mountain can prove very problematical. Poor snow conditions have been the cause of many accidents and if embarking on one of the easier snow/ice climbs it is worth aiming to be on the summit at sunrise, where the party will experience one of the best panoramas in the range. Many of the routes stand as a tribute to the superlative icecraft of Armand Charlet, and the first ascent remains one of the most historic occasions in the Golden Age of Alpinism.

**90**     **WHYMPER COULOIR**

AD+

76

The first ascent of the route is unknown as Whymper traversed L out of the couloir at ⅓ height, but it was descended by R Fowler with M Balmat and M Ducroz, 17 Sept 1865

*The classic and most frequented route to the summit. Difficulties and dangers vary enormously and are minimised in cold snowy conditions. After 9am the couloir generally becomes very prone to avalanche and stonefall, so speed and fitness are of prime importance. It is thus recommended as a means of descent early in the morning or during late evening when the snow has refrozen. If arriving on the summit towards midday it is best to wait, if possible, at the Col de la Grande Rocheuse for the return of colder conditions, or take another descent route. The couloir steepens gradually and attains 55° for the last 100m. A serious route.*

From the Couvercle Hut head N over slabby rocks to the Talèfre glacier and go up it in a curve alongside the Moine-Cardinal chain until beneath the broad couloir coming down from the Col de la Grande Rocheuse (2hr). Cross the rimaye well to the R (often tricky) up against the rocks of the Grande Rocheuse, and go up a narrower secondary couloir (stonefall danger) parallel to and R of the main couloir. As soon as possible reach and climb the rocky crest on the L then traverse L across another couloir coming from the Grande Rocheuse to a broader snowy ridge on the R side of the main couloir. Continue up this and the main couloir to about 150m below the col where, if conditions are deteriorating, it is possible to traverse across to the L side and climb snowy rocks to the main ridge. A sharp and elegant snow crest leads up to the summit. 600m, 5–7hr from the hut.

In descent it is possible to make 12–14 rappels from in situ anchors down the rocks on the L bank. Thereafter a common mistake made is in not going far enough to the L (E) in the bottom section (allow 4hr to the hut).

**91**     **GRANDE ROCHEUSE BUTTRESS**

AD

R Fowler with M Balmat and M Ducroz, 17 Sept 1865

*This route is generally taken as a sure way up or down the mountain when the Whymper Couloir is too dangerous and the Moine Ridge too snowy to allow a comfortable climb. It is both steeper and more difficult than the latter. See Photo 76*

Climb up the first rocky ridge mentioned in the description of the Whymper Couloir then cross the couloir on the R and work up the sound rocks of the S buttress of the Grande Rocheuse. Having skirted 1 gendarme on the L, turn a second on the same side to reach the crest of the buttress and climb up it to the final steep step. Trend L up some chimneys then climb direct to the main ridge about 20m R of the summit. Cross the summit, descend a steep rocky ridge to the col then continue up the classic snow crest to the Aig Verte. 600m, 6½–8½hr from the hut.

Much safer though more difficult is to follow the crest directly. Start just L of the steep couloir leading up to the Col Armand Charlet then work up L on easy rock to a 40m chimney (III). Climb this and slabs above to the crest and follow it easily to join the route above (AD+, 7–9hr from the Couvercle Hut.

**92**    **MOINE RIDGE**

AD    G Hodgkinson, C Hudson and T Kennedy with M Croz, M Ducroz

76    and P Perren, 5 July 1865

*A classic mixed climb that becomes considerably harder under snowy conditions. After mid-season dry conditions make this the safest, simplest and most popular descent from the mountain when the Whymper Couloir is too dangerous.*

Follow Route 90 towards the Whymper Couloir and reach the base of the large rocky promontary at the lower end of the Moine Ridge. Up in the L corner of the glacier a snowy couloir, facing SE, slants R up the face. Reach the base of this in c2hr from the Couvercle Hut. Above the rimaye (c3480m) slant up L (almost horizontally L at first on easy ledges) towards a gap in the NE ridge of the Cardinal. Cross beneath a couloir 50m below the ridge, zig-zag up R and reach the crest at a small gendarme near the top of the snowy couloir. Go onto the R side of this secondary ridge on mixed terrain reaching the main ridge steeply at a small gap (c3800m). Continue up the ridge turning any difficulties on the R side. About 20m above an obvious pointed pinnacle regain the crest via a short chimney and follow the final snow ridge to the summit. c750m, 6–8hr from the hut in good conditions; c5hr in descent.

**93**    **Y COULOIR**

D    A Mummery with A Burgener, 30 July 1881. Winter: M Bertinotti and D Grevoz, 14–15 March 1971

*This obvious line on the SW (Charpoua) face offers a varied and interesting snow/ice climb. Unfortunately it is seriously exposed to stonefall and requires very cold and icy conditions to render a safe ascent.*

*Most of these have taken place during the night with a dawn arrival on the summit ridge. Fitness and speed are as important as technical competence. A serious undertaking.*

From the Charpoua Hut follow the crest of the scree ridge onto the glacier and go up it (badly crevassed) to the foot of the couloir (1½–2hr). Access to the couloir is barred above the rimaye by a huge rock wall and it is best to cross the rimaye at its L extremity and slant up R on the rocks of the Aig Sans Nom and Pt Croux to reach the snowy bed above this. It is also possible to climb tricky ice runnels in the rock wall itself. The couloir is set at a reasonable angle of 45° steepening to 50° in the L branch that leads to the summit snow crest. c800m, 7hr from the hut

The R branch gives a more direct and elegant finish but is more difficult (D+).

## 94   SANS NOM RIDGE

**D+**

**80**

G de Longchamp with M Bozon and A Charlet, 21 Sept 1926. The traverse the Aig Sans Nom and Aig Verte had been completed by R Broadrick and A Field with J Ravanel and J Démarchi, 24 Aug 1902 but they took a different route to the Aig Sans Nom. Winter: M Flouret and J Sangnier, 12–14 Jan 1971

*Undoubtedly the finest ridge on the mountain and one of the best of its type in the Alps. It is however a long, committing and serious undertaking which is not often climbed. The couloir leading to the Brèche Sans Nom is fairly safe in cold snowy conditions but otherwise it is seriously exposed to stonefall. A very early start is essential to complete most of this before dawn and to avoid a bivouac before reaching the Couvercle Hut. The W face of the Aig Sans Nom remains in the shade and gives strenuous climbing on excellent, if often icy, granite.*

The most expedient route up the badly crevassed glacier leading to the base of the Brèche Sans Nom Couloir varies from year to year and can take up to 2hr from the Charpoua Hut. Either a) climb the couloir directly (2–3hr); or b) after 100m climb out R crossing the ridge and continuing up the R flank by easy scrambling until ledges below a steep wall lead back into the couloir c200m below the top (2–3hr); or c) just above the level of the little rock rognon climb a large crack in the SSW spur of the Aig Sans Nom, then go easily up rock steps to the R flank of the ridge mentioned above. This method avoids most of the stonefall but can be difficult in the dark (3–4hr).

The Pic Sans Nom (3791m) can be climbed directly from the brèche. See Route 106.

Above the brèche is the triangular W face of the Aig Sans Nom, 250m high. Start 10m back down the couloir again, climbing a short overhanging chimney (III) and the slab above (IV) to a platform. From the Rhand end descend a few m and climb a chimney (10m, III) and the series of easy steps that follows for 40m, to reach a vertical wall split by chimneys not far from the L edge of the face. Traverse R round a ridge for 50m then climb a steep wall followed by 3 successive chimneys (IV then III, 50m) to a ledge below the fourth chimney. Traverse L and up a vertical wall (IV+) for 5m followed by a deep and icy chimney (20m, IV) to a stance L of an overhang. Traverse L across a slab (12m, IV) and climb a short chimney. Easy ground leads to a large rock on the ridge. Turn this on the R and continue to the summit block which is climbed on the L side (3–4hr).

Rappel down the wall facing the Aig Verte and continue along the ridge, turning a gendarme on the R by a rope move. Turn further obstacles by terraces on the R and continue along the snow/ice ridge to the gap between the 2 summits of Pt Croux (4023m). Climb the sharp crest to the snowy dome of 'The Calotte' and so reach the summit of the Aig Verte (3hr; all this section is delicate and exposed). 10–12hr from the hut.

This route has been used to extend the classic traverse of the Dru to the summit of the Aig Verte, first done in 1935 and, over a week in Aug 1973, continued to the Col des Cristaux.

**95**
TD
82

**NANT BLANC FACE DIRECT**

D Platonov with A Charlet, 22 Aug 1935. Winter:R Desmaison and G Payot, 4–7 Feb 1964.

*An outstanding mixed route, arguably the best on the mountain and undoubtedly one of the finest of its kind in the range. It is almost impossible to find the face in perfect condition; when the rocks are dry the lower slope will be hard ice, or if the slopes are straightforward névé the rocks will be verglassed and difficult. Winter ascents have normally had to contend with hard black ice. The lower section of the route is potentially exposed to minimal stone and icefall but this austere face receives little sun until late afternoon. See also Photo 81*

When approaching from the Grands Montets station, it is possible to make a reasonable bivouac halfway up the rognon at the foot of the rock spur coming down from Pt Farrar in the Grands Montets Ridge (above Pt 2989m). A very comfortable bivouac exists on top of the isolated rock rognon below the base of the rocky spur taken by Route 110.

Cross the rimaye (c3200m) and climb the initial ice slope (50°) to a narrowing at 200m. The slope steepens slightly and after 150m meets the foot of the rock band that supports the long rocky spur on the L edge of the upper ice slope. Slant up L to a small snow ridge and follow it to the L side of the rock band. Climb directly through this barrier in 3 or 4 steep and difficult pitches, then continue up the crest of the spur above, or the edge of the huge ice slope just to the R, to reach the snowy dome of the 'Calotte'. It is sometimes possible to avoid the serac barrier above on the L but it often gives a long and steep pitch. Cross a small rimaye (often quite hard) and reach the summit. Average angle 53°, 950m, 8–10hr from the rimaye.

**96**  **GRANDS MONTETS RIDGE**
D  P Dalloz, J Lagarde and H de Ségogne, 9–10 Aug 1925. Winter: F
82  Audibert and C Jaccoux, 9–11 Jan 1964

*This is a long, serious and classic expedition where one is unlikely to meet other parties. As far as Pt Farrar the rock is quite poor and the climbing can become a trifle tedious. Above, the granite is excellent and the quality of the climbing almost matches the superb situation high above the Nant Blanc and Argentière glaciers. The 'Calotte' is renowned for its potential to windslab avalanche and although it is usual to begin at the Grands Montets station, it is advantageous to bivouac in the vicinity of the Pt de Ségogne. This allows the final slopes to be climbed in the early morning when they are at their best and also avoids a late descent from the summit. See also Photos 79 and 86*

From the Grands Montets station follow Route 116 to the shoulder on the NW ridge of the Petite Aig Verte (½–¾hr). Go up for 100m then descend slightly to the R and follow a conspicuous series of ledges that lead across the Nant Blanc face level with the base of the gendarmes above. Keep alert as at one point a fairly obvious narrow couloir needs to be descended for 20m to a point from which it is possible to re-ascend the other side and continue traversing again at the same level. The ledge line disappears near Pt Farrar and it is necessary to climb some chimneys to the gap immediately to the N of this point. Turn it on the L and reach a gap below the Aig Carrée (3716m) where there is a good bivouac site (2–3hr). Climb a deep chimney on the N face (25m. IV) then continue up the R side of the ridge to the top (IV). Descend on the Argentière side keeping as close as possible to the SE ridge (short rappel to finish) and reach the first step of the Pt de Ségogne. Traverse L to a narrow vertical icy couloir and climb it by cracks on the R side (IV) to regain the ridge at a group of 3 small gendarmes. Turn these on the L (IV) and reach a gap below the second step. Climb a magnificent and exposed slab (IV+, sustained) and follow the easy ridge above to the summit of Pt de Ségogne (3797m). Rappel down the Argentière side and follow ledges across to the Col du Nant Blanc (3776m, 4–5hr).

Climb the steep snowy slopes of the 'Calotte', keeping on the L side, to the summit. 900m, 9–11hr from the Grands Montets station.

It is also possible to reach the ridge quite easily from the Argentière glacier by climbing a snowy couloir directly below the Pt de Gigord (3531m) and at ⅔ height slanting L on easy rock to a notch halfway between this and PtFarrar.

*Aiguille Verte continued on page 166*

---

# Aiguille Verte: Cordier Couloir

Situated on the NE (Argentière face). A very serious ice route which was an outstanding achievement at the time. Today the seracs on the Original Route have become far more complex and menacing. In the lower section there is considerable danger of icefall from the hanging glacier and stonefall from the rocky flanks to the R is not uncommon. A very cold night and early start are desirable.

**97**
D+/TD–  **ORIGINAL ROUTE**
H Cordier, T Middlemore and J Oakley-Maund with J Anderegg, J
**78**  Jaun and A Maurer, 31 July 1876. Winter: B Macho and D Marquis, 19 March 1973

The foot of the couloir can be reached from the Grands Montets station in 1hr or from the Argentière Hut via the foot of the NE spur of the Grande Rocheuse (good bivouac site) in 2hr.

Cross the rimaye (c3150m) on the R and slant up L into the couloir. After 300m it narrows and 3 delicate ice pitches (underlying rock) lead to an easing in angle where it is possible to cross the couloir and climb over steep bulges to reach the snow slopes below the 'Calotte'. Slant L to reach the snow ridge above the rock triangle on the NE face. Climb directly to the summit crossing or turning serac barriers and keeping alert on the upper slopes which are prone to windslab. Average angle for the most part of 55°. 1000m, 7hr from the rimaye. See also Photo 79

**98** **VIA COL DU NANT BLANC**
D   P Dalmais with A and G Charlet, 13 July 1935. Winter: M
[78]   Michellod and D Triollet, 19–21 Jan 1972

Instead of traversing L, climb directly up the R side of the couloir. It is possible to slant L high up to reach the ridge above the col. Follow Route 96 to the summit. This is technically easier and somewhat safer than the Original Route but still serious. 6hr. See also Photo 79

**99** **DIRECT ROUTE**
TD   J Boivin and P Gabarrou, 24–25 Sept 1975. Winter and second
[78]   ascent: G Comino, 12 March 1978

The upper section of the Original Route can be reached directly by climbing the steep ice couloir between the rock triangle and the rocky rib descending from the serac barrier. The last 120m give very difficult climbing on mixed terrain (60°–80°). Serious, 12hr

## Aiguille Verte: North-East Face Rock Triangle

A number of lines have been created on this 600m buttress which leads onto the easy upper slopes of the Cordier Route. Two are described below.

**100** **CLASSIC ROUTE**
TD–/TD   P Labrunie and J Martin with A Contamine and G Payot, 26 Aug
[78]   1962. Winter: E Chrobak, M Gryczynski, J Michalski, J Surder and
R Szafirski, 9–13 March 1965

*This is a fine safe route which gives difficult and often verglassed rock climbing. In snowy conditions it may be advantageous to bivouac on top of the Triangle so as to complete the upper slopes early the following morning. Easy access has ensured a number of winter ascents.*

From the Argentière Hut follow the main path W down to the glacier and cross it passing between the rock rognon 2866m and the foot of the NE spur of the Grande Rocheuse (good bivouac site). Traverse W in an arc to the lowest point of the Triangle in the centre of the face (3077m, 2hr). Or alternatively from the Grands Montets station descend to and traverse the Rognons glacier to the foot of the route (1hr).

Climb the R side of a couloir at the base of the Triangle for 100m then slant L and climb a chimney filled with blocks for another 100m (V). Continue up to a large smooth rock ridge and gain a huge dièdre on the L side (IV). Climb the dièdre for 200m then slant L across slabs to reach a small icefield (V). Climb up R and follow an icy chimney (IV+) to the ridge. Climb along the E flank of the ridge for 100m (IV and V). Reach the crest and follow it more easily (III and IV) to the snowy ridge below the slopes of the 'Calotte' (6–8hr). Climb directly to the summit, joining the upper part of the Cordier Route. 1050m, 9–11hr from the foot of the face.

It is easier if, after climbing the huge dièdre, the long couloir L of the ridge is followed rather than climbing up to the crest. The rock here is frequently poor but the overall standard is reduced to D+/TD–.

| | |
|---|---|
| **101** | **GABARROU-VOGLER ROUTE** |
| TD | P Gabarrou and R Vogler, 29–30 Aug 1981 |
| **78** | |

*This takes a parallel line L of the previous route. As with other variations on the flanks of the Triangle, the rock is not altogether sound in parts and an ascent under such very cold and snowy conditions such as are found out of the summer season would give a more enjoyable climb.*

The initial rock buttress is climbed almost directly via a system of cracks and couloirs in the upper part. Ice then mixed/rock climbing leads to the base of the large icefield high up on the L side of the Triangle. Climb the L side and the ridge above to the summit of the Triangle (15 pitches, sustained IV+/V with 1 pitch of V+, 11½hr). Finish up Route 100 to the summit. 1050m, 14hr from the rimaye.

---

*Aiguille Verte continued*

| | |
|---|---|
| **102** | **COUTURIER COULOIR** |
| D | Using the rocks on the L side of the Rock Triangle and finishing as |
| **78** | for the Cordier: B Washburn with G Charlet, A Couttet and A |

Devouassoux, 2 Sept 1929. First direct ascent of the couloir: M Couturier with A Charlet and J Simond, 1 July 1932. Winter: M Bertotto and A Bonomi, 26–27 Jan 1964

*An established classic. Although the easiest route on the Argentière face, it is the most aesthetic, taking the line of least resistance directly to the summit. The sun strikes the face very early and can sometimes produce avalanche conditions in the couloir, so it is worth climbing most of the route before dawn. It is thus a serious undertaking, despite moderate difficulties (51° for the first 200m, 55° for the next 300m and thereafter 45°) but one that is frequently accomplished. See also Photo 79*

Reach the foot of the couloir from a bivouac at the Grands Montets station in 1hr (beware serac falls from the Cordier Couloir when traversing the Rognons glacier). When conditions are bad in the middle section of the couloir, one can traverse R atc300m above the rimaye and take a snow band slanting steeply R across the upper section of the rock triangle. Finish up the snow slopes of the 'Calotte'. 900m, 4–8hr from the rimaye.

Near the top, the Bettembourg Finish, which lies to the R of Route 104, climbs 6 sustained ice pitches of 75° up the obvious narrow gully. Good rock protection, TD/TD+

**103**   **JARDIN RIDGE**
AD+/D–   First complete ascent: G de Longchamp and A Jacquemart with A
**80**   Charlet, 19 Aug 1926

*As with all routes to the summit of the Verte, this is a serious undertaking at high altitude. It is the longest route from the Couvercle Hut and although an established classic is not often done nowadays. Splendid situations and very varied climbing make this ridge second only to the Sans Nom. The most delicate section is usually the crossing of the exposed ice crest of the Col Armand Charlet.*

Follow Route 84 to the summit of the Aig du Jardin (6–7½hr). Continue along the narrow rock crest and down a snow ridge to Pt Eveline (4026m) then cross the long and very thin ice ridge of the Col Armand Charlet to the foot of a gendarme. Turn this by a rising traverse on the Talèfre face then continue up the mixed ridge to the Grande Rocheuse (2–3hr). Descend the steep rocky ridge to the col beyond and follow the exposed and often corniced snow ridge to the summit. 550m, 9–12hr from the hut.

## Aiguille de la Grande Rocheuse 4102m

Traversed when following the Jardin Ridge to the Aig Verte. See Route 91 for the easiest means of ascent. Descent can also be made via this route or the Whymper Couloir. The N face offers 2 magnificent climbs that have rarely been repeated.

**104**    **NORTH-EAST FACE DIRECT**
TD    P Bourges and R Mizrahi, 20–21 Feb 1975

**78**

This climbs the L side of the Couturier Couloir to gain a steep and shallow ice runnel leading to the summit rocks of the Grande Rocheuse. There are pitches of 70°–75° (Scottish 3 and 4) similar to the crux of the Swiss Route on Les Courtes. In good conditions there is no objective danger. 900m

**105**    **NORTH-EAST SPUR**
TD–    M Azéma and G Fraissinet, 12–14 July 1946

**79**

*A long and fairly interesting route with magnificent views across the N faces of the Verte and Droites. It is easier but similar in style to the NE Spur of Les Droites and 1 bivouac will generally be necessary.*

Reach the foot of the spur, above the rock rognon 2866m, where there is a good bivouac site (1½hr from the Grands Montets). 100m above its base slant L onto the ridge then follow the crest to the foot of the main step (III, 2hr). Climb this slightly R of the crest (250m, mixed, pitches of IV, 4½hr). Go up the ridge, turning or climbing a group of 3 towers, to the second step (1hr). Climb this on the R flank but near to the crest, on sound rock (IV). Continue along a horizontal section then turn 2 gendarmes on the R to a third steep section. Follow broken rock on the L side for quite a long way into a shallow couloir and where this becomes steep and narrow, climb a chimney (25m, V) back to the crest. The ridge now becomes broken. Work up L on mixed ground to reach the crest of the ridge that lies on the R side of the NE Couloir of the Col Armand Charlet. Climb this ridge and finally the summit of the Grande Rocheuse. 1200m, 15hr from the foot of the spur.

# Pic Sans Nom 3791m

E Carr, G Morse and J Wicks, 28 July 1890

A thumb of excellent granite situated at the end of the Sans Nom Ridge. The summit is rarely reached by any means.

**106**    **EAST RIDGE**
IV+    First ascent party

A short ascent from the Brèche Sans Nom. Climb the crest of the ridge directly with a 15m pitch of IV+ at ½ height. 65m, ½hr. Descend by rappel.

**107**  **NORTH-WEST FACE**
ED2  M Boysen and N Estcourt, 9–10 Aug 1967

82

*Hard strenuous rock climbing in a remote and harsh situation. Although there was considerable competition for the first ascent, it has subsequently received hardly any attention. Very dry conditions are needed to avoid verglassed rock as the face sees minimal sunshine.*

From the Dru Rognon climb the couloir leading to the Col des Drus but break out L early and slant up to a shoulder on iced-up rock (IV and IV+). Above, a very prominent chimney line leads up for nearly 300m to a small but conspicuous triangular ice slope. Climb the buttress on the L which has a hard overhanging crack to start (VII) but then continues more easily via cracks and chimneys to the ice slope (V and VI). Climb up L to a break in the wall above and follow it (V+) to reach the next step. Climb out L (V) and from a good ledge descend and traverse L to a crackline, climbing it (IV) until a tension traverse L can be made into a series of icy chimneys. Continue up these to the final block and climb it by a shallow dièdre (VI and A2). Slabs lead to the summit (IV). 800m, 20hr

**108**  **WEST PILLAR**
ED2  J Brossard and R Mizrahi, 14–16 Aug 1973

82

This takes a line parallel to the previous route. Start up the prominent chimney line but then break out R and climb a series of very sustained cracks and chimneys on excellent granite (V+, VI and A2, strenuous) before rejoining the NW Face Route at the final block. 800m

## Aiguille Sans Nom 3982m

Duke of the Abruzzi with J Petigax, L Croux and A Simond, 17 Aug 1898

An important secondary peak of the Aig Verte with an impressive N face overlooking the Nant Blanc glacier. The summit is rarely climbed for its own sake and is a serious proposition as, realistically, the easiest descent is to continue along the Sans Nom Ridge and over the summit of the Aig Verte. Otherwise reverse Route 94 which will generally require a large amount of rappeling.

**109**     **SOUTH RIDGE**
D          M Davaille and B Denjoy, 1–2 Aug 1955

*Although very rarely done, this appears to give an interesting but not sustained rock climb on excellent granite once the ridge is attained. The traverse across the S face is exposed to stonefall.*

Using alternative starts (b) or (c) in Route 94, reach the crest of the SSW spur of the Aig and traverse across the S face in a wide arc, slanting up R below an enormous gendarme, to reach the S ridge. Follow this, with a detour R at ½ height, to the summit (pitches of III and IV taking the line of least resistance). c750m

# Aiguille Sans Nom: North-West Face

*There are 5 climbs on this inspiring face overlooking the Nant Blanc glacier. All give difficult mixed climbing of high quality. Those on the L, whilst shorter and less sustained than the N face of Les Droites, are very similar in style though technically a little more difficult. Generally, objective dangers are slight and although there have been few subsequent ascents, this face offers some of the best ice/mixed climbing in the range.*

**110**     **BRITISH ROUTE**
TD+/ED1 J Brown and T Patey, 11 Aug 1963

82

*A varied and extremely interesting climb with some difficult icy rock in the upper section. The exit onto the ridge is 80m above the Brèche Sans Nom. See also Photos 81 and 85*

From the Grands Montets station reach the good bivouac site on the rocky island below the base of the spur in 1½hr. Climb the R flank of the spur by a chimney (III, poor rock) and reach the crest on the L after 100m. Climb the crest for 2 pitches (IV−). Turn the next section on the R returning to the ridge via a series of steep cracks (IV). 80m higher, turn a tower on the R via a letterbox then traverse easily below the crest to the large ice slope or take the smooth slabs above (short section of V) to the col below the ice slope (3½hr).

Turn the large seracs on the R and climb up the slope for 200m to the rocks of the Pic Sans Nom. Climb alongside these until 100m above the base of the couloir leading to the Brèche Sans Nom. Follow a band of snow R to a steep buttress on the L side of the couloir (3hr). Cross a steep icefield on the R (80m at 60°) to a small pointed flake in the middle of the wall. Climb the steep chimney above (45m, VI, icy). Continue up cracks on the L (15m, V). Traverse R and climb up to easy ledges (20m, V+). On the L climb a wide chimney for 100m (IV and V) to a shoulder and continue up a couloir of icy rocks for 60m to the ridge. Traverse R onto the W face and follow Route 94 to the summit. 1100m, 14hr from the foot of the face

## 111 DIRECTISSIMA

ED3  P Gabarrou and P Silvy, 5–7 Aug 1978

**81**

*This appears to epitomise the ultra-modern Alpine mixed route involving high standard rock climbing and hard serious ice work. Subsequent parties have confirmed this to be one of the finest and most varied routes they have ever climbed. Normally, the climbing will be objectively safe, belays are good and the technical pitches are well protected. See also Photo 82*

Start directly below the summit at a 300m high rock pillar with a shattered gully running up the R side. Start just L of this gully (stonefall) and trend L on mixed ground followed by slabs and grooves (45m, VI) onto the front of the pillar. Climb the shallow groove system above for 2 pitches (VII– then VI) and surmount an overhang (VI). Continue up slabs on dubious rock (VI, strenuous) followed by cracks and grooves (VI, A1) to the top of the pillar where there is a palatial bivouac site between this and the serac barrier (6hr, 7–8 pitches total). The difficulty of the serac barrier varies. Above, the ice slope is 50° then steepens to 60°–65° at the base of the headwall (300m). Traverse L for 3 pitches on a rampline below a very steep wall, then ascend loose flakes to an icy corner and climb it (Scottish 5/6) to a small ledge. Traverse 5m R and climb over a bulge into a shattered groove. Climb the groove and when it overhangs, the crack on the L wall (A1/A2). Surmount a bulge on the R and swing into an ice gully. Climb this for 4 long pitches (Scottish 5) then continue for a further 5 pitches on more open mixed terrain to finish just L of the summit. 950m, 18–20hr

1 rappel down the S face leads to a good bivouac site.

## 112 FRENCH DIRECT

ED2  J Boivin and P Vallencant, 3–4 Aug 1974. Winter: J Bolton and D
**81**  Robinson, over 6 days in late Dec 1975

*An excellent mixed route to the L of the Direttissima. Unfortunately the superb couloir at the start is threatened by ice fall from the serac barrier, though above this the icefield and sound granite headwall have little objective danger. See also Photo 82*

The initial couloir is separated from Route 95 by a snowy rock buttress. Initially there are thinly iced slabs (70°–75°). Thereafter the angle eases until a difficult ice pitch (Scottish 4/5) leads onto the large ice slope. Climb this for 300m (55°). To the L of the Direttissima a vague rocky spur descends into the ice slope. Climb up the L side and reach a terrace on the crest where there is a good bivouac site. The rock wall above is overcome using some icy cracks (V, mixed). Slant up L on mixed ground then follow icy chimneys and couloirs on the R through the second rock band (Scottish 4/5) to the summit slopes. Climb these in 5 tricky mixed pitches to finish just L of the summit. 900m, 16–20hr from the foot of the face.

## 113 NANT BLANC FACE – BRITISH ROUTE

ED1

82

G Cohen and R Collister, July 1976. Winter: R Turnbull and D Morgan, 1983

*This route is sustained at a reasonable level for most of its length. The initial rock buttress provides an alternative and by far the safest start, to other routes in the immediate vicinity. Cold and snowy conditions are a prerequisite for this climb. See also Photo 81*

Start on the L side of the snowy rock buttress immediately R of the start to Route 95. Climb the snowy ramp that slants up to the rounded crest on the R and follow this up and back L to the top (Scottish 3). Continue up the ice slope (50° then 55°) to the top L corner of a snow bay, R of a prominent pillar in the upper wall. Climb up the depression above to the R of the pillar (the first 6 pitches are Scottish 4 and 5) taking the line of least resistance until easier mixed climbing leads out onto the main ridge. 850m, 12hr

## 114 NORTH PILLAR DIRECT

ED1/2

See description

81

The N Pillar lies L of the upper section of the previous route and was first climbed in 1928 by A Charlet and C Devouassoux via a long diagonal approach from the couloir leading to the Col du Dru. On 10–11 Aug 1982 M Miller and S Richardson reached the crest of this pillar via the rock buttress start to Route 113 and after climbing some difficult iced-up cracks and chimneys (Scottish 5) reached the couloir on the L and followed it in 4 steep pitches (Scottish 4, then easier) to an exit just R of Pt Croux. This is probably the safest line on the face and has good rock belays throughout. 850m, 12–14hr

# Aiguille Carrée 3716m

This granite gendarme, traversed on the Grands Montets Ridge, gives a strenuous crack climb on the face overlooking the Nant Blanc glacier.

**115**
V+/VI
**82**

**WEST FACE**
E Martin with R Desmaison, Y Masino and G Payot, 17 May 1963

From the Nant Blanc glacier climb a mixed slope to the top of a narrow rotten rock ridge then traverse R to the foot of the Aig (1½hr). Climb 3 pitches up a dièdre (IV+) then an overhanging wall via a wide crack (VI with some aid). Continue up the dièdre for 2 pitches (IV+), a huge slab (3 pitches, V) and more cracks (2 pitches, V) to the summit. 500m, 8hr from the glacier. TD to the summit of the Verte. See also Photo 86

# Petite Aiguille Verte 3512m

J and R Charlet with P Charlet, Sept 1886

A small summit and a magnificent viewpoint. It gives an excellent introduction to snow and mixed climbing and is strongly recommended as a first Alpine route. Rapid and straightforward access from the Grands Montets station has made this one of the most frequented peaks in the range.

**116**
F+/PD−
**82**

**NORTH-WEST RIDGE**
First ascent party. Winter: A Charlet and C Devouassoux, 20 March 1927

*The normal route, a classic and delightful little excursion. Although this climb can be easily done from an early téléphérique, it can be unbelievably crowded! More romantic alpinists will attempt an overnight bivouac near the station in order to avoid the rush.*

Cross the gentle glacier. Climb the rimaye and short slope above to an obvious shoulder. Continue up the ridge, easy snow at first then several rock steps (move of III) to the very exposed summit. c100m, 1hr

**117**
PD

**NORTH-WEST FACE**
A Contamine, 1959

The steep snow/ice slope provides a fine little training climb and is taken direct. 100m, 1hr

**118**
PD

**NORTH-NORTH-EAST RIDGE**
unknown

**79**

*An interesting alternative and less frequently climbed.*

Climb onto the ridge crossing the rimaye towards its Lhand side. Continue, climbing over or around the various rock towers to the superb curving snow crest of the 'Demi-Lune'. Follow this to the summit rocks. 150m, 1½hr

**119**
PD+

**EAST-NORTH-EAST COULOIR**
H Cameré and P Chevalier, 23 Aug 1930

**79**

In good conditions this is a steep but straightforward snow/ice climb (50°–55°) leading directly to the summit from the Argentière glacier. c300m, 1½hr

## Col & Aiguille des Grands Montets 3233m & 3297m

There are some excellent practice climbs on the little pinnacles W of the Col and about 20 1-pitch routes on the SE flank of the Aig which are reached in a couple of mins from the station. They are graded according to the following colour code: green III, blue IV, red V and VI.

## Pointe de Bayer 3010m

The Arête de Bayer runs due W from the Aig des Grands Montets towards the Aig à Bochard (2669m). Routes have been climbed all over the flanks of this ridge but the best and most popular are concentrated on or around the Bayer Spur. They give short, non-serious modern rock routes with in situ protection on the hard pitches.

**120**    **SOUTH (BAYER) SPUR**
V    A Comte, R Ravanel and J Roche, 23 June 1976
31

From the Grands Montets station descend Route H6 to the edge of the glacier. Continue close under the arête on a scree-covered ledge until below a prominent spur, just R of the rocky couloir falling from the vicinity of Pt 2766m. The climb follows the crest of the spur. 250m

Descent: either (a) down the N side to the Pendant télécabine terminus and continue down the path to the Lognan in 1hr, or (b) along the ridge E to the Grands Montets glacier, or (c) rappel. Route 122 is equipped for this purpose.

**121**    **GRENADINE**
V/V+    E Deschamps and M Ravanel, 1983
31

Perhaps the best of the easier routes and a popular climb on the wall just R of the spur. 200m

**122**    **LE SONGE DE KRONOS**
VI+    E Deschamps and M Ravanel, 19 July 1984
31

A difficult bolt-protected slab and wall climb. 170m

## Aiguille à Bochard 2669m

This is easily reached from the terminus of the Pendant télécabine in ½hr and offers a number of short rock routes. Worth noting are the 120m E face at V/V+, the 150m NE spur and 200m NNE spur at V/VI.

## Pyramide d'Argentière

This is the name now given to the rocky rognon 2866m at the foot of the NE spur of the Grande Rocheuse. It offers some short rock routes of medium difficulty which are quite popular and worth doing en route to the Argentière Hut.

An easy descent is made to the col where snow slopes lead down on either side to the base of the routes.

**123**    **NORTH-EAST RIDGE**
V     A and F de Finance with R Ravanel, 3 Aug 1977

`79`
`32`

Climbs the R side of the crest on wonderful granite. 200m

**124**    **EAST FACE**
V     J Charlet, R Ravanel and party, c1974

`79`
`32`

Joins the above for the easier upper ridge. 200m

## Les Drus 3730m and 3754m

Grand Dru: C Dent and J Hartley with A Burgener and K Maurer, 12 Sept 1878. Petit Dru: J Charlet-Stratton, P Payot and F Folliguet, 29 Aug 1879. Winter traverse of both summits: A Charlet and C Devouassoux, 25 Feb 1928

Quite possibly the most famous granite pyramid in the world. Seen from Montenvers it presents one of the most inspiring sights in the range, with a summit of fairytale sharpness. There are 2 tops, the Grand and Petit Dru separated by a small gap, the Brèche des Drus. The Petit Dru is nothing more than a shoulder but its walls provide the great climbs for which the mountain is justly famous. Historically almost every major route climbed was a landmark in the progression of mountaineering and hard new eliminates are still being created.

## Les Drus: Grand Dru

**125**    **SOUTH-EAST SIDE**
AD    First ascent party

`83`

*The normal route in ascent and descent and a good safe climb on sound rock. Route finding is quite intricate both on the mountain and in the approach via the Charpoua glacier. The upper part of the E ridge can be slow to clear after bad weather. Serious*

From the Charpoua Hut follow the scree crest to the end of the rognon and head NE up the badly crevassed glacier. At c3100m contour round to the L and go up a steep snow slope towards the Col des Drus (1–2hr). Cross the rimaye which can often be extremely difficult. Approach the base of the couloir descending from a gap situated immediately R of the Grand Dru and L of a pointed gendarme. Above, a vague rib splits a steep slope 20m high. Climb the groove on the R then traverse into the one on the L and so reach the couloir; or climb a vertical chimney on the L and slabs above to the same point.

Now slant L up a huge system of scree ledges before working back R to cross the couloir again. Continue towards a gendarme that is situated just L of the Col des Drus and when below this slant up L to just below the crest. Continue L on ledges, passing beneath the pointed gendarme, to the couloir which is joined 15m below the gap in the E ridge. Climb the L side of the couloir for 8m to a large ledge, the 'Pendulum Platform' (3½hr).

Reach another ledge c3m below and to the L, then slant up a vague couloir, traversing L on some ledges below a steep wall to reach a Rward slanting chimney. Climb this (8m) and the 3 successive chimneys above to reach a zone of short walls and ledges that lead L to a deep chimney. Climb it (30m, III) to a large scree terrace. Go R to reach the E ridge just above its large step, finishing with a short chimney on the ridge itself. Climb up the ridge for 100m to the summit. c430m, 6hr from the hut.

In descent it is more convenient to rappel the difficulties from in-situ anchors. Locating the short chimney on the ridge can often be tricky. Make 1 rappel down this and 2 down the chimneys below the large scree terrace. Traverse to the 'Pendulum Platform' (a short wall of IV in this direction). Make a diagonal rappel into the couloir. One can either reverse the route of ascent or rappel the L bank of the couloir, crossing to the R near the base for the final rappel over the rimaye. 4–5hr to the hut.

*Grand Dru continued on page 181*

# Grand Dru: South Face

This, the 'forgotten side' of the Drus, is split into 3 pillars, which, though well defined in the lower half of the face, merge into two higher up. They give magnificent and rather underrated free climbing which has been somewhat neglected in favour of more prestigious undertakings on the W face. The climbs get the sum for most of the day, the granite is excellent and descent takes one back to the same glacier. This means that fast parties can climb the routes without the encumbrance of sacs full of bivouac gear, which are a prerequisite for most parties attempting the other great rock routes on the mountain.

**126    VOIE PIERRE**

ED1    G Brenas and M Raquin, 8 Aug 1981 and 20 July 1982

83

*This direct line up the Rhand pillar is considered to be equal in difficulty to the great routes on the W face. The crux is a wide crack near the top of the route.*

From the Charpoua Hut follow Route 125 up the glacier until it is possible to traverse horizontally across it to the base of the pillar where a large ledge system runs L across the face (¾–1hr). About ⅓ of the way up the initial pillar is a tower. Start on the R by easy rocks and a Lward slanting ramp (IV+), then climb straight up (IV+ to V+) to reach easier ground just to the R of the couloir that descends from the tower. Climb up to a vertical wall. A thin crack, twin grooves and a very strenuous crack to finish (80m, VI/VI+) lead to the crest. Follow this, mainly on the R side, until a smooth dièdre (15m, V+) and chimney (V) lead to the top of the step. Reach the foot of the huge gendarme above, L of a quartz ledge in 3 easy pitches (it is possible to escape R here onto the normal route). Climb up an easy-angled slab on the L (IV+) then return R via flakes (V+) to the crest of the gendarme. Traverse 15m across a slab then climb a crack on the L, descend another on the R (IV) then go up a system of grooves (V) to a little platform on the R side of the gendarme. One more pitch (VI) leads to its top.

Rappel, then climb up L for 2 easy pitches to a col at the foot of a red pillar 80m high. Climb the crest of the pillar to a smooth wall then traverse R across a slab (2 pitches, V+ and VI). Climb a white corner (VI−), traverse 10m L along a narrow ledge then work up R to the top of the pillar (V+). Above is another red pillar split by 3 cracks. Climb the widest crack (40m, VI+) then move L and climb a strenuous chimney (VI). 2 further pitches (V+ and VI−) lead to the summit of the Grand Dru. 700m, 14hr.

**127    SOUTH PILLAR**

TD    M Bastien and A Contamine, 30 June 1952. Winter: C Bougnard, F

83    Diafra and M Poencet, 8–10 Jan 1976

*The classic route which has gained recent popularity as a fine safe and relatively unexposed crack climb on excellent granite. In fact it does not follow any of the pillars but takes rock inbetween, clearing quickly after*

*bad weather, except for the initial cracks which can remain icy.*
*Fortunately the route has not suffered desecration by an abundance of*
*pegs and in the top half the correct line is not obvious. Escape is possible*
*onto the normal route at half-height though there is also a well-equipped*
*rappel descent from this point.*

At the base of the central pillar is a large terminal gendarme. Slant
L on slabs (IV) crossing the couloir coming down from the gap
behind the gendarme to a terrace below a 80m wall and in the
depression R of the central pillar. Level with a detached flake,
climb a chimney on the R using 2 parallel cracks (V+) then take a
crack on the L, turning an overhang on the R (IV+). Climb a thin
crack (V+), traverse R across a slab, then take another crack (V+)
to the edge of a very large couloir in the upper section of the
buttress. Get into it and climb straight up a series of dièdres (IV+)
as far as a narrow couloir that slants down to the L. This is the same
point as that reached on Route 128 climbing directly up the central
or Stembert Pillar.

  Cross the couloir and take a double crack (V) up to the foot of
a dièdre on the L. Climb the dièdre (25m, IV/V) and successive
cracks and corners (IV and V) up to the base of the 'Trident'.
Follow a ledge R and climb a short chimney (V) to a window
through which one can see the Charpoua glacier. This is the top of
the second step. Slant up R for a pitch (IV) then cross a wet
chimney (IV) to a large block. Climb a slab (IV), chimney (IV) and
dièdre (V+) to a terrace on the R. A thin crack and a wall (V) lead
to a large and often snowy terrace at the foot of the final step. Climb
up then R towards the 'Red Pillar' and, passing under an overhang,
turn a large block to reach the crest (IV). A 30m dièdre on the R
leads to a ledge (IV+). From the R hand end climb a short overhang
(IV) and some exposed grooves (V) to a series of dièdres which lead
to the final ridge (IV+). Follow this (II and III) to the summit.
650m, 8–9hr from the hut.

**128**  **STEMBERT PILLAR**
TD   E Beyer, M Debaecke and P Masschelein, 18 Aug 1982

**83**  *This straightens out the previous route by a very fine piece of climbing up*
*the crest of the central pillar and the walls above. After 13 sustained*
*pitches Route 127 is joined at the window.*

Start by climbing an 80m dièdre on the crest of the pillar (V and
VI). Move R and climb up just R of the crest (VI−) to a good ledge.
Round the corner, climb up to a roof (V) then move back R across

179

the crest and climb directly for 2 pitches (V+) into the narrow couloir where the classic route is crossed. Continue up the couloir for a pitch (IV) then work out L finally turning an overhang on the R to a good ledge (V). Move R into the open corner system on the L of the huge gendarme and follow it to the window (V/V+). Continue up Route 127 to the summit. 650m, 10hr from the hut.

**129 TRIDENT PILLAR**
TD   D Collangettes and J Frachon, 21 Sept 1978

**83**

*This takes the Lhand pillar with a prominent triple-headed tower, the 'Trident', in the upper half of the face. Probably the best route on the face leading directly to the summit and giving magnificent free climbing which although sustained is never extreme. Stances are good and the rock is excellent; however the cracks and chimneys climbed on the W side of the 'Trident' can often remain very icy. See also Photo 80.*

Reach the foot of the pillar in 1hr from the Charpoua Hut. Start L of the crest and directly below a huge dièdre in the upper part of the initial pillar. Climb easily up for 5 pitches and reach the crest of the pillar on the R (III to V−. Climb up for a pitch (V) then move L and climb up the R wall of the huge dièdre for 2 pitches (V and V+) to a roof. Turn it on the R and climb up through a chimney/tunnel (V) to a large terrace. From the Lhand extremity of this terrace climb slabs on the L of a chimney (V). Move L to a dièdre and follow it (V) over an overhang and up an easy corner onto the W flank of the ridge. Climb up this side in icy chimneys and dièdres (V) to a small gap and follow the ridge to the foot of the summit block of the 'Trident' (easy escape here onto the S Pillar Route). Turn it on the L in a deep icy chimney (V) and reach the gap behind the 'Trident'.

Move R down some ledges then climb up a chimney on the R side of a huge block in the buttress above (V+). From behind the block climb a short dièdre to a sloping slab and descend it, to avoid an overhang, to some terraces (V). Climb a dièdre but leave it at mid-height by a delicate Lwards traverse (V+) to reach the top of the buttress via a window (IV). Climb the final buttress by the Lhand of 2 parallel cracks (V+, sustained), the chimney that follows (V) and above that, another icy chimney on the R (V+). Surmount 2 successive overhangs and reach some terraces (V+). Take the line of least resistance through the bulges above (V) to the summit. 650m, c25 pitches, 14hr from the hut.

*Grand Dru continued*

**130**    **NORTH FACE**

ED2    H and P Lesueur, 25–27 July 1952. Winter: A Parkin and T

**87**    Renault, 10–13 Jan 1983

*A tremendous exploit in impressive surroundings that was obviously well ahead of its time. There have been few subsequent ascents, all by technically gifted parties who confirmed the high level of sustained difficulty in the icy cracks of the central section. The climb is very rarely in amenable condition and is an obvious target for a winter ascent, albeit of the highest order.*

The climb begins at a small icefield 60m to the L of Route 142 and from the top R corner climbs a couloir chimney (IV and V, mixed) to the crest of a spur beneath steep walls (this point is reached easily from the classic N Face Route on the Petit Dru). On the R climb cracks and chimneys (V and VI) which are themselves on the R of a huge black chimney. Reach the obvious diagonal line that runs across the N face and gives hard mixed climbing in cracks and chimneys. Cross the NE couloir just below the narrows and continue up the final wall of the Grand Dru on delicate verglassed terrain. 850m, 15–20hr

# Petit Dru

**131**    **SOUTH FLANK AND SOUTH-WEST RIDGE**

D–    First ascent party

**83**

*The normal route and an established classic of the range giving safe, strenuous yet interesting climbing on sound rock. It is quite popular and is generally combined with a traverse of the Grand Dru. Above the shoulder on the Flammes de Pierre Ridge, the climbing is continuous with typical short steep 'Chamonix-style' cracks interspersed with good stances and belays. Normally used in descent by parties completing routes on the N and W faces. In the afternoon there is some danger of stonefall below the shoulder. See also Photos 80 and 86*

From the Charpoua Hut follow Route 126 across the base of the S pillars of the Grand Dru and descend into a huge couloir coming down from the SW ridge of the Petit Dru (1hr). Slant up L across a spur and climb a second couloir to the Flammes de Pierre Ridge. Just below the top climb a chimney on the R (III) to a gap in the ridge immediately SE of the prominent gendarme 3361m (1½hr).

Cross the R side of the gendarme to join the level section of the main ridge and follow it to the shoulder (½hr) where the angle suddenly steepens. Traverse R for 30m along the upper edge of a snowpatch and climb a short chimney to a secondary ridge. Follow this up to the main ridge again and climb large blocks and the deep vertical chimney above (IV+) until a ledge on the L leads into a couloir. Climb the couloir in its entirety, finishing via some steep chimneys (50m, IV) to a huge flat platform on the crest of the ridge.

Trending slightly L climb a succession of cracks and chimneys in the slabs above (40m, IV, several large pegs). Follow a ledge L to the edge of the large couloir slanting down towards the Bonatti Pillar. Above, take the Lhand of several chimneys (IV, icy) then follow a scree slope R to the Charpoua side and climb steep walls to a large horizontal ledge, the 'Quartz Ledge' (IV). Climb a series of strenuous cracks (IV) then traverse horizontally R past a detached flake to a short rib. Climb it (5m, IV) to an easy couloir which leads to the summit block (4hr). 700m, 7hr from the hut

In descent make 10 or 12 continuous rappels down the line of the route from the many slings in place. Avoid going too far R into the steep couloir alongside the Bonatti Pillar. Reverse the route of ascent going down the large couloir immediately after Pt 3361m. At the base it is possible to reach the Charpoua glacier directly in 2 rappels but it is very crevassed at this point and it is usually better to follow the horizontal ledgeline back L (E) under the 3 pillars and set foot on the glacier as high as possible. c5hr to the hut.

**132**  **TRAVERSE OF LES DRUS**

D+  Although the Grand Dru had been reached from the Petit Dru years previously, the route now followed was first traversed by E Giraud with J Ravanel and A Comte, 6 Sept 1903. In the reverse direction when the difficulties can be rappeled: H Dunod with E Rey and F Simond, 31 Aug 1887

*A classic ridge traverse and one of the most famous in the range. In recent times it has been a little neglected due to the overall length and commitment, but it remains a highly recommendable outing giving good rock climbing in a superb situation.*

From the Charpoua Hut reach the summit of the Petit Dru in 7hr by Route 131 and descend easily to the Brèche des Drus. The W face of the Grand Dru is short and steep. Climb a 6m crack (IV), traverse R along an exposed ledge and slant L up a wall to reach a horizontal crack which leads L to the W ridge (III). One is now at grips with the famous Z pitch. Go up 5m to a black terrace (IV) then slant up R until below the big overhang where an exit is made L to the W ridge (IV). From a small terrace on the N face climb cracks to a deep chimney and follow it Lwards to a large platform on the W ridge (IV, icy). The ridge is easy and leads to the summit block which is climbed via an ice slope on the L (1hr).

Descend Route 125 to the Charpoua Hut. 12hr for the round trip. In the reverse direction the traverse becomes AD+.

**133    SOUTH-WEST (BONATTI) PILLAR**

TD+    W Bonatti, 17–22 Aug 1955. Winter: R Guillaume and A Vieille, 15–17 March 1961

85
35

*The first ascent of this magnificent rock climb constitutes one of the most remarkable exploits in the history of alpinism. Once the most difficult route in the Western Alps, it is now a popular and established classic With pitches of V+ and A1 and a victim of excessive pegging. Most parties will use these pegs from time to time and climb the 50m wall entirely on aid, but in 1982 M Pedrini and C Camerani freed the whole route with a crux, the dièdre just R of the aid crack in the 50m wall, a phenomenal layback (ED3 with pitches of VIII).*

*There are 2 ways to approach the foot of the pillar. The obvious couloir below the W face gives a short approach from the Dru Rognon but is notorious for its serious stonefall. It should only be considered in very cold and snowy conditions such as winter/spring. The rappel descent from the Flammes de Pierre is considerably safer but on poor rock. Crampons at least are indispensable for crossing the couloir at the foot of the pillar.*

From the Charpoua Hut follow Route 131 to the Flammes de Pierre, crossing the ridge to the L (W) of Gendarme 3361m where there are excellent bivouac sites (2hr). Below, a shattered rocky ridge, forming the L bank of the couloir below the W face, leads down towards the Dru glacier. Scramble down 50m then make 5 rappels to a small gap just before a conspicuous gendarme. Make 4 more rappels down the loose icy chimney on the R. 1 pitch across the couloir (40°) leads to ledges at the foot of the pillar (3hr). In case of retreat it is possible to climb back up to the Flammes de Pierre (III and IV), taking a line to the R of the rappel descent in the upper section.

About 600m from the foot of the pillar. A reasonable time for an ascent of the pillar to the summit is 14–18hr. Only the fastest parties will avoid a bivouac. Good bivouac sites appear more

183

frequently than one would expect and they are excellent in the vicinity of Pitch 12 and below the shoulder.

Above the 50m wall it is possible to escape R by a long and difficult traverse (IV and A1) onto the normal route. It is also possible to descend from the shoulder by following ledges to the R (E) making 2 long and exposed rappels down the back of a very steep couloir to some ledges. Follow these E for 100m or more to gain the normal route by a short ascent.

**134**   **ABSOLU**

ED3   P Camison and P Grenier, 3–5 Aug 1986

**85**

The L side of the SW pillar is taken by this extremely difficult mixed free and aid route. VIII–/A2, 600m

L again is the bolt extravaganza of the Gross Route which contains 10 difficult pitches A2–A3 and some 68 bolts. It was completed from 20 April to 8 May 1975

**135**   **FRENCH DIRECTISSIMA**

ED2   H Giot and H Sachetat, 20–21 Sept 1982. A winter ascent was made

**85**  as far as the junction with Route 136 by S Long and J Silvester in

**34**  Feb 1987, but was thought to have been climbed by a continental party prior to this date.

*A direct line up the immaculate red shield to the R of the grey rockfall scar in the centre of the W face. The granite, whilst brittle and needing care lower down, improves by mid-height. The red shield gives sustained artifical climbing with plenty of in situ gear, an obvious target for future free climbing attempts.*

The route begins from the huge central terraces that work up L from the couloir below the W face. Although only 20–25m above the foot of the couloir, the safest approach is still via the Flammes de Pierre, making 3 more rappels below the point gained on the approach to the Bonatti Pillar, then crossing the couloir to the ledges. Once established on the route, which starts up an 80m Rward facing dièdre L of a smooth grey wall, there is no objective danger. Bivouac sites exist above pitches 11 and 18. 800m

**136**   **AMERICAN DIRECTISSIMA**

ED3   J Harlin and R Robbins, 10–13 Aug 1965. Winter: P Malinowski,

**89**  M Piekutowski, Z Wach and J Wolf, 25 Feb–5 March 1976

**34**

Without a doubt one of the most demanding routes in the Alps. Originally climbed almost entirely on aid, it was free climbed with one or two rest points by M Pedrini on 9 July 1983, a truly tremendous effort (ED4/5 with some VIII+). Most parties will still use a considerable amount of aid (A3/4, mainly small wires) and find the route a very serious undertaking due to the steep sustained climbing on poor rock. There are large and worrying unstable sections around the Great Roof and some hard off-width cracks. Very fast parties will still require one bivouac and 3 or 4 are not uncommon. Good ledges exist above pitches 6 and 13. Not surprisingly the route has had few ascents and there is not a lot of in situ gear. 600m to the shoulder. See also Photo 86

**137**  **WEST FACE ORIGINAL ROUTE**
TD+
**85**  F Bérardini, A Dagory, M Lainé and G Magnone, 1–5 July and 16–18 July 1952. Winter: J Couzy and R Demaison, 10–14 March 1957

The ascent of this face was a post-war tour de force and one of the earliest examples of extensive use of artificial aid in the Western Alps. As far as the upper terraces, below the huge rockfall scar, the route is seriously exposed to stonefall. Even above this the climbing is very loose and unpleasant and for these reasons has almost totally been abandoned in favour of the Direct Start, which joins the Original Route at the Jammed Block. Retreat or escape from the upper part is quite difficult and despite an excessive number of pegs the route is a serious undertaking. 1000m from the foot of the couloir, 600m of climbing above the terraces, 12–14hr from the terraces.

**138**  **AMERICAN DIRECT**
ED1
**85**  G Hemming and R Robbins, 24–26 July 1962. Winter: A Bellica and I Koller, 28 Feb–5 March 1976
**33**

This major rock climb of exceptional quality has become one of the most popular modern classics in the range. The line is elegant with minimal stonefall danger and that only near the base. Commitment below the junction with the Original Route is not great as a direct descent via very well equipped rappel points presents little problem. In fact most parties nowadays terminate the route at the Jammed Block and descend by this method. The wall clears quickly after bad weather although the upper part and exit onto the N face can remain quite icy. The route is generally completed in 2 days with a bivouac just above or below the 90m Dièdre. There is a considerable amount of in situ protection (or aid) but the route can be climbed completely free, the hard sections consisting of strenuous jamming in sound granite cracks. 1050m, 14–18hr. See also Photo 86

**139    GENEVA ROUTE**

ED2    N Schenkel and B Wiestlibach, 1–2 Aug 1982 (to the Jammed
85    Block only)

*An entirely free climb, using only nuts for protection, that runs parallel to the American Direct. It follows a fairly direct line to the R side of the Jammed Block and gives very sustained crack climbing with considerable exposure. Treat the pitch grading circumspectly as it appears the standard of climbing could well be higher than that suggested by the first ascent party.*

Start midway between Route 138 and the Bonatti Couloir. Climb a small but well defined corner (20m, VII). Move R along a terrace and then climb up and pendulum R to an obvious crack system. Follow this for 200m (V+ to VII), generally bearing R, to reach the large lower terraces on the W face. There is a prominent crack line halfway between the American Direct and the Bonatti couloir. Climb a chimney just R of this and continue to a thin crack system leading up R. Climb this (VI+/VII) with a exit onto a slab. Climb a crack and corner on the R (40m, VI/VI+) followed by a poorly protected offwidth (VI+) to a small ledge. Traverse L and climb the L side of the huge dièdre that leads to the Jammed Block (V+ and VI). 600m

**140    PASSAGE CARDIAC**

ED3    M Piola and P Steiner, completed 2 July 1986
85

A demanding addition to the free climbing offered by the W face. The route takes the bolt-protected slabs immediately above the traverse ledge taken on the first pitch of the American Direct. There are unavoidable moves of VII but climbed free the second pitch is VIII. Above, the character changes and steep strenuous cracks lead up directly with an exit onto the Niche des Drus. The crux is an VIII+ offwidth! c600m to the N face.

**141    C'EST ARRIVE DEMAIN**

ED1/2    P Berhault, C and Y Remy, 15–16 July 1979
89

Dry conditions are needed for this rock climb on the N face. It starts at the Lhand side of the W face and reaches the terraces by a crack system that lies above the top R corner of a smooth triangular slab L of some roofs. The line thereafter lies between Routes 142 and 143 and has several pitches of VI, one of VI+ and a short section of A1 before joining the Original Route for the last chimneys. 1000m, 22hr. See also Photo 85

**142**     **NORTH FACE ORIGINAL ROUTE**

TD     P Allain and R Leininger, 31 July–1 Aug 1935. Winter: G

**89**    Devouassoux, Y Masino and G Payot, 8–9 Jan 1964

*One of the 6 classic N faces of the Alps and at the time of its first ascent considered the most difficult climb in the range. Whilst the main difficulties are on rock (a succession of strenuous and often brutal cracks and chimneys) the upper section is often icy and crampons can prove useful. Stances and belays are excellent, there is little exposure and almost no objective danger save in the lower section which is slightly threatened by any stonefall coming from the Niche des Drus. Difficulties augment considerably in bad conditions and in winter this route provides an exacting mixed climb of high quality. See also Photo 87*

From the Dru Rognon go up the glacier and, skirting the foot of the Dru, head up the snow slope in the direction of the Col des Drus. Reach the first couloir on the R (½hr). Cross the rimaye (often difficult) and climb the deep couloir on easy broken rock for 100m to reach boulder-strewn terraces. In certain dry years the glacier shrinks leaving a smooth wall below the couloir. In this case climb steep cracks on the R for 1 pitch (V+) then slant up L to the terraces. Make a rising traverse R and climb some cracks and chimneys (100m, III and IV) on the L side of a large triangular pillar to a point where the pillar meets the smooth walls above. Climb diagonally R up cracked walls (IV) and follow a steep crack (15m, IV+) to an exposed ledge. From the R hand edge of this ledge climb a vertical crack in the wall above, the Fissure Lambert (10m, V). Turn an overhang on the L and follow the icy couloir-chimney above (IV) to the bottom of the Niche.

    Slant up R crossing several couloirs to rocks on the R side of the Niche and climb these easily to a large terrace overlooking the W face. Another couloir, with large blocks, leads to a second terrace. Traverse 12m to the L and climb a vertical chimney (20m) and the dièdre that follows to a ledge. Climb a short crack to another ledge, then take the dièdre that lies just L of the wide crack above (IV) to a stance overlooking the Niche. Climb a vertical crack (20m, III and IV) then the steep wall above either direct, starting with a flake (V) or L, following a vague ledgeline (V). Both methods lead to the Fissure Allain (30m, VI/VI+ climbed free) which was taken by the first ascent party. It is now avoided by traversing R through a letterbox then slanting up R using a wide crack in the steep slabs above. This, the Fissure Martinetti, becomes steeper and narrower near the top where a difficult exit is made L (V) to a good platform. Climb a flake crack on the L (V) then a 4m strenuous wall (V) to a third terrace overlooking the W face.

Climb a series of steep cracks on the L (40m, IV) to a snowy ledge. The climbing now becomes more mixed. Slant up L crossing a wall to reach a line of chimneys that lead to a second ledge 150m below the summit (IV). Slant L again and reach a wide chimney with large blocks at the start. Climb this for 60m (IV+) to the Quartz Ledge c60m below the summit. It is possible to follow this R and, passing through a hole on the S face, reach the normal route (131) in 2 pitches. Otherwise, traverse L and climb an icy chimney for 2 pitches (IV+) to the summit. 850m, 8–12hr from the Dru Rognon.

## 143 NORTH FACE GUIDES ROUTE

ED1/2    M Feuillarade, C Jager, J Paris and Y Seigneur, 8–15 Feb 1967

**89**

*Though originally climbed in winter, subsequent summer ascents have experienced very little stonefall and considerably reduced the number of aid points. This serious undertaking has seen few ascents. Apart from one or two pitches the rock is surprisingly sound if often wet and the upper section can be heavily iced. See also Photo 87*

Climb up the boulder-strewn terraces at the start of Route 142 to the steep walls below the Niche. Climb almost directly up a couloir-chimney system followed by cracks for 4 pitches to a detached flake (IV and V). Work up R in a series of overhanging dièdres (VI and VI+) to a couloir which leads in 2 easier pitches to the bottom of the Niche. Work up the L side (50°) and take the obvious hard loose dièdre just L of the rockfall scar and R of a vague pillar (VI and A1). Climb a further 4 pitches in this dièdre line with excursions onto the pillar (A1 at the start, then more free climbing) on generally sound but icy rock. A series of capped grooves on the L lead to the summit. 850m, fast parties will complete the route in 2 days using a good bivouac site at the top of the Niche.

## 144 NORTH FACE DIRECTISSIMA

ED3    P Gabarrou and A Long, 26–28 July 1986

**87**

*Unrepeated at the time of writing, this takes an elegant direct line up the true N face. It begins on the L of Route 130 and crosses both this and*

*Route 143 before reaching the summit ridge. Objectively safe and on excellent granite, it presents free climbing of the highest order with several aid pitches on verglassed rock, which would probably go free after a prolonged dry spell. The difficulties are sustained with pitches graded from V to VIII−. See also Photo 89*

Start at the top of the icefield as for Route 130. Climb a system of dièdres on the L to easy terraces. Slant up these and drop down R to the foot of 2 dièdres. Climb the one on the L and continue to a second set of terraces. Climb the huge compact buttress above via the obvious central crack, crossing roofs directly, to easy ground. In the upper buttress climb the second dièdre on the R and the wall above (bolt) moving L to follow a big dièdre to mixed ground. Several more pitches lead to a huge set of overhangs. Continue up the dièdre or climb the cracks on the R. Cross the roofs and continue up to an impressive chimney capped by an enormous block. Above this, work L to an enormous dièdre and climb the walls for several pitches until easier mixed ground leads to the ridge L of the summit. 800m, 30hr

Several more routes have been explored on the walls to the L. In the centre of the face, a direct line taken by J Semen and J Slavik, 28–30 July 1979 (VI and A1) emerges in the vicinity of the Brèche des Drus. The rock just R of the NE Couloir is taken by the Polish Route (J Kukuczka, W Kurtyka and M Lukaszeweski, 12–14 Aug 1973, mainly IV and V with some A1).

**145    NORTH-EAST COULOIR**

ED1

87

W Cecchinel and C Jager, 28–31 Dec 1973. Direct ascent: R Accamazzo and T Sorenson, Aug 1977

*Commonly referred to as the Dru Couloir, this magnificent enterprise, coming straight after the revolution in ice climbing equipment, was hailed as the hardest and most sustained ice climb ever achieved in the Alps. The difficulty, though not the quality, was quickly found to be overrated (generally Scottish 4) and the climb is now a modern classic, with the hardest section probably below the Nominé Crack. Surprisingly it is not a suicidal undertaking in summer for the route is only prone to ice and stone fall in the easier lower section which should be climbed at night. However retreat from the upper half of the route would be quite problematical and it is no place to be caught in bad weather.*

*In Aug 1977 J Roberts and S Shea climbed the vertical ice chimney directly to the upper couloir but retreated in a storm (5 pitches; Scottish 5/6 and A2). The route was completed several days later by a different pair, and is rarely in condition.*

From the Dru Rognon work up the glacier to the foot of the couloir coming down from the Col des Drus (1hr). Climb the couloir for 6 long pitches (55° then 60°) to where a vertical ice chimney on the R leads directly to the upper couloir descending from the Brèche des Drus. Continue in the main couloir line for 3 more mixed pitches then slant up R for 2 hard pitches on thinly iced slabs to flakes at the base of a 60m vertical wall. Climb the thin crack in the wall (the Nominé Crack, 40m, V and A1, many pegs). Slant R across a steep wall of blocks and loose flakes for 1 pitch (icy V and V+). Climb a further mixed pitch straight up to the base of a chimney-couloir (IV and V). Climb the chimney as far as a yellow curving crack (V), make an exposed traverse R and continue more easily (III) before climbing diagonally Rwards behind a large detached flake for a further 15m. Now move down R to the upper couloir. Follow this for 6 pitches with good spike belays (Scottish 3 and 4) to where it eases. The Crux is a 15m high 'narrows' of 75°–80°. 2 further pitches at 55° lead to the brèche. 700m, 14–18hr

| 146 | **COL DES DRUS** |
|---|---|
| ED2 | C Tuccinardi and E Schmutz, 27–30 Oct 1975 |
| **89** | |

First reached from the S by C Dent with A Burgener and another guide in 1874. The N side is a steep and sustained mixed climb on poor rock and has 2 difficult chimney pitches in the upper section (VI and A2). 550m

# Flammes de Pierre Ridge

The traverse of this ridge provides a very long and entertaining scramble on excellent granite over or around the numerous gendarmes. The flanks above the Charpoua glacier provide hard sustained climbs in the modern idiom that have yet to gain popularity.

| 147 | **POINTE 3280m** |
|---|---|
| VI+ | P Belmastro and U Manera, 5 July 1970. Winter: H Bouvard and M |
| **80** | Piola, 4 Feb 1989 |

*This lies in front of Pt Michelle-Micheline and offers a triangular face of immaculate granite overlooking the Charpoua Hut. This excellent free climb takes the Lhand spur of the face, broad at the base but narrowing towards the summit. It gives a succession of steep jamming cracks similar to the S Pillar of the Grand Dru.*

Climb the crest of the spur to the L end of a prominent red overhang and reach a terrace above (mainly IV with some sections of V+ and A1). Starting with an overhanging dièdre (VI+) climb 60m up steep smooth walls (V and VI) then leave the spur and work up R, climbing steep red slabs (V) and a steeper couloir line (V+) back to a shoulder on the crest. Follow it easily (III) and climb the summit buttress by a series of dièdres (V). c550m, 12hr

Rappel and traverse towards the Dru keeping below the crest of the Flammes de Pierre and reach the normal route (131).

# Point 2699m

Much good climbing is to be found in the vicinity of the Charpoua glacier snout, reached in 2½hr from Montenvers. The S face of the conspicuous rock triangle gives several excellent free climbs.

**148**  **SOUTH FACE 1984 ROUTE**
VIII  B Cormier, D Lavigne, D Radigue and Y Toupin, during 1984

**80**  Start in the centre of the face below a high R ward slanting roof. On the L climb up to the R hand end of the roof in 2 pitches (VI+ and VII+). Climb round the R side (VIII) and continue up walls above (VII) crossing 2 ramps to a scree-covered terrace. The final pyramid in 'the Diamond' is climbed on the R side (VI−). Descend the route by rappel. 14 pitches with unavoidable moves of VII+. Route-finding is easy as the line is well-endowed with fixed pegs and bolts. c400m

**149**  **SOUTH FACE 1986 ROUTE**
VII+  C Carli and J Chassagne, 5−6 Aug 1986

**80**  This follows the very obvious crack line to the L of the huge roofs and gives 12 pitches of strenuous climbing with unavoidable moves of VI/VI+ and a 5m section of A1. Finish on the scree ledges below the diamond. 300m

# Le Cardinal 3647m

First ascent of W top: W Davidson with C Klucker and S Innerkofler, 18 Aug 1897

A sharp and spectacular granite spire when seen from the Charpoua side. It has 2 tops, the E (3647m) a 6m high monolith that is rarely climbed, and the W (3642m) – the usual objective.

**150    SOUTH-EAST FACE**
PD    First ascent party

**76**

*The normal route from the Couvercle Hut. A short interesting and fairly popular training climb.*

Follow Route 92 as far as the rimaye (2hr) then make a rising traverse L across broken rock to the foot of the final wall, which lies above and to the R of the S Brèche du Cardinal (a gap in the S ridge to the R of 3 prominent gendarmes). Slant up R and climb 2 successive chimneys (III) that lead back to the S ridge. Follow it, crossing or turning gendarmes and passing round the base of the E top to the W summit. c250m, 4hr from the Couvercle Hut.

**151    WEST FACE AND SOUTH RIDGE**
PD    M Kurz and K Steiner, 12 Aug 1909

**88**

*The normal route from the Charpoua Hut. A classic and very popular excursion. It is better than the Couvercle Route and is normally used in descent after climbing the rock routes on the SW face. See also Photo 80*

Go up the Charpoua glacier and climb the wide and mainly snowy couloir that comes down from the S Brèche du Cardinal on the R of the peak. It is 350m high, steepens to 45° and is climbed on the R side to the gap, just L of the group of 3 prominent gendarmes (2½hr). Climb up the S ridge until it is possible to traverse R across the E side to reach the chimneys mentioned in Route 150. Follow this route to the summit. 500m, 4hr from the Charpoua Hut.

**152    SOUTH FACE**
V+    G Javelle, J Madesclaire and A Zagdoun, 26 July 1964

**88**

*A nice little climb on good granite. It overlooks the upper part of the couloir taken by the normal route.*

Follow Route 151 and c70m below the brèche work up L to a huge but shallow dièdre that falls from the SW ridge. Start on the R at some grooves that are themselves to the L of a stony couloir. Climb these grooves (III) then a series of cracks (IV+), passing a leaning block, to reach a huge platform overlooking the couloir. Climb a grey slab (IV) then traverse L to a series of open chimneys that lead up to a red wall (IV+ and V). Traverse L and climb a crack (10m, V+), then vertical walls on the R (V+), to a good platform. An easy chimney leads to the ridge which is followed to the summit. c200m, 6hr from the hut.

**153**
V+

**88**

**SOUTH-WEST PILLAR**

J Guichard and G Magnès, 3 Sept 1973

*This takes a direct line up the pillar that appears in profile from the Charpoua Hut and is R of the huge central dièdre on the SW face. Although a prominent feature on the approach, it is surprisingly ill-defined at close quarters. The route is sustained and has had few ascents.*

Follow Route 151 to ²/₃ height in the couloir then traverse L and reach the base of the pillar by an easy Lward slanting ramp. Climb a crack to a shoulder then move up over a rocking block (IV) and overhang above (V) to a series of cracks. Follow these for 1 pitch (V+) and reach the top of a slanting chimney (V, strenuous) leading to a ramp. Climb the ramp (III) and crack above (V with several aid moves) to a wide chimney. Follow this to a dièdre and climb it for 1 pitch (V+) to an exposed ledge. Follow the ledge (IV−), make a diagonal rope move and climb up to the SW ridge on the L (V+). Just below the ridge climb a wide crack (V+). Regain the ridge and follow it to the top. 250m, 6hr from the hut.

**154**
V+

**88**

**SOUTH-WEST FACE**

P Allain, F Aubert, A Fix and J Rousseau, 5 Aug 1949

*The Original Route but still a very fine climb, and an easier proposition than Route 153. Sustained, exposed and on excellent granite.*

Start towards the R side of the face at the base of some cracks and chimneys. This point is reached in 1¾hr from the Charpoua Hut by following the couloir of Route 151 to mid-height then slanting L across mixed ground.

Climb the cracks and chimneys (V then IV). Slant L and take a dièdre (V), then a short narrow chimney turning the overhang on the L (V+ with a few aid moves). Continue up smooth walls and easy steps to a large platform below an equally large dièdre. Climb the dièdre for 25m (IV+) then move L and climb a crackline to rejoin the dièdre higher up (IV+). Climb a short wall on the R (V) and a short dièdre that leads over a roof (IV+). Climb a loose block on the R and above, a crack leading round onto the S face in full view of the S Brèche du Cardinal. Traverse R to a huge couloir and climb it for 60m (IV and V) to a small gap on the SW ridge. Follow

193

the ridge turning several gendarmes on the N side (IV and V) and continue up to the W summit. 350m, 7hr from the hut.

**155**    **WEST FACE**

V+/A1    J Midière and J Reppelin, 11 Aug 1963

**88**

One or two ascents and variations have been completed on this face up the conspicuous line of dièdres that lie just to the L of the SW ridge. Reach it by following the easy ramp (mixed rock and snow) up L from the bottom of the face, then return R up a couloir to a gap between a huge pinnacle and the face. The dièdres themselves are probably best climbed on the L side before working R to reach the groove in the final wall. They give difficult climbing on friable rock and have not become popular. 400m, 8hr

# L'Evêque 3469m

E and M Pasteur, E Carr, C Pasteur and C Wilson, 7 Aug 1892

A popular little peak, suitable for Alpine novices or early season fitness. There are some very worthwhile rock routes above the Charpoua glacier.

**156**    **SOUTH FACE**

AD–    First ascent party

**90**

*The normal route of ascent and descent. It gives a safe and interesting climb that can be a little prone to verglas. See also Photo 76*

Reach the Brèche Nonne-Evêque by Routes 162 or 163. Descend slightly L then slant back R to the foot of a long chimney system. This can be climbed in its entirety though it is slightly easier in the lower section to avoid a vertical square-cut chimney on the R (III, sometimes icy). Reach a gap in the Rhand ridge then slant L across the face to the SW ridge. Follow it for a short way before moving onto the L side. Return to the crest c15m below the summit where some delightful climbing leads to the highest point. 3½hr from the Couvercle, 5½hr from the Charpoua Hut.

**157**    **SOUTH-WEST RIDGE**

D–    G Garrigou and M Legris with A Contamine, 1 Aug 1950

**80**

*An established classic with all the requirements for a high quality outing: interesting climbing, excellent rock and protection, in a fine position and*

*objectively safe. The wild cirque of the Charpoua adds a feeling of
remoteness despite the route overlooking the hut.*

Go down from the Charpoua Hut and follow Route 163 towards the
couloir of the Brèche Nonne-Evêque. Slant up a snow patch and
climb the couloir between the main spur on the R and a subsidiary
spur on the L. After negotiating 3 short overhangs and a 25m
chimney (IV+) some easy terraces are reached. Leave the couloir
and traverse R to the crest, following it for several pitches (IV) to a
buttress. Turn this on the L in an open dièdre (IV) and continue up
the ridge turning a gendarme on the R. Descend a chimney on the
R (20m, IV) then slant up R for 40m to a couloir. Climb the R side
via a chimney, dièdre and steep wall (IV) and continue up a rocky
spur. After 20m reach a couloir on the R which comes down from a
spur at the base of a prominent buttress. From some terraces above,
take the spur to the R of the gendarme that has now been
completely turned and follow chimneys back L to a window on the
ridge (IV+). Climb a wall then a 25m chimney just R of the crest
(IV) and avoid another indistinct gendarme by a crack on the R
(III).

Move onto the L side and climb up to the foot of a gendarme
with a huge block on top (IV). From the top of the block move up L
via a flake (V) and descend to a little gap. Continue up the crest (III)
passing a more distinct notch and climb the dièdre above (IV). Turn
several gendarmes on the L and go down some ledges leading to the
base of 2 large chimneys in the summit buttress. Take the Lhand
chimney to an overhang (IV) then slant up R on the wall
overlooking the Rhand chimney (V) and reach the crest of the ridge.
Shortly after, move 20m to the R of the crest and climb a line of
chimneys (IV) to a large terrace below the summit. Climb round on
the R of a gendarme and go up blocks to the top. 700m, 6hr from
the hut.

**158  DIRECT ROUTE**
D/D+  A Melchior and B Moreau, 16 Aug 1974

The crest of the ridge has been followed almost throughout. Both
gendarmes that were turned on the R side can be climbed directly
by cracks and steep walls (V+). 9hr

**159  WEST PILLAR**
V/VI  A Giorda and M Ogliengo, 25 Aug 1982

This is the prominent red pillar to the R of Route 160 and very
obvious from the Charpoua Hut. It gives 250m–300m of very

sustained climbing on excellent granite. On the first ascent the climb was terminated at the top of the pillar and a rappel descent made of the couloir separating it from the main body of the Evêque. 8hr

**160  WEST FACE**
TD–  J Loustau-Chartrez with R Charlet and R Fournier, 19 Sept 1970

**88**

*A direct and worthwhile climb on excellent granite. It is best attempted after a good spell of dry weather as certain ledges hold the snow and the 120m dièdre can be extremely difficult if at all wet or icy. Few ascents.*

From the Charpoua Hut go up to the top of the rognon and cross the glacier to the foot of the face. Start where the snow reaches its highest point against the rock walls at c3000m and directly below the summit (½hr).

Climb R on poor rock for a pitch (III) then take a short dièdre on the R (IV+). Climb another on the R, again that slants back L to an area of snowy rock. Cross this in 3 pitches to its top L corner (III/IV) which lies below the second step and traverse R for 15m to a huge dièdre, 120m high (III). Climb the dièdre in 3 pitches (V+ and VI) to a snow patch and above this slant up R on mixed ground (III/IV) until a ledge leads back L into the dièdre. One is now parallel and R of the huge red dièdre clearly visible from the hut. Climb the dièdre, finishing with a traverse L to the top of the red dièdre (V+). Climb up to a platform on the L (IV and V). Traverse 12m to the L (IV) then move up and R to a detached flake which is climbed on the L side (A1 then V+). Climb the dièdre above (V+) then move up R over an overhang (IV+). Another dièdre leads to the main ridge 10m to the R of the summit. c470m, 9hr from the hut.

## Pointe 3014m

The various lower buttresses on the peak offer a number of short and hard free climbs. This Pt is the subsidiary spur below the SW ridge.

**161  SOUTH-WEST SPUR – L'EMINENCE GRISE**
VI  O Rathenux and T Renault, 30 Aug 1987

**80**
**36**

A very fine free climb starting 30m to the R of the crest of the spur and reached in 20min from the hut. Difficulties on the last pitch can

be substantially reduced with a little aid (VIII free). From
summit block make 9 rappels down the line of ascent. 250.

## Brèche Nonne-Evêque 3306m

First traverse: E Carr, C, E and M Pasteur and C Wilson, 7 Aug
1892

Usually reached from the Talèfre side on the more standard routes
to or from the Evêque and Nonne.

**162**
F+
**90**

### TALEFRE SIDE
Follow Route 90 along the W edge of the Talèfre glacier and climb
the broad snowy couloir to the brèche. 2hr from the Couvercle Hut.
See also Photo 76

**163**
PD
**80**

### CHARPOUA SIDE
From the Charpoua Hut descend the path for 200m then cross the
glacier, going round the foot of Pt 2704m to reach the long couloir
that descends from the brèche. Climb it for 500m to the gap. 3hr
from the hut.

This is generally taken in descent after completing the harder
routes on the W side of the Evêque or Nonne.

## La Nonne 3340m

C, E and M Pasteur and C Wilson with A Cupelin, 23 July 1890

Another well-frequented summit with an exposed rocky crest. The
summit, at the S end of the crest, is a triple tower.

**164**
AD−/AD
**90**

### TRAVERSE OF MAIN RIDGE
S ridge: First ascent party. N ridge: T de Lépiney and party, 8 Sept
1922

*A delightful and consequently popular training climb on good rock. The
classic excursion follows a S to N direction.*

From the Couvercle Hut go up the Talèfre glacier to the base of the
first narrow couloir that lies to the R of the bigger couloir
descending from the Brèche Moine-Nonne. Climb 30m up a rib on
the L side, then reach the couloir and climb it on good rock to the
main ridge, a little above the brèche. Climb the ridge, a little on the

p between 2 gendarmes. Cross the Lhand gendarme
0m on the Charpoua side. Slant up L on broken rock,
d regain the ridge on the R (III). Above is the
d by 3 rock fingers. Turn the first on the L. The
hest can be climbed at V/V+ but the third (most
ly IV. (3½hr from the hut).

d the crack and go along ledges to reach the horizontal
section of the N ridge. This is sharp and smooth and may well have
to be crossed, in part, à cheval. Reach easy ground and follow it,
turning a line of gendarmes by ledges on the Talèfre side, to a
shoulder above the Brèche Nonne-Evêque. Descend easily to the
gap (2hr). From here it is possible to climb the Evêque and return
to the gap in 2hr. Descend Route 162 to the Couvercle Hut. 7hr for
the round trip. Allow 9–10hr if the Evêque is to be included.

**165**  **WEST PILLAR**
TD    P Jassaud with R Fournier, 3 Sept 1971

Starting 60m to the R of the Nonne-Evêque Couloir, this route
follows the crest of the prominent pillar, composed of 3 main
buttresses, finishing directly to the summit. Unfortunately the
climbing is not very homogeneous, with hard pitches (up to VI and
A2) separated by easier sections where the rock is not altogether
sound. 550m, 15hr on the first ascent.

## Aiguille du Moine 3412m

E Lloyd and I Stratton with J Charlet and J Simond, 22 Sept 1871.
Winter: Germain, J Tricou, M Vetillard and J Willemin with J
Demarchi, Feb 1918

Standing in the middle of the range at the end of the ridge running
SSW from the Aig Verte, the summit of this rocky pyramid offers
the most fantastic panorama. Easily accesible from the Couvercle
Hut, it holds a number of good rock climbs and is one of the most
frequented mountains in the massif. When descending the normal
route, special care is needed in locating the correct line.

**166**  **SOUTH FACE**
PD    First ascent party

90

*The normal route, one of the most popular in the range and highly
suitable for novice alpinists. Surprisingly the face is rather featureless, the*

*climbing straightforward and not particularly interesting. The route is quite short and an early start is unnecessary.*

From the Couvercle Hut follow a good track W to the little Moine glacier and go up it to the S face where a huge couloir leads up to a point a little R of the summit (1hr). Climb up the couloir for a short distance to a platform on the R and leave the couloir, slanting up R in 2 wide chimneys to a grassy terraced slope. A vague path goes up this slope first R then L to a small buttress overlooking the couloir. Climb a short chimney to a shoulder (III). Climb the R side of the couloir easily for 50m then take 2 successive chimneys (III) to reach a large platform on the L. Slant up L, crossing the couloir by a fine ledge, then take cracks and a ramp to an enormous terrace from where the summit can be seen. Slant up R and follow the R flank of a long rocky spur crossing 2 scree terraces before returning L across the spur to easy ground. Go up slabs and grooves for 100m to a huge ledge and continue directly to the summit. c450m, 3½hr from the hut.

## 167 SOUTH RIDGE

AD–

E Bruhl and L Valluet with A Ravanel and F Belin, 2 Sept 1928

90

*A delightful little climb, short, safe and highly recommended for the technically competant. It provides a useful introduction to Alpine rock, reaching the upper part of the ridge via a diagonal approach from the Moine glacier.*

From the base of the huge couloir of the normal route and just above the rimaye, climb steeply to a large ledgeline leading L for 200m. Where it ends climb up R on easy ground. Work L to the S ridge and reach it at a gap below a striking pinnacle resembling a double-headed hammer. Reach a big terrace and climb to an obvious horizontal ledge which leads L to a dièdre. Climb a crack in the back (4m, IV) and the chimney above (III) then follow the ridge for a long way to a terrace below a vertical wall. Climb this direct (V+) or by a crack on the L (IV) and continue easily up the long rocky ridge to the summit. 450m, 4½hr from the hut.

## 168 SOUTH RIDGE INTEGRAL

D–

W Birkenmajor, J Bujak, B Chwacsinki and W Ostrowski in 2 parts on 7 and 13 Aug 1932

90

*An established classic giving a long and sustained outing on excellent granite. The climbing, on open faces and cracks, is more delicate than strenuous and very well protected. Highly recommended, especially to the more experienced route finder.*

Cross below the Moine glacier to reach a couloir-chimney leading to a gap at the foot of the S ridge just N of Pt 2858m where there is a conspicuous arrowhead of rock and a metal sign (¾hr). Climb the couloir to the gap (III) and move R where a chimney on the E face (III) leads up to the ridge. Follow the crest to a rock table (IV). Traverse across the E flank of the ridge to a notch (IV) then continue across a slab (IV) finally climbing a crack to the crest (IV+). Cross the deep gap beyond by a diagonal rappel then climb the crest on the far side (IV) and jump across a small gap. Continue along the ridge to the foot of a gendarme and climb it on the L side (IV). Go down the ridge on the R side to a shoulder (IV) and reach the platform below (III). Walk along a big flat slab and go down to a notch. Climb out the other side by an overhanging chimney round on the L (IV+).Continue easily along the ridge turning the first gendarme on the L and the second on the R. Reach a narrow gap and rappel 25m to an easy couloir on the W face running parallel to the ridge. Climb it to the ridge, finishing via a chimney and a through-route under a huge chockstone (IV). Slant up the R side of the ridge to the large gendarme and turn it on the L via a chimney with overhanging blocks (35m, IV+). Continue along the ridge, generally traversing on easy ground below the crest, first on one side then the other, returning to the ridge each time by steep dièdres (IV). Reach the gap below the pinnacle resembling a double-headed hammer where Route 167 is joined. Follow this to the summit. 600m, 7hr from the hut.

**169    SOUTH-WEST RIDGE**

TD    J Asper, M Bron, I Gamboni and R Habersaat, 9–10 Aug 1958

*This is a very long and sustained rock climb of high quality in a surprisingly remote situation. It has seen very few ascents, no doubt due to the fact that the best approach lies directly from Montenvers. A bivouac is unavoidable and the whole enterprise a lengthy and committing undertaking.*

Reach the foot of the ridge in 3hr from Montenvers by a tedious ascent of the grassy slopes and broken rock above the Mer de Glace. In the first half the ridge is well-defined and the route keeps fairly close to the crest. The upper section bristles with sharp gendarmes and is climbed mainly on the R flank. Route finding is often tricky and as many variations are possible, a full-blown description is unnecessary. There are many pitches of IV and V with a few short sections of A1. 600m, Allow 16–18hr from Montenvers to the summit.

| | |
|---|---|
| **170**<br>AD<br>**91** | **NORTH RIDGE**<br>H Kuntze and G Hasler with J Ravanel and E Simond, 19 Aug 1902 |

*Although seldom done, this climb is not uninteresting and allows a straightforward traverse of the mountain. In descent the 3 main steps are easily rappeled.*

Reach the Brèche Moine-Nonne by Route 164 descending the ridge at the end to reach the gap. Climb the first step on the crest (III) then avoid the gendarmes on the horizontal section that follows by scrambling across the R flank. Return to the ridge below the second step (pitch of III) and climb the latter directly via an open chimney (IV). The third step can also be climbed direct (V) or turned on the R via snowy rocks to an open couloir, the L side of which is followed easily to the summit. c300m, 4½hr from the hut.

| | |
|---|---|
| **171**<br>VI<br>**91**<br>**37** | **EAST FACE DIRECT**<br>A Contamine and P Labrunie, 25 July 1954 |

*This is the best route on the face and an established classic. It takes a direct line on excellent granite with the crux occurring on the first pitch. The face is steep and receives a lot of sun ensuring that the climb rapidly comes into condition after bad weather. See also Photo 90*

Start at the foot of an open dièdre 50m high and capped by a roof that lies to the R of 2 high parallel chimneys. Reaching the rock can often be difficult due to the state of the glacier (¾hr from the Couvercle Hut). 400m, 6hr

| | |
|---|---|
| **172**<br>V<br>**91**<br>**37** | **EAST FACE – AUREILLE-FEUTREN ROUTE**<br>J Aureille and Y Feutren, 2 or 3 Aug 1942 |

*Easier, not as good as the previous route, and taking longer to dry out, this is still a worthwhile outing which will certainly not be crowded. The major difficulties occur in the first 80m while the upper section gives pleasant crack climbing.*

Start at the foot of the large couloir L of the summit fall line. There is usually a thin high snow cone and the climb begins with a thin crack slanting up to the L (¾hr from the Couvercle Hut). 400m, 5hr

## Col d'Argentière 3552m

First traverse: S Winkworth with A, F and P Simond, 22 June 1861

Lying S of the Tour Noir this is a fairly easy link between the French and Swiss sides of the range but is rarely used for this purpose.

**173** **WEST (FRENCH) SIDE**
F+ *An easy glacier walk or ski ascent during the winter months.*

**92** From the Argentière Hut follow the path SE (red paint markers) to the Argentière glacier and reach the foot of the Tour Noir glacier. This is flat at first and relatively uncrevassed. Higher it becomes steeper and has long crevasses that need wide detours before an easier slope leads to the broad saddle. 3hr from the hut.

**174** **EAST (SWISS) SIDE**
PD/PD+ *A complicated glacier approach followed by steep shattered rocks in a wild and unfrequented environment.*

From the A Neuve Hut go down the path then traverse W across moraine to reach the glacier close to Pt 2753m. Cross the badly crevassed glacier to Pt 2971m. Up to the L a long rocky rib comes down from a point a little above the col. Reach it and climb the crest to the Passage d'Argentière (3620m) just N of the col. 3½hr

## Tour Noir 3837m

E Javelle and F Turner with J Moser and F Tournier, 3 Aug 1876

An attractive rocky peak with straightforward access. It is climbed regularly in summer and not infrequently in winter. The classic ascent from the Argentière Hut involves traversing the mountain, up the W or most often the N ridge and down the SE flank. The Swiss approach, being longer and more difficult, is rarely used and cannot really be recommended. As with other high peaks in the vicinity, the view is both magnificent and extensive, not only across the Argentière Wall but also over the Valais and distant Oberland.

**175** **SOUTH-EAST FLANK**
PD First ascent party

**92** *The normal route though generally used in descent after a traverse of the mountain. Numerous variations are possible. Recently a large rock fall*

*has occured above the 'Vires Javelle' which presently receives frequent stonefall. The crest of the S ridge may now provide the safest means of ascent.*

From the Argentière Hut follow Route 173 to the Col d'Argentière and go up for 200m to the Passage d'Argentière. Go up the L side of the ridge on blocks and snow turning a pointed gendarme to reach a steep buttress. Move R along the 'Vires Javelle', a system of broken ledges, then cut across the SE face c100m below the summit. After c80m, a conspicuous rock rib is reached. Climb a slabby couloir for 12m and gain the rib on the R (moves of II). Follow it to where the angle eases then move R again to a spur of easy blocks. Follow it to the gap between the 2 summits. The N summit is the highest. 4½hr from the hut.

When descending this route beware of continuing too far down the scree below the Javelle Ledges. It is also possible, after reaching the gap between the two summits, to traverse S on the A Neuve side and rappel to the normal route at the 'safe' end of the Javelle Ledges. 2hr to the hut.

| | |
|---|---|
| **176** | **WEST RIDGE** |
| AD | H Hoessli, M Kurz and K Steiner, 30 July 1909 |
| 92 | *Although not well known, this gives a pleasant and worthwhile climb of nearly 300m.* |

The ridge is well-defined and rises steeply above the Col des Améthystes (3563m). Reach it from either side, although the approach via the Améthystes glacier (Route 178) is probably more convenient (2½hr). Follow the ridge crest turning any major difficulties on the R (moves of III). The middle section can give delicate mixed climbing. Near the top slant R and climb the couloir to a gap between the 2 summits. 6hr from the Argentière Hut.

| | |
|---|---|
| **177** | **NORTH RIDGE** |
| PD | L and T Aubert with M Crettez, 23 July 1898 |
| 92 | *Shorter, easier and far more popular than the W ridge. The usual ascent route when making the traverse. There is however, a fair amount of poor rock and the approach couloir is exposed to stonefall.* |

From the Col Sup du Tour Noir follow the ridge as near to the crest as possible. It is quite impressive but easier than the shattered rock on the flanks. c300m, 1hr

# Col Supérieur du Tour Noir 3690m

**178**    **FRENCH (WEST) SIDE**
PD    *A short couloir with stonefall danger.*

92

From the Argentière Hut follow the good track up the crest of the moraine on the L side of the Améthystes glacier. Continue up the L side of the glacier then walk across in the upper section to reach the base of the couloir. Climb the snowy bed or rocks on the L side to the top. c160m, 3hr from the hut.

**179**    **SWISS (EAST) SIDE**
PD    *Wild and unfrequented.*

From the A Neuve Hut go up the glacier towards the Grand Lui then work L passing below the Col de l'A Neuve until it is possible to head S and climb the shattered rocky buttress on the R side of the couloir coming down from the col. 4½–5hr from the hut.

# Pointe Inférieure des Améthystes 3273m

C Joublet with R Charlet and M Burnet, 24 July 1907

An entertaining little excursion to the minor summit that marks the final bastion in the long W ridge of the Tour Noire. Suitable for a short day's training.

**180**    **SOUTH FACE**
F    From the Argentière Hut reach a very narrow gap on the ENE ridge

92

by a snow slope above the Améthystes glacier. Move onto the S face and follow scree-covered ledges to the summit. 2hr

# Pointe 3130m

Standing at the foot of the W ridge, this gendarme is reached in 30min from the Argentière hut and offers several nice short rock climbs.

**181**    **SOUTH PILLAR**
IV/A1    F Audibert and F de Siéyes, 3 and 4 July 1969

92

*Suitable for a pleasant afternoon's enjoyment. The granite is excellent. Although originally described with a fair amount of aid, this has almost*

*certainly now been pruned to a minimum to give a high standard free climb.*

Start round to the R of the lowest point and directly below the summit. Climb up L in a dièdre (IV−) then continue direct (A1 then III) crossing an overhanging 10m wall (A1). After 50m reach a quartz ledge. Slant up R for 100m (IV+) then back L for 60m (IV, A1) to a large terrace. Climb a crack (A1 and IV) onto the ridge and so reach the summit. 200m, 4hr from the hut.

Descent: On the S side a narrow gully (slight stonefall) leads down to the glacier.

**182**    **SOUTH FACE**
VII+    Climbed on 12 and 13 Aug 1985, party unknown

*A hard free climb with all the necessary protection in-situ. The route follows the slabs on the R side of the face.*

Start at an arrow on a ledge that lies above a conspicuous hole in the rock. Climb the grey slabs towards the R side of the face and continue up this finishing on the E ridge. 180m, unavoidable moves of VII−/VII.

# Aiguille de l'A Neuve 3753m

A Barbey and L Kurz with J Bessard and J Simond, 11 Aug 1888

A rarely visited summit just N of the Tour Noir. The rock tends to be poor but in good conditions the N face can provide pleasant snow and ice work.

**183**    **SOUTH-WEST FACE**
PD    First ascent party

**92**

*The normal route and easiest means of ascent and descent. The couloir is exposed to stonefall and should be completed early in the day.*

Follow Route 178 to below the SW face of the mountain. A prominent couloir in the middle of the face slants from R to L and gives the line of ascent – easy climbing on snow and broken rock to reach the ridge just R of the summit. c200m, 3hr from the Argentière Hut.

**184**    **NORTH FACE**
D−    M Kurz and K Steiner, 29 July 1910

84

A moderately steep ice route with a mixed finish. The situation is remote and despite a straightforward approach from the Saleina Hut (2hr) or even the Albert Premier by crossing the Fenêtre du Tour(4hr), it is seldom climbed. Allow 3hr for the face and another 1hr for the main ridge running due S to the summit. The shortest descent to the Saleina glacier reverses the NE ridge to the Col de l'A Neuve (poor rock) but this is not easy to follow and has a step of IV in ascent. It is safer but longer to follow the easy crest S to the Col Sup du Tour Noir (½hr, PD−), descend Route 179 and reach the Col de l'A Neuve. 550m

## Col de l'A Neuve 3406m

First traverse: L and T Aubert with M Crettez, 22 July 1898

This can provide a useful passage for parties climbing routes on the Grand Lui and Aig de l'A Neuve.

**185**    **NORTH SIDE**
PD    A short steep snow/ice slope. 200m, 3½hr from the Saleina Hut.

84     **SOUTH SIDE**
PD    *A crevassed glacier approach.*

From the A Neuve Hut go up the glacier towards the Grand Lui passing N of the rocky island 3040m. Continue W and descend a wide open couloir to the glacier bay below the col. Reach the latter easily by a gentle slope. 3hr from the hut.

## Col du Tour Noir 3535m

First traverse: H George and R Macdonald with M Anderegg and C Almer, 22 July 1863. Winter traverse: J Sanseverino, 12 Feb 1959

An impressive pass between the Aigs de l'A Neuve and d'Argentière. It does not afford an easy passage between France and Switzerland so is rarely crossed.

**187**    **SOUTH-WEST (FRENCH) SIDE**
F
A straightforward walk up the Améthystes glacier. 3hr from the
**93**   Argentière Hut. See Route 178. See also Photo 92

**188**    **NORTH-EAST (SWISS) SIDE**
AD+
A steep ice slope. 350m, 5hr from the Saleina Hut.
**84**

# Grand Lui 3509m

V Attinger, E Colomb and L Kurz with F Biselx and J and J
Bessard, 3 June 1889

An easy snow peak and delightful viewpoint. Routes on this
mountain provide an excellent introduction to Alpine climbing for
parties based on the Swiss side of the range and will not be
overcrowded. Relatively popular in winter as the base of the
mountain is easily reached on ski.

**189**    **SOUTH FLANK**
F
First ascent party

*The normal route from the A Neuve Hut. An easy but crevassed glacier
approach.*

Follow Route 186 towards the Col de l'A Neuve. When level with
the Col de Saleina and after passing several enormous crevasses,
head N and climb the snowy rocks directly to the summit. 3hr from
the A Neuve Hut.

**190**    **WEST SIDE**
PD
**84**   J Kugy with D Maquignaz and J Proment, July 1896

*This is probably the easiest approach from the Saleina Hut and the
normal route in winter.*

Follow Route 238 towards the Col du Chardonnet and at c3000m
start contouring the glacier to the SE in the direction of the Col de
l'A Neuve. When opposite the Grand Lui go up L to a snowy
couloir on the W face and climb it direct to the summit. 3½hr from
the Saleina Hut.

**191**    **NORTH-WEST RIDGE**
PD
First ascent party
**84**
*A well-defined ridge, short but steep in parts. It descends to a snow
shoulder before the rocky peak Pt 3255m.*

Follow the previous route towards the W face and climb a short slope to reach the snow shoulder from the W side. Follow the snowy crest directly to the summit. 3½hr from the Saleina Hut.

**192**    **NORTH FACE**
AD–    J Duchosal and R Gréloz, 12 Oct 1937

**84**

The lower part of this little snow/ice face is cut by a rock barrier. Difficulties increase markedly if this is not well-covered in snow. The face can be approached directly or via the snow shoulder on the NW ridge. 4hr from the Saleina Hut.

**193**    **EAST-SOUTH-EAST RIDGE**
PD–    E Monod-Herzen with O and E Crettez, 19 Aug 1902

The Col du Grand Lui is reached easily from the Saleina or A Neuve Huts by short couloirs from the respective glacier basins (3hr or 2hr). The ridge is very straightforward and can be used in either direction to effect a traverse of the peak. 1½hr

## Petit Darrey 3508m

V Attinger, A Barbey and H Pascal with J and J Bessard, 31 July 1890

An undistinguished summit which is best combined with a traverse of the Grand Darrey.

**194**    **NORTH-EAST RIDGE**
F    L Courvoisier-Haas and H Rieckel with G Coquoz, 28 Aug 1894

*Perhaps the best of the normal routes to the summit.*

From either the Saleina or A Neuve Huts, use Route H24 to reach the Darrey glacier. Go up it and get onto the NE ridge at any convenient point on the R. A short but interesting rock crest leads to the summit. 3hr from the Saleina Hut, 4hr from the A Neuve Hut.

**195**    **EAST-SOUTH-EAST RIDGE FROM GRAND DARREY**
I/II    First crossing: V Fynn and F Biselx, 25 Aug 1896

c400m in length, this rocky ridge allows a complete traverse of the Grand and Petit Darrey. 1hr of scrambling in either direction.

## Grand Darrey 3514m

L Kurz with F Biselx, 7 Aug 1885

Slightly more interesting climbing than on the Petit Darrey.

**196**    **SOUTH-EAST RIDGE**
PD+    E Rossier with O Crettez and S Copt, 1900

*A delightful little climb and thoroughly recommended as the most interesting route to the summit.*

From the A Neuve Hut use Route H24 to reach the Col Sup des Essettes at the foot of the ridge (1¼hr). Climb up the ridge to a buttress and ascend this by short walls with steep cracks (III+) on the R of an area of smooth slabs. Continue along the ridge turning any difficulties on the R side and cross a fore peak before reaching the top. 400m, 3½hr from the hut.

**197**    **NORTH-EAST RIDGE**
PD    First ascent party

*This is the normal route from the Saleina Hut and the easiest descent from the peak.*

Follow Route H24 to the Planereuse glacier and go up the Darrey glacier to the entrance of the upper cwm (2hr). On the L climb a snow/ice slope and rotten rocks to the NE ridge and follow it, at first snowy and narrow then rocky, to the summit.
     3hr from the Saleina Hut.

The complete NE ridge can be climbed at the same grade by reaching the prominent saddle W of Pt 3191m from the Darrey glacier. The huge gendarme on the ridge can easily be avoided.

**198**    **SOUTH-SOUTH-WEST FACE**
AD    J Busio and R Gréloz, 10 Sept 1950

A short and direct rock route on good granite. The climb finishes on the fore summit, starting from the top of the tiny glacier bay in the centre of the face. c250m, 4hr from the A Neuve Hut.

## Pointe des Essettes 3160m

A long ridge runs S from this point and overlooks the A Neuve Hut. The SW face, reached in a few minutes from the hut, has a host of pleasant little rock climbs on excellent granite.

## Grande Pointe des Planereuses 3151m

V Attinger, E Colomb and L Kurz with F Biselx, 10 July 1892

A minor peak, easily accessible from the Saleina Hut. The climbing is short and the peak can be attempted at almost any time of the day. A traverse gives the most satisfying outing.

**199**    **SOUTH-WEST RIDGE**
F    First ascent party in descent

An easy ascent from the Col des Planereuses over broken rock. See Route H24. 1¾hr from the hut, 1hr in descent.

**200**    **NORTH RIDGE**
PD–    A Dubois and L Kurz with J Copt, 15 July 1893

*An interesting little scramble.*

Reach the foot of the ridge from the E side at a gap beyond the rocky rognon Pt 2932m. Climb on the W side of the crest to the summit. 2hr

## Grand Clocher des Planereuses 2806m

V Attinger and L Kurz with F Biselx, 11 July 1892

Even more accessible from the Saleina Hut, this minor rock peak gives some pleasant training on generally good granite.

**201**    **SOUTH-EAST FLANK**
F    First ascent party

From the Saleina Hut head up to the Col du Grand Clocher which lies on the ridge just S of Pt 2835m. Reach it by a scree couloir. Move R onto the flanks and climb directly to the summit. 1hr from the hut.

**202**    **NORTH-WEST RIDGE**
PD      E Blanchet and A Martin with F Veillon, Sept 1910

Go down the path from the Saleina Hut and reach a gap in the NW ridge between the Grand and Petit Clocher. Avoid the first buttress on the L and regain the ridge by a series of chimneys. Follow the crest to the top. 1hr from the hut.

The W ridge is reported to be worthwhile at about the same grade.

**203**    **EAST RIDGE**
PD      E Blanchet and A de Ribeaupierre with C Veillon, 27 July 1916

By crossing the Col du Grand Clocher (see Route 201) it is possible to reach the E ridge at c2500m. It gives interesting scrambling on sound granite. 2hr from the hut.

## Petit Clocher des Planereuses 2699m

E l'Hardy with M Crettex and E Revaz, 14 Sept 1896

The best climbing close to the Saleina Hut lies on this fine little obelisk.

**204**    **WEST FLANK AND NORTH RIDGE**
PD+      First ascent party

The easiest route to the summit descends the hut path for ¼hr and climbs the huge couloir on the W flank of the N ridge. There are 2 summits. Turn the first to reach the gap beyond then descend, on the W side, to a ledge. Follow it and climb up on good rock to a scree ledge below the final steep wall. Climb this to a point just L of the summit via a chimney (IV). 2½–3hr from the hut.

**205**    **SOUTH-WEST PILLAR**
V+/A2      G Genoud and D Troillet, 10 Sept 1969

*A short difficult rock route that clears immediately after bad weather. First climbed with about 20 points of aid, it is an obvious target for a high-standard free ascent.*

The pillar is obvious and lies a few minutes above the path. Begin 10m R of the crest by climbing up to a sloping terrace (A1, IV+). Take a crack on the L (A1), the 40m dièdre above (V+ and A1) and passing to the R of an overhanging flake (A2) reach a little ledge.

Climb over a block (V) and up R for 40m (A1 and V) to a dièdre/chimney. Climb this (V and V+) then work up R for 40m to easier ground (V, friable rock). Reach the foot of a buttress (III and IV). Climb a wall on the L and the chimney above (V) to a gap in the ridge close to the summit. 200m, 5hr from the hut.

Descent: From the gap in the ridge rappel down a chimney on the S side to a large sloping terrace. Follow this into a couloir on the R and descend it (rappel) to easy ground leading down to the path (1hr).

## Amône Slab

Although only a roadside crag, it is worth mentioning this wonderful and popular 400m slab climb situated opposite the village of L'Amône just down from La Fouly. 16 pitches of immaculate compact limestone give delicate climbing with large cemented belay pegs. Mainly V with moves of VI−. Unfortunately the climb follows a dried-out watercourse and in a storm the route can be quickly transformed into a waterfall with serious stonefall. The route is direct and easy to follow with a scrambling descent to the R.

## Aiguille d'Argentière 3902m

A Reilly and E Whymper with H Charlet, M Croz and M Payot, 15 July 1864. Winter: M Cottier with M Crettez, 9 Jan 1910

One of the most frequented high snowy mountains in the range with a wide variety of quality routes in all grades. The summit is renowned for its outstanding views over the Argentière basin and towards the famous peaks of the Valais. The rock walls of the Jardin ridge overlooking the Améthystes glacier have recently become as popular for hard free climbing as almost anywhere in the range. Pride of place however must go to the N face with its selection of first-class ice routes.

**206**    **SOUTH-WEST FLANK (MILIEU GLACIER)**
PD−/PD    Descended by L Dècle and Y Hutchinson with A Imseng and L
**93**    Lanier, 14 Aug 1880, but not ascended until 1895

*The normal route and strongly recommended to those visiting the Alps for the first time. An elegant and scenic glacier expedition taking a direct line to the summit between the 2 long parallel ridges that descend to the Argentière glacier. For good reason it is extremely popular and it will be rare indeed to ascend untrampled snow.*

From the Argentière Hut follow a broken track NW to the moraines on the R side of the Milieu glacier (20mins). Go up the centre of the glacier, then closer to the L side where there are fewer crevasses. Climb a steep slope at the top to reach the summit ridge just R of the W top. Follow the delightful crest 100m to the main summit on the R. 950m, 4hr from the hut.

The upper slope deteriorates rapidly in the morning and any descent of this route should be made fairly early. The risk can be reduced by keeping close to or on the rocks at the side.

**207**     **WEST SUMMIT VIA SOUTH-WEST (STRATON) RIDGE**
TD
93   The first complete ascent of the route described below has not been recorded, but the ridge was first climbed by H Heiner and L Wanner with J Charlet-Straton, 11 Aug 1881, who avoided most of the difficulties on the R side.

*This monstrously long and serrated ridge on the L side of the Milieu glacier has seldom been climbed in its entirety. It gives a superb outing with climbing similar to a complete traverse of the Aigs du Diable. Although the difficulties are greater, they are not sustained and the exposure and commitment are much less, with escape possible at a number of points. A shorter and more feasible alternative climbs up onto the upper part of the ridge just below the Chapeau Fort (3774m) at AD+.*

Cross the Milieu Glacier and reach a small cwm on the L side of Pt 3306m. Climb a narrow couloir to the ridge and continue up it to a 3-pronged gendarme (2hr). The ridge can be climbed from its base (c2700m) to this point (several pitches of IV). Climb to the summit of Pt 3640m (IV, 2½hr). Continue along the ridge climbing all gendarmes fairly close to the crest by the line of least resistance. Short rappels are made to gaps on the far side, and after a very serrated and exposed section, a large snowy col is reached below the Chapeau Fort (IV and V with at least 3 pitches of V+, 9hr).

    Avoid the first tower on the L then climb cracked walls and chimneys (IV+) on this flank of the Chapeau Fort to reach its summit. Rappel 40m down to the snowy col below the final buttress

213

and follow the steep but easy ridge to the summit. Complete ascent 750m, 15–16hr from the hut.

The shorter but pleasant alternative follows the Milieu glacier until a little below the point where one is level with the Chapeau Fort. Climb up L to the hanging snowfield following this and the rocks above (IV and V) to the ridge, 2 or 3 pitches below the top of the Chapeau. 300m

There are now many first-class rock climbs between 20–30m high on the SE flanks of this ridge above the Milieu glacier. On the W side of the ridge, approached directly from the Chardonnet glacier, the W spur of Pt 3040m gives an excellent line to the summit (8 pitches, IV and V, 180m. Rappel descent into the couloir to the R).Similar but not sustained is the W spur of Pt 3250m (11 pitches, V/V+ with in-situ protection. Rappel the ascent route). Both climbs can be reached in about 1½hr from the Grands Mulets station.

## 208    WEST FLANK AND NORTH-WEST RIDGE

PD/PD+    First ascent party

**97**

*The easiest means of reaching the summit when coming from the Swiss side. It is a much safer means of descent when the upper slopes of the Milieu glacier are in poor condition and surprisingly, it is not that much longer.*

From the Argentière Hut follow Route 237 up the Chardonnet glacier and take the R (S) branch. From the Saleina Hut cross the Col du Chardonnet by Route 238 and descend to the same point. Go up the glacier, at first on the R side, then on the L to avoid a zone of crevasses. At the top climb a rocky rib between 2 steep couloirs, or the couloirs themselves, onto the NW ridge. Follow the ridge easily until it peters out into the snow slopes of the N face. Either follow these or the rocks (good belays) on the R, to the vicinity of the W summit. 4½hr from the Argentière Hut, 5hr from the Saleina Hut.

*Aiguille d'Argentière continued on page 216*

---

# Aiguille d'Argentière: North Face

A classic snow and ice face in a somewhat lonely situation rising above the head of the Saleina glacier. Unfortunately the face has changed over the years from a straightforward snow slope to a complex and dangerous hanging glacier. The Direct Route, first climbed in 1930, is unjustifiably dangerous, and the most interesting routes nowadays lie on the NNE face a little to the L. The face can be reached in 3–3½hr from the Argentière Hut by first crossing the the Col du Chardonnet, in 2hr from the Saleina Hut via Route 238 or in 3½–4hr from the Albert Premier Hut by crossing the Fenêtre du Tour where there are comfortable bivouac sites.

**209**     **ORIGINAL ROUTE**
D–     J Lagarde and H de Ségogne, 2 Aug 1926. Winter ascent: J Braunet
97     and A Meir, March 1966

The classic line which gives objectively safe climbing to the R of the hanging glacier. The average angle is 50° and in good conditions succumbs to straightforward cramponing. Once above the seracs on the L either slant up to the summit ridge or continue via the shoulder on the NW ridge. 700m, 4–5hr

**210**     **BETTEMBOURG DIRECT ROUTE**
TD–/TD     G Bettembourg, 13 April 1973
97

This takes the steep couloir to the L of the central rock buttress which is itself L of the hanging glacier. The top of the buttress is reached after 300m and ice walls in the upper section of the face are climbed directly to the summit. The route is threatened throughout by serac fall and both difficulty and danger will vary from year to year. A serious climb, 700m, 5–8hr

## Aiguille d'Argentière: NNE Face

**211**     **MESSNER ROUTE**
TD–     H Holzer, S Mayerl, G and R Messner, 6 Aug 1967
97

*A highly recommended and elegant line that gives enjoyable and varied climbing. Steeper and more difficult than the N face but without objective danger. In recent years it has become quite popular and is now considered the best route on the wall.*

Start below the rock spur that lies to the L of the central buttress and is almost in a direct line with the summit. Climb the ice slope on the L of this spur for 150m and before it steepens slant up R onto the crest. Climb it to the upper icefield (Scottish 2/3) and follow this for 300m (50°) to the triangular rock buttress at the top of the slope. Climb it direct on large flakes or by the obvious gully on the R and finish up the narrow NE ridge to the summit. 700m, 5–7hr from the rimaye.

The ice slope L of the rock spur was climbed directly (75°) onto the upper icefield by C Scott and D Haston in 1972.

| | |
|---|---|
| **212** | **GABARROU-JOUVE ROUTE** |
| TD– | P Gabarrou and B Jouve, 15 Sept 1977 |
| 97 | |

This begins in the same place as the Messner Route then takes a L ward slanting rampline to reach steeper ground. 2 difficult mixed pitches (70°) lead to the small upper snowfield and from the top of this, the NE ridge is gained via a 55° gully. The few subsequent ascents have confirmed this to be a quality mixed climb with no objective danger. 700m, 5–6hr

---

*Aiguille d'Argentière continued*

| | |
|---|---|
| **213** | **NORTH-EAST RIDGE INTEGRAL** |
| D– | R Dittert and F Marullaz, 13 Aug 1944 |
| 97 | |

*Rarely climbed although the upper part of the ridge is often followed to the summit after completing climbs on the E and NE flanks. See also Photo 84*

The base of the ridge takes the form of 2 rocky spurs split by a deep snowy couloir. Start 30m to the L of this couloir and climb up the crest of the spur for 50m. Continue on the L flank steeply, on good granite, and cross a couloir to reach the crest of the ridge at a small gap above the spur. Follow the ridge at a fairly gentle angle over snow and rock until a final narrow crest leads to the summit. c800m, 6hr from the rimaye.

| | |
|---|---|
| **214** | **BARBEY COULOIR** |
| AD | A Barbey with J Bessard, 27 June 1884 |

*This is the wide Rward slanting couloir on the E face that gains the NE ridge at a point just below ²/₃ height. It is frequently climbed from the Saleina Hut but due to its aspect a very early start is necessary and the route cannot be recommended as a means of descent. A classic snow gully of average angle 42°.*

At c3000m on the Saleina glacier slant L passing round the foot of the NE ridge and reach the E face. Climb the wide snowy couloir bearing R all the way (it is often possible to use the rocks on the R) to reach the NE ridge in 2½hr. Continue up the ridge to the summit (1hr). 600m, 5½hr from the Saleina Hut.

**215 EAST FACE DIRECT**
AD    H, J and P Hadjilazaro and P Maehly with O Crettex, 17 July 1902

*A more logical conclusion to the Barbey Couloir.*

Start up the Barbey Couloir but then slant up through a rock barrier on the L to follow snow slopes on the R of a central rocky rib, directly to the summit. 600m, 5½hr from the Saleina Hut.

**216 EAST FACE LEFT SIDE**
AD    G Bonfanti and R Quagliotto, 13 Oct 1985

Really no more than a variation on the Direct Route, starting on the L of the broken central rock spur and climbing alongside this on 50°+ snow slopes to the summit. Very snowy conditions will make the mixed climbing through the lower rocks more enjoyable. 600m, 5½hr from the Saleina hut.

**217 EAST-SOUTH-EAST (FLECHE ROUSSE) RIDGE**
AD    G Morse, J Wicks and C Wilson, 3 Aug 1893

93    *An established classic that appears to have been rather neglected in recent years. It offers continuously interesting climbing in an airy situation. See also Photo 94*

Follow Route 187 towards the Col du Tour Noir and slant up to gain the ridge just above a group of 3 gendarmes (3618m, 3hr). Go up the ridge turning a tower on the R and crossing, or turning on the L, the next group of gendarmes to reach a stony section. Climb a snow/ice couloir on the L which leads up to a snowy saddle on a secondary ridge in front of the prominent tower of the Flèche Rousse. In bad conditions one can climb the rocks on the R side or even avoid the couloir altogether by using the L flank of the secondary ridge (3hr).
      Climb up above the snowy saddle, trending R on easy ground, towards the summit of the Flèche Rousse. Turn a large overhang and the leaning arrowhead of rock that follows, on the L side, to reach the top (3879m). Go down to the gap beyond by a scramble and a 15m rappel over a vertical step. Follow the ridge above, at first on rock then snow, to the summit. c450m, 7½hr from the Argentière Hut.

**218**

AD

94

**Y COULOIR**

H Cameré, July 1922

*A classic snow and ice climb somewhat reminiscent of the typically deep and enclosed 'Scottish gully' (average angle 45°). It is exposed to stonefall, especially near the base, and an early start after a well-frozen night is essential. Despite this, it has become a very popular undertaking and in high season one is most unlikely to be on the route alone. See also Photo 93*

From the Argentière Hut follow Route 187 up the Améthystes glacier and reach the foot of the Y Couloir on the L (2hr). It is possible to climb directly into the couloir but this is steep and most parties enter by using the spur on the R, climbing onto the crest via a steep chimney. Above the steep section of the couloir, cross it to the L side and climb up to the fork. The normal route follows the R branch which is deeper and less exposed to stonefall and leads to the saddle on the ESE ridge above the Flèche Rousse (3hr). The L branch is steeper at first then more rocky in its upper section where it is better to move to the R. It terminates on the SW ridge which is followed easily to the summit. 450m, c5½hr from the hut.

**219**

TD–

94

**FLECHE RIDGE**

H Mazeaud and J Pellissier with J Charlet and G Belin, 27 Aug 1947

*A sustained rock climb over the various towers that make up this very steep ridge. There have been relatively few subsequent ascents.*

Start well to the R of the small spur used by Route 218 where a ledge slants up to the L on the flanks of the ridge. Above is a red gendarme. Climb up to the overhang (IV) then, moving R, climb a series of chimneys and cracks (IV to V+) into an easy couloir and follow it for 100m to the ridge. Climb the crest, continuing over a number of towers (IV and IV+) with short rappels on the far side until an 80m couloir on the L leads up to the top of the Flèche Rousse. Follow the ENE ridge to the summit. 500m, 8hr from the hut.

**220**

D

93

**JARDIN RIDGE**

M Azéma with A Charlet, 27 Aug 1942

*Running SW from the S summit of the Argentière is this long narrow granite ridge with numerous isolated gendarmes. It ends at Pt 3177m overlooking the snout of the Milieu glacier. The various spurs and buttresses, of generally first-class granite, rising from the Améthystes glacier give many worthwhile climbs. They are easily and quickly reached from the Argentière Hut, clear rapidly after bad weather and catch the sun for most of the day. The situation is not overly serious and descents are short.*

*Recommended is a traverse of the ridge itself, a long and entertaining expedition which enjoys a certain popularity. Some of the gendarmes can be climbed or easily avoided and parts of the ridge may often be followed by teams completing harder routes on the flanks. See also Photo 94*

From the Argentière Hut go round the base of Pt 3159m using the moraine and reach a gap to the N of this Pt via a rocky couloir. Climb diagonally up the face on the R, using grooves on the E side (II) or a dièdre on the W (40m, III) to an area of smooth slabs. Follow these onto a little ridge leading to the plateau (III) – a huge area covered with big blocks. Continue up this, crossing a deep notch by a 20m rappel and climbing cracks (III) on the far side to the upper section of the plateau. The ridge gradually narrows and leads to a group of gendarmes – the '3 Guards' and the Yatagan (3510m). Cross a small notch (rappel) and climb the first 'Guard' by a crack on the L (IV). Follow the ridge over the top (III) and make a short rappel into the gap beyond. Rappel 25m down the Améthystes flank, traverse easily to some huge slabs and climb a steep crack on poor rock (25m, IV+) then easy rock back to the ridge. Exposed climbing leads to the top of the second 'Guard' (IV). Rappel 25m and scramble down to the gap before the Yatagan. Turn this on the R, passing between it and a gendarme just N of the Minaret and reach the foot of the Casque (4½hr).

Traverse across broken rock to the gap between the Reine and the Casque. Continue the traverse descending to the foot of a split tower and pass behind it, going down and across for 15m to a letterbox. Climb the narrow chimney (10m, IV) then slabs and cracks (IV) to a terrace. Reach the ridge above, R of a small gendarme, via slabs and a chimney (IV) and follow it to the top of the Casque (3668m, 2hr). Slant down R for 10m then make 2 rappels of 25–30m each and traverse into the gap below the final ridge leading up to the S summit. Follow it, crossing a small tower (20m, rappel) and avoid the first two of a group of gendarmes by ledges on the R, climbing the third directly. A narrow easy-angled snow ridge leads to the S summit. 900m, 9hr from the hut.

**221**     **TOUR JAUNE**
VI/A1    J Bellin, G, P and R Ravanel, 27 June 1968

94

*A detached pyramid (3700m) of excellent granite lying just to the L of the Y Couloir. A prominent crackline splits the face of this tower from top to bottom and the climb attempts to follow this with various deviations to one side or other. A little aid was used on the first ascent but it should now be possible to free climb most of the route.*

Reach the base of the route in under 2hr and scramble up easily towards the spur. After 100m climb up a couloir/chimney on the L (80m, IV) to a terrace with a small tower on the L side. The crackline in question now lies above and to the R. Descend by the same route (9 rappels). 400m, 5–6hr to the summit.

**222**     **SOUTH SUMMIT CENTRAL ROUTE**
TD–    U Manera and D Rabbi, 28 July 1974

94

*Lying to the L of the Tour Jaune, this face is easily distinguished in the lower section by a great rounded granite pillar 150m high. Several routes of varying difficulty climb this face but the one described below has become most popular. After the initial pitch the rock is compact and very solid.*

From the Argentière Hut reach the foot of the route in under 2hr and scramble up to a very large dièdre in the rounded pillar. Start on the R then slant up L in chimneys and cracks (V/VI). Continue on the L of the couloir above for 30m then traverse R to a large smooth slab and climb it (IV) to a vertical wall. Traverse 10m and climb the wall to a good ledge (IV+). Climb straight up steps to the horizontal ridge joining the tower to the wall above and move up to the R where there is another red tower with a couloir on its L. Starting on the L, climb more or less on the crest of the tower finishing steeply to the top (V and V+). Climb up rocky steps for 35m (mainly IV) then slant up L (IV+) to reach an open dièdre. Climb the crack on the L of the dièdre (V) then 2 short overhanging walls (V+ with some aid) to easier ground. Slant L for 3 pitches in rocky couloirs (III and IV) until below the summit ridge. Climb red slabs to the crest (IV+) and follow it over a small tower (IV) to reach the S summit. Continue easily to the main summit in ½hr. 500m to S summit, 8–10hr from the hut.

# Le Casque 3668m

The first major tower on the Jardin (SW) Ridge below the S summit. Although the short rock face above the Milieu glacier has been climbed, it is the SE flank where the high-quality free climbing will be found.

**223**
IV/V
94

**SOUTH-EAST SPUR**

F le Guern with G Rébuffat, 5 July 1967

*Nice climbing on the crest in a series of cracks and dièdres which are sustained at a reasonable standard. The final buttress can often be damp due to melting snow on the summit ridge.*

The spur, which is very obvious on the approach, lies on the R side of the SE face and is reached from the Argentière Hut in 1½hr. Climb this crest, a succession of 3 buttresses separated by large terraces, to a slender gendarme. It is possible to avoid this on the R though a short ascent gives a fine pitch of V+ and A1. Reach the gap below the final buttress by a rappel and climb a series of cracks to the top. 400m, 5–6hr from the hut.

**224**
V/V+
94

**SOUTH-EAST FACE**

P and R Mazars with G Bettembourg and H Thivierge, 29 July 1974

This offers some excellent and often strenuous climbing up a series of steep cracks. The face lies directly above the Brèche Casque-Reine and is reached by following the icy couloir on the R (E) side of the Minaret then continuing on easy broken ground via Route 220 along the Jardin Ridge to the brèche. Take a fairly direct line up the steep walls above the brèche for 250m to the summit. Sustained climbing.

Descent: from the summit follow the ridge to the W then make 4 rappels to the col between the Casque and the Yatagan. Reverse the icy couloir on the E side of the Minaret (2 rappels) to the Améthystes glacier.

# Le Roi

This is one of the 3 gendarmes that make up the Echiquier group lying SW of the Casque. It gives a short rock climb on excellent granite with a well-equipped rappel descent.

**225**
IV/V
**95**

**SOUTH-WEST FACE**

G Bettembourg and J Charlet, 8 July 1970

This overlooks the icy couloir to the R (E) of the Minaret. Follow this couloir until directly below the summit of the Minaret then climb the obvious huge dièdre on the SW face of the Roi for 150m to the summit block. Climb this on the exposed SE face. 180m, 3½hr from the Argentière Hut.

Descent: rappel 40m into the gap between the Roi and the Cavalier, then make 3 rappels directly down to the Améthystes glacier.

**226**
VI

**TRAVERSE OF ECHIQUIER**

First traverse of the group: P and R Mazars and P Jullien with G Bettembourg, H Thiverge and J Charlet, 28 July 1974

After climbing Route 225 and reaching the Brèche Roi-Cavalier, it is possible to climb directly to the summit of the Cavalier via some cracks (IV at the start, A1 and V to finish). Make 1 huge rappel to the foot of the Reine and reach the gap between it and the Casque. Starting on the W flank, climb it by a spiral movement to finish up the N ridge (VI with a little aid.

It should be possible to continue via Route 224 to the summit of the Casque and thus reach the Aig d'Argentière, but this would probably need a bivouac.

# Le Minaret 3450m

M Azéma and G Fraissinet, 13 Aug 1945

A beautiful pinnacle below the Yatagan. Of all the routes on the SE flank of the Jardin Ridge, those on the Minaret are probably the finest. The climbing is steep, sustained, continuously interesting and on perfect granite. The foot of the 300m high SE face can be reached in 1hr from the Argentière Hut, and it has become very popular.

**227**
V+
**95**
**38**

**SOUTH-EAST SPUR**

R Mazars with G Rébuffat and P de Cléry with H Cretton, 26 July 1966. Winter: M Berreux and M Bessat, 1 March 1975

The modern classic and undoubtedly the finest route on the peak with plenty of in situ protection. The lower tower of very red granite has a distinct shoulder at ⅔ height and dropping from this is a narrow chimney widening at its base. The climb follows this in its entirety, starting up easy ledges to reach the L side of a detached flake. The second tower sports the only section of artificial climbing but the finest free climbing is reserved for the exposed crest of the final tower. 270m, 5–6hr

## 228 MINE ADOREE
VI+    B Domenech, C and Y Remy, 7 Aug 1984

95
38

This takes the very prominent chimney line to the L of the previous route. From the base of the second tower the route follows cracks and flakes on the L of the ridge to gain a wonderful dièdre directly below the summit. All the necessary protection pegs etc were left in place. 300m, 5–6hr

## 229 SOUTH FACE DIRECT
V+    P Beylier with G Crétin and G Rébuffat, 1 Aug 1968

95
38

Sustained free climbing, steep and exposed with a few aid moves, and well worth doing. The start takes a vague groove line directly below the large chimney system of Route 228. Starting near the Rhand end of the large terrace, climb a system of cracks and chimneys in the wall above joining the SE spur for its last 2 excellent pitches. 300m, 5–6hr

Descent: either rappel the route of ascent (Mine Adorée has well-equipped rappel points) or make 2 rappels from the summit to the gap between the Minaret and the Yatagan. Traverse across to the icy couloir that descends NE from this gap alongside the Minaret and descend it (2 rappels) to the Améthystes glacier.

# Le Plateau

The lower section of the Jardin Ridge is a broad flattish area of large blocks and there are many rock routes on the fine granite walls below this Plateau. The final bastion, overlooking the Milieu glacier, is Pt 3177m. The Lhand side of the SW face is a lovely pyramid of excellent granite that has been the focus of considerable attention in recent years. The foot of the face can be reached in 20min from the Argentière Hut. With a warm and sunny aspect at most times of the year, the cliff can be treated in the same way as a (somewhat larger) British crag.

**230**    **SOUTH RIDGE**
IV/V    H Feissner and R Ravanel, 20 Aug 1974

`96`
`39`

The easiest route on the face and a delightful climb on slabs and in dièdres. It is not really strenuous and is rapidly becoming a modern classic. 300m, 3–4hr

After Pitch 5 the 'Diagonal Route' (P Raddat and R Ravanel, 18 Aug 1974, IV/V) wanders up across the walls on the R, via cracks and corners, to the Plateau.

**231**    **CENTRAL DIEDRE**
VI+    F Simatos with R Ravanel, 29 June 1972

`96`
`39`

The route of the face and an established classic with plenty of in situ protection. A few points of aid will reduce the difficulty of Pitch 2 and make the climb more homogeneous in standard. The rock on the last few easy pitches is not altogether sound. 300m, 5–6hr. See also Photo 92

**232**    **SINGE BLEU**
VI+    E Arbez-Gindre and M Ravanel, 11 March 1984

`96`
`39`

Sustained climbing up a series of steep Rward-facing corners and the most difficult climb described here. The necessary pegs are in place but the climb has some unavoidable moves of VI/VI+. There is a fixed rappel descent back down the route. c280m, 6hr

**233**    **DIAGONAL CRACK**
V/V+    P, R and R Ravanel, 19 June 1967

`96`
`39`

The obvious feature on the L side of the face. The climbing is quite easy lower down but gives a few interesting sections of V and a little A1 in the upper Rward slanting crack. c280m. See also Photo 93

**234**    **FUREUR DE VIVRE**
VI+    E Deschamps and M Ravanel, 30 July 1984

`96`
`39`

Difficult slab and crack climbing to reach the crest of the Lhand ridge and even then the difficulties are not over! All necessary pegs and bolts are in place and the route can be rappeled from in situ anchors. c280m

Descent: Either rappel one of the ascent routes or continue E along the Plateau to a cairn. Directly below is a chimney leading down to the R. Descend it for 40m and follow a sloping ledge L (E) under red walls to reach slabs leading to the top of the couloir used on

Route 220. Descend the couloir to the moraine of the Améthystes glacier. 1hr back to the hut.

# Le Plateau: Pointe 3159m

This Pt lying to the S of the Plateau has more than half a dozen routes on its lower buttresses and is just behind the Argentière Hut.

**235**     **GENEPI RIDGE**
V     H Biondi, P Darout and R Ravanel, 7 Sept 1977

93
41

An excellent little climb and modern classic which takes the SE face and finally S ridge of a subsidiary pyramid of rock to the S of the main summit. Conspicuous at ½ height is a huge terrace with big blocks. From the brèche on the far side of this pyramid (Pitch 8) either descend an easy couloir on the R to the moraine or continue along the ridge (III/IV with 1 free rappel) to the summit of Pt 3159m. Reach the gap beyond and descend the couloir on the E side to the moraine. 250m, 4hr. See also Photo 92

A very direct line was climbed up the centre of this face to the summit of the Pyramid by a U C P A party on 24 Aug 1986. 200m, VI+

Harder routes were done on the S face on 13 and 29 Aug 1985 by R Ghilini and O Ratheaux, 180m, VI+ and VI+/VII.

The Oreilles de Lapin (2928m) give numerous practice climbs on the excellent granite that lies just above the hut.

**236**     **GERMAIN-MOLLIER ROUTE**
VI/A1     J Germain and C Mollier, 21 June 1961

93

This route follows the line of the single crack that splits the steep, front face of the smaller pyramid to the L of Route 235. The first ascent party reduced the free climbing difficulty to VI by climbing several sections with aid (A1). This aid has almost certainly been reduced in modern times but details are not available. 130m. See also Photo 92

# Col du Chardonnet 3323m

First traverse: S Brandram and A Reilly with A Albrecht, J Carrier and H Charlet, 24 Aug 1863

A fairly simple glacier pass that is frequently crossed. Combined with the Fenêtre de Saleina and the Col du Tour it forms the classic Three Cols Route, very popular with spring skiers.

**237**
F+
**101**

**SOUTH-WEST (FRENCH) SIDE**
From the Argentière Hut follow moraine to the R side of the Chardonnet glacier. Work up into the centre (very crevassed) taking the L branch, which is less steep, to the col (2½hr).
　　From the Grands Montets Station it is best to reach the moraine on the L side of the Chardonnet glacier directly and follow this onto the glacier at c2850m (3hr to the col). See also Photo 93

**238**
PD–
**97**

**NORTH-EAST (SWISS) SIDE**
From the Saleina Hut follow a small track SW down onto the glacier and go up it passing to the R of the rock island 2944m. Curve round under the Grand Fourche and climb the final 60m slope (50° often icy) or steep rocks on the R side to the col (2½hr).

# Aiguille du Chardonnet 3824m

R Fowler with M Balmat and M Ducroz, 20 Sept 1865. Winter: before 1914

A very beautiful peak and despite the fact that there is no really straightforward route to the summit, it is a very popular ascent from the Albert Premier Hut. The N side offers an extraordinarily fine variety of snow/ice routes while the S and W flanks are quite rocky and have been somewhat neglected. Nowadays the mountain is frequently traversed, descending by the W ridge.

**239**
AD–
**98**

**WEST RIDGE IN DESCENT**
P Thomas with J Imboden and J Lochmatter, 1 Aug 1879

*Although traditionally the normal route it is nowadays invariably used in descent. In the upper section the correct line is not all that obvious from above. Snow conditions can make the climbing precarious after midday so an early start is preferred. See also Photo 101*

From the summit follow the W ridge for 80m to a forepeak where the gradient increases. Descend SW a short distance to a large

226

couilor on the Argentière side and go down it for 150m before reaching the rocky rib on the R. Descend this mixed ground to a wall overlooking the shoulder. Slant down R, passing the top of a big icy couloir, then back L on snowy rocks to rejoin and descend (several rapels) the lower half of this couloir to the shoulder (3587m). Go down a snowy ridge to the Col Sup Adams Reilly (3478m) then head N down the glacier which is steep (45°) to start with and often has a rather large rimaye which may require a rappel or an heroic jump! Pass to the R of the rock rognon 3214m. A direct line to the Albert Premier Hut is badly crevassed and it is wise to head towards the foot of the Aig Forbes, keeping a watchout for any ice fall from the seracs above. Return via Route 240. 3½–4hr to the hut.

**240**   **EAST RIDGE (FORBES ARETE)**
AD   L, H and T Aubert with M Crettez, 30 July 1899

**98**

*An established classic and undoubtedly one of the finest expeditions of its class anywhere in the Alps. It is now the most popular means of reaching the summit and combined with a descent of the W ridge gives a splendid traverse. At present the seracs guarding the approach to the 'Bosse' are fairly safe, but in some years they can be very unstable. In that case it is preferable to approach via the NNE ridge. It is equally possible to start from the Trient Hut, crossing the Col du Tour, or from the Saleina Hut climbing the E facing snow couloir (100m, 45°) to the Fenêtre Sup du Tour (3458m).*

From the Albert Premier Hut walk SE onto the Tour glacier and, passing L of Signal Reilly (2833m), work up below the Col du Tour. Bear R to reach the rocky buttress at the end of the NW ridge of the Aig Forbes (3490m, 2¼hr). Go up the snowy cwm on the R, which may be crevassed and threatened by seracs to reach a plateau below the Fenêtre Sup du Tour. Slant up R below a small group of seracs to reach an ice ridge and follow this to a steep bulge, the 'Bosse'. Climb it (50m, 53°) and follow easier slopes up to the ridge, gaining the crest at a gap just above the gendarme 3703m (1¼hr).

Climb over the first gendarme by a chimney crack and groove (III) then continue along the narrow, exposed and often corniced crest. Turn the last gendarme on the L and climb a chimney to the summit. 600m, c6hr from any of the 3 huts; in less than perfect conditions the ridge can take considerably longer.

If the 2 areas of seracs mentioned earlier are found to be in a dangerous state then it is best to avoid them on the L. Cross the Aig

Forbes and continuing up the NNE ridge until one can slant R, above the upper serac barrier, to the E ridge.

**241**    **NORTH FACE**

D

98

P Chevalier, H de Se[c]gogne and E Stofer, 7 Aug 1929. Winter: W Cecchinel, G Crémion and C Jager, 11 Jan 1972

A steep glacier face that is very exposed to ice fall from the various serac barriers that threaten the route below ½ height. The amount of difficulty and danger will vary from year to year and a closer inspection will be needed before attempting the route. c550m, 4–6hr

**242**    **NORTH BUTTRESS**

D–

98

A Migot with C Devouassoux, 28 July 1929. Winter: B Schare with D Bertholet, 18–19 Jan 1964

*A popular classic, taking an elegant line up the crest of the N spur that leads directly to the summit. Not surprisingly many parties consider this to be one of the best mixed climbs in the Alps. It makes an ideal introduction to the middle-grade mixed routes of the range. From time to time the seracs at ½ height may threaten, but otherwise the climbing is continuously interesting and good rock belays are possible throughout the mixed section. The top slope is generally icy.*

From the Albert Premier Hut follow Route 240 towards the Forbes Arête then traverse R to the foot of the buttress (2hr). Climb up the snow slopes on the R (some stonefall danger) until easy mixed ground leads up L to the crest of the spur. Climb the steepening snow ridge then icy rocks and short narrow couloirs on the R. Bypass the big serac barrier by slanting R up snow-covered slabs to an easy-angled snow ridge (the crest of the spur can be followed in its entirety, safer but slightly more difficult). Continue to the final slope and climb it (100–150m, 50°) to the summit. c450m, 6hr from the hut.

**243**    **NORTH COULOIR**

TD–

98

J Aureille and Y Feutren, summer 1942. Winter: J Beaugey and J Dupraz, 5–6 March 1973

*A very worthwhile ice climb that has become increasingly popular. Cold and snowy conditions are necessary for the route to be fully iced. With less covering the central section can give very steep and problematical mixed climbing. Good rock belays and, more recently, bolts, are to be found throughout the ascent.*

Cross the rimaye wherever possible and reach the bottom of the narrow couloir via a 50° slope. Climb up for 2 long and sustained pitches (Scottish 4) and continue up 55° then 50° slopes to the summit. 450m, 6–7hr from the hut.

**244**    **NORTH-WEST BUTTRESS DIRECT**
TD–    P and P Gabarrou, 11 Sept 1977

`98`

A good covering of well-frozen snow and ice will facilitate progress on this safe and enjoyable mixed climb that starts with a narrow 100m gully to the R of the N couloir. 450m, 6–8hr

**245**    **NORTH-WEST BUTTRESS**
D    J Escarra with E Borgeat and E Payot, 29 Aug 1929

`98`

Although somewhat superseded by the obvious couloir line to the R, good mixed climbing can be found on the Rhand crest of the NW buttress. The initial snow ridge can be approached from either side and above easy climbing in the same line leads to a 100m step at about ½ height. Several pitches of IV on good rock are climbed to gain the steep mixed ground above. 400m, 6hr from the hut.

**246**    **NORTH-WEST FACE 1979 ROUTE**
D    P Gabarrou and J Michod, 1979

`98`

The obvious icy ramp/couloir that slants up L to an exit onto the upper slopes of the N buttress a pitch or two below the summit. The climbing appears to be objectively safe and enjoyable with good rock belays throughout, making this a short and worthwhile outing. c400m, 6hr from the hut.

**247**    **NORTH-WEST COULOIR**
TD–    G Bettembourg and J Charlet, 15 July 1972. Winter: J Charlet and
`98`    D Pugnat, 1 March 1980

The start is identical to the previous route and is gained by slanting L up snow slopes before reaching the Col Sup Adams Reilly. The couloir on the R is very steep (Scottish 4), widening to an exit on easier snow slopes where the descent route can be joined after a traverse to the R. Instead, slant up L on mixed ground for 200m to the summit. c400m, 6–8hr from the hut.

**248**    **WEST-SOUTH-WEST RIDGE**
D+    G Bettembourg and J Mangeot, 10 April 1972

`101`

The long ridge above the R side of the Adams Reilly glacier has been climbed entirely along its crest to a junction with the W ridge at the shoulder. The base of the ridge at c2700m can be reached in 1½hr from either the Grands Montets Station or the Argtentière Hut. Mainly III and IV with several pitches of V. 1100m to the summit, 12hr

**249**    **CAPUCINS BUTTRESS DIRECT**
D+    G Bettembourg and J Charlet, 17 Aug 1971

**101**

*Perhaps the best of the long rock climbs on the SW face. Sustained climbing on excellent granite following the crest of the pear-shaped buttress above the little Trident glacier.*

Reach the lowest point of the buttress, at the top of the Trident glacier, in 2hr from either the Argentière Hut or Grands Montets Station. 30m to the L of the base is a dièdre. Climb it (IV) then continue for 20m (IV) to reach a large dièdre slanting to the R. Climb this to the top of the pear-shaped buttress (IV and V). Reach the top of the next step by a dièdre on the R (60m, IV+). Go up a wall and traverse R to the crest of the spur (IV+) which is followed to a terrace. Climb the step above on the R side (40m, IV+) and continue up the ridge to reach a small gap below the Petit Capucin. Go R and reach the gap between the 2 Capucins via a corner (V) and more easy ground. Reach the foot of the Trident (c3570m) and either climb it in 3 pitches or turn it on the Argentière side.

A delightful snow crest now leads to a 200m high buttress. Climb up the centre for 2 pitches to a detached block. Turn it on the L (IV) and continue directly for 2 steep and strenuous pitches (IV+) to a large terrace on the L. Climb some cracks and a dièdre (sustained V) then slant R for 2 pitches (IV+ and V) to the top of the step. An exposed and rocky ridge leads to a gendarme. Descend on some good ledges to the foot of the forepeak and climb it slightly on the R via large blocks (IV). Go along the ridge for 80m to the summit. 700m, c10hr from the hut.

**250**    **POINT 3026m SOUTH-WEST SPUR**
VI+    Unknown

**101**

*This is the first gendarme at the base of the SW ridge that lies on the R of the Chardonnet glacier.*

Reach the top of the moraine on the R bank of the Chardonnet glacier in about 1½hr from the Grands Montets station. Climb a grassy dièdre (III and IV) then continue in a fairly direct line up the L flank of the spur to some terraces. Climb up R via a red wall and follow a fine yellow dièdre on the crest of the spur (VI/VI+).

Continue up the crest, negotiating various offwidth cracks, to the summit. 200m. Rappel descent.

**251**  **WEST COULOIR**
AD  K Richardson with J Bich and E Rey, 5 Sept 1890

**101**  This is the obvious snowy couloir on the SE face that runs from the Chardonnet glacier just S of Pt 3442m to the E ridge a short distance below the summit. It forms the easiest means of descent on this side of the mountain but its aspect and exposure to stonefall mean that it must be completed early in the day. Near the top, break out L and reach the summit directly via a short snow crest. c550m, 3hr

**252**  **EAST COULOIR**
AD  E Monod-Herzon with O and E Crettex, 16 Aug 1902

**93**  The parallel couloir to the R becomes a bit vague after 250m and it is just about possible to climb up anywhere onto the E ridge via little rocky spurs and gullies. c500m to the summit, 3–4hr. see also Photo 101

## Gendarme 3660m

A fairly indistinct summit on the continuation of the E ridge running down to the Col du Chardonnet. The various pillars give some nice rock climbing with rather a long approach.

**253**  **SOUTH PILLAR**
V+  J Charlet and R Ducroz, 3 July 1979

**101**  *Fine climbing on good granite but not sustained at the grade.*

The climb is approached directly from the upper Chardonnet glacier and takes the third spur to the L of the Col du Chardonnet. At the base of the pillar there is a huge cairn. Climb onto the pillar from the R and follow the crest for 3 pitches (IV). After a 20m section of V+ and A1, continue up the crest avoiding the final buttress by climbing the R flank (V+). 400m, 8hr

**254**    **EAST PILLAR**
V/A1    J Belin and J Charlet, 16 July 1971

*This lies just to the R of the frontier ridge, overlooking the Saleina glacier. The line generally follows a huge dièdre-couloir splitting the SE side of the pillar and is mainly free climbing with a number of aid moves.*

From the Col du Chardonnet turn the first 2 large towers of the SE ridge on the L side. Climb the wall and broken rock above until a huge scree terrace can be followed R for 40m onto the face overlooking the Saleina glacier (the scree terrace can be reached directly from the Chardonnet glacier by climbing a snowy couloir to the N of the gendarmes on the SE ridge) (c1hr).

Follow the line of cracks and dièdres directly above to reach the gap between the 2 gendarmes at the top of the pillar. Cross onto the other side and climb an overhanging dièdre to the top of the pillar (5hr). Follow the ridge to Pt 3660m (1½hr). c300m, c10hr from the Argentière or Saleina huts.

Descent: The easiest descent on reaching the Forbes Arête is to reverse the NNE ridge to the Fenêtre Sup du Tour. However it is possible to climb down the SE ridge starting in a couloir on the S side. Continue on this flank via cracks and large blocks until it is possible to cross the ridge to a couloir on the E side and descend it to the huge scree terrace (several rappels).

## Aiguille du Passon 3389m

L and M Kurz with J Joris, 10 Aug 1905

A sharp pyramid of broken rock to the NW of the Aig du Chardonnet. Gaining the summit is easier than it looks and can be approached from the Albert Premier Hut by heading S across the Tour glacier until nearly at the Col du Passon. Beware many hidden crevasses!

**255**    **NORTH-EAST COULOIR**
AD–    G Delyle with J Charlet and J Ducroz, 11 July 1953

**98**

This is the wide open couloir rising up to a gap in the NW ridge on the R of the N summit (3383m). Heavy consolidated snow makes the ascent straightforward; otherwise the top half gives steep mixed climbing over broken rock. c250m, 3hr

**256** **DESCENT VIA NORTH-EAST FLANK**
PD  Go down the NW or SE ridges easily until it is possible to scramble
down the NE flank of the mountain on broken rock to the Tour
glacier. 2½hr to the Albert Premier Hut.

## Col du Passon 3028m

First traverse: L Dècle with D Balleys, Aug 1882

A useful and straightforward (F) crossing point between the
Argentière and Tour glaciers, especially during the winter to spring
months. See Route H16.

## Fenêtre du Tour 3336m

First traverse: F and W Pollock with F Couttet and E Tournier, 2
Sept 1867

Situated between the Aig Forbes and the Grande Fourche at the
head of the Tour glacier. It provides the shortest route between the
Albert Premier and Saleina Huts and allows routes climbed from
either glacier to be accomplished conveniently from either hut.

**257** **NORTH-WEST(FRENCH) SIDE**
F  A glacier walk from the Albert Premier Hut following Route
240 towards the Aig Forbes until a short slope of snow and rocks
leads to the saddle. 2hr

**258** **SOUTH-EAST (SWISS) SIDE**
F/F+  From the Saleina Hut follow Route 238 towards the Col du
Chardonnet and climb a long snow/ice slope or rocks on the L to the
saddle (2½hr). When coming from the Argentière Hut it is possible
to reach the saddle in 1–1½hr from the Col du Chardonnet.

## Grande Fourche 3619m

H Whitehouse with H Copt, 18 Aug 1876. Winter: R von
Tscharner, 1922

An isolated summit at the head of the Tour glacier. It is an excellent
viewpoint and despite uninspiring climbing on the normal routes it
is reasonably popular. It offers 3 short yet useful training routes.

233

**259** **WEST-SOUTH-WEST RIDGE**
PD    A Brun with P Charlet, 1882

*The normal route on the French side.*

Well above the Fenêtre du Tour on the WSW ridge is a prominent shoulder. Directly below a snowy col on the R of this is a couloir. Reach the foot of this in 2hr from the Albert Premier Hut and climb it for 100m to the col. The route now follows more or less the crest of the ridge until higher up it becomes impracticable. Cross onto the Saleina side and climb cracks, returning L and crossing snowy rocks on the Tour side to the last rock step. Climb it on the R steeply, via blocks and cracks, reaching the crest just below the top. 200m, 4½hr from the hut.
     The ridge can be followed all the way from the Fenêtre du Tour which is far more interesting. Either climb the Chandelle via chimneys on the N side or turn it completely and the gendarmes that follow, to reach the shoulder. 5½hr from hut to summit.

**260** **SOUTH RIDGE**
PD    First ascent party

*The normal route from Switzerland. A rocky scramble.*

Reach the foot of the ridge via Route 238 in 2hr from the Saleina Hut. Go up the glacier on the L and climb rocks on the R of a broad snowy couloir, crossing a scree slope to reach a shoulder. Traces of a path up some easy rock steps lead to the S ridge. Climb a couloir on the R side for a short distance then finish up an easy buttress on the L. c400m, 3½hr from the hut.
     The ridge can be climbed directly from its base at a slight increase in standard.

**261** **NORTH-EAST RIDGE**
IV    P Morizot and A Pontet, 23 July 1953

*An entertaining little rock climb on sound granite.*

From the Col des Fourches go up the ridge turning the first rocky pyramid on the L side. Continue up slabs and dièdres to the summit. c200m, 3hr

**262** **NORTH-WEST PILLAR**
IV/V    J L Bernezat and a group of CAF students

Climb fairly directly up the spur towards the L side of the face in a series of cracks and chimneys that can often be icy. 200m, 3–4hr

**263 NORTH-WEST COULOIR**
AD–  P Gérard, G Martin and students, 2 Aug 1973

*This is the quickest and most interesting route to the summit on this side of the mountain.*

Climb the snow/ice couloir to the R of the NW Pillar. Where it terminates, slant up L on mixed ground to the top of the pillar and follow the easy horizontal ridge and broken rock above to the summit. c200m, 2½hr

**264 PETITE FOURCHE 3520m**
F  A pleasant little pyramid giving short and easy ascents from almost any direction. The NW ridge – a nice snow crest – seems the most popular.

**265 TETE BLANCHE 3429m**
PD/PD+  A small peak to the SE of the Col du Tour and very easily accessible from the Tour glacier. It has an excellent little training route on the N face, overlooking the Trient glacier that is generally in condition. 50°–55° snow/ice, c150m.
  The best descent follows the ridge S until it is easy to walk down onto the Tour glacier.

## Col du Tour 3282m

First traverse: R Heath and A Wills with A Balmat, E Bell and F Cachet, in 1858

Frequently used as a passage between the Tour and Trient glaciers. The last in the classic Three Cols Route from the Argentière glacier which crosses the Col du Chardonnet and Fenêtre de Saleina.

**266 WEST (FRENCH) SIDE**
F  Reached by a straightforward walk up the crevassed Tour glacier as for Route 240. 2hr from the Albert Premier Hut.

**267 EAST (SWISS) SIDE**
F  An even easier glacier walk. 1hr from the Trient Hut.

99

235

## Aiguilles du Col du Tour 3355m and 3359m

There are many short rock climbs on the S side of this ridge which give high-quality routes on excellent granite. Descent is made either by rappeling the route or climbing easily down the ridge to the Col du Tour. The S pillar of the E summit leading to the ridge a little R of the highest point has pitches of IV, V and A1. A direct route up the S face to the W summit has climbing of V+ and A1/A2 on the lower third but becomes much easier higher up. Slightly to the L another line, sustained at III to IV+, appears to offer better climbing than either of the routes mentioned above. Further L obvious pillars give more hard lines. All these climbs are no more than 150m high and can be completed in 2–3hr.

## Pointe 3332m

**268**    **SOUTH FACE**
IV+    P Martin and R Ravanel, 17 Aug 1965

This lies just N of the Col Sup du Tour (3289m, another easy crossing point) and has a long rocky projection into the Tour glacier, terminating with Pt 3250m. A very good rock climb takes the S face of this Pt starting with a dièdre in the centre of the face (IV with a few aid pegs). Reach a ledge and follow it L for 2 pitches. Climb cracks and chimneys (IV and IV+) to a gap in the ridge just R of the summit and continue easily along the crest to Pt 3332m. This is recommended as a very good way to start the Aig Purtscheller S Ridge. 2–2½hr

## Aiguille Purtscheller 3478m

L Purtscheller, 17 June 1890

A distinctive rock pyramid S of the Aig du Tour. Routes on the impressive triangular W face are now obsolete due to a series of rock falls. The rock on the S ridge, however, is good.

**269**    **SOUTH RIDGE NORMAL ROUTE**
IV    R Aubert, R Dittert and F Marullaz, 16 May 1943

**99**

*Similar to routes on the Aig de l'M, this excellent little classic comes into condition quite rapidly after adverse weather. Due to the ease of access*

*from the Trient Plateau, it is often climbed during winter/spring. A late start is quite acceptable and may well avoid the crowds. It is well worthwhile continuing to the summit of the Aig du Tour via the S ridge.*

From either the Albert Premier Hut via the Col du Tour or the Trient Hut, reach the Trient Plateau and cross it to a V-shaped notch in the S ridge above a group of gendarmes (3396m). Climb the crest of the first tower on the ridge for only 8m (III) then traverse round the L side to reach the gap behind it at a huge jammed block. Climb up the crest of the second tower a few m. then traverse R across a wall (IV) and go straight up to regain the crest of the tower at a little shoulder just below the top (III). Go over or turn on the L side the top of the tower and reach the gap below the last and biggest tower. Traverse R on good ledges for 1 pitch and climb up to the base of a deep chimney (IV). Follow it all the way to the final gap (III). An 8m dièdre on slightly shaky rock (III) leads to the summit. 150m, 3hr from the Trient Hut, 5¼hr from the Albert Premier Hut.

**270    SOUTH RIDGE INTEGRAL**

V+

99

A Berthoud with R Marcoz, 31 July 1958. Winter: F Trêves and M Sirvin with R Marcoz, 17 March 1962

*A complete ascent along the crest is not often done. The climbing is excellent but a trifle difficult on the final tower. The most popular combination is to climb the first 2 towers direct but revert to the Normal Route on the final tower. This gives a homogeneous route at IV+.*

Climb the first tower up the middle of its S face for 12m then traverse to the ridge on the R (V−). Climb this to the top (IV+) and rappel 15m to the huge jammed block. Climb directly up a crack on the R of the crest (IV+) and reach the top of the second tower. On the third tower, climb some grooves on the R (IV). Move R along a ledge (IV) and climb a dièdre (V+) that finishes on the R of a tunnel crossing the tower close to an overhang. Traverse L to the ridge and move up to a shoulder (IV). Climb the buttress in front directly (V+) and a small step above (V+, with an awkward rounded finish) to a horizontal ridge. Follow it, crossing a little gap (IV) and turn a small gendarme on the L to reach the final 8m dièdre leading to the summit. 4hr from the Trient Hut.

Descent: Climb down steep loose rock in a vague couloir on the NE face or alternatively make 2 30m rappels. Go down a snow slope to the Trient Plateau. 1½hr to the Trient Hut.

237

# Pain de Sucre du Tour 3441m

A small gendarme just N of Col Purtscheller.

| | |
|---|---|
| **271**<br>IV+ | **SOUTH-WEST SPUR**<br>A Contamine, G Robino and R Thomas, 21 June 1951 |

*A little gem!*

Start 15m to the R of the base of the spur on the E wall (1½hr from the Albert Premier Hut). Slant up for a pitch above some big overhangs to reach the base of a huge slab (IV). Climb the slab diagonally Rwards (IV+) then move straight up to a terrace near the crest of the spur (IV). Follow a chimney-couloir on the R (IV+) then keeping close to the crest reach the summit. c130m, 3hr from the hut.

| | |
|---|---|
| **272**<br>IV+ | **SOUTH RIDGE**<br>K Gurékian, 1950 |

Follow the crest from Col Purtscheller with its delightful slabs and delicate moves (IV+) onto the shoulder just below the top. This gives a pleasant little outing completed only too quickly!

Descent: Either by rappel or down-climbing the N ridge (II) to the Trient Plateau.

# Aiguille du Tour 3544m

C Heathcote with M Andermatten, 18 Aug 1864 (S summit).
Winter: C Cunningham and guides, 10 Feb 1882

Eminently suitable for the Alpine beginner with several classic short routes in the easy grades. There are 2 quite distinct summits separated by a deep gap. The best climbing tends to lead to the S and lower summit (3542m) while the N summit is usually crossed when traversing the main ridge. On all routes the easy ground lies over typically shattered granite and the novice should generally be on his guard. The peak is very popular indeed during the summer months and is not infrequently climbed in winter when an easy approach can be made on ski. Summiteers will be rewarded by a magnificent panorama over the N flanks of the range.

**273** **EAST FLANK**
F    First ascent party

**99** *The normal route, not only from the Trient Hut but also from the Albert Premier Hut by crossing the Col du Tour. A very straightforward and popular ascent.*

It is usually best when leaving from the Trient Hut to walk towards the Col du Tour and then skirt round below the frontier ridge to the base of the peak (1hr). Halfway up the NE ridge, between the deep gap separating the 2 summits and the S top, is a shoulder. Climb the face directly to this and follow the crest to the top. 2hr from the Trient hut, 3½hr from the Albert Premier.

**274** **SOUTH RIDGE**
F+   A Brun, before 1891

**99** *The shortest route from the Albert Premier Hut and a straightforward continuation after climbing the Aig Purtscheller.*

From the Albert Premier reach the Col Purtscheller (3383m) via a steep snow slope and rocky couloir in 1½hr. It is possible to walk onto this from the Trient Plateau (F, 1hr from the Trient Hut). Turn the Pain de Sucre du Tour on the R and scramble easily up the crest to the top. 2hr from the Albert Premier Hut.

**275** **TABLE COULOIR**
PD   First ascent unknown

**99** *A classic snow climb and one of the most popular ascents from the Albert Premier Hut. Highly recommended.*

This is the couloir that lies to the R of the SW spur. It gives a straightforward snow climb with an exit of 50° onto the upper section of the W ridge. From here the summit is easily and quickly reached. 3½hr from the hut.

**276** **SOUTH-WEST (TABLE DE ROC) SPUR**
PD   M Dreyfus, A and R Duval, P Henry and M Ichac, 18 July 1926

**99** *Another established classic which is well-frequented. The crossing of the Rock Table, a conspicuous granite block perched on the crest of the ridge, is a unique experience which should not be missed. The vague lower section of the spur provides useful practice in route-finding.*

Following the initial section of Route 240, reach the glacier bay between the W ridge on the L and the SW spur to the R. Climb up R in the first couloir lying on the L side of the spur (III). Reach the poorly-defined spur and follow the narrowing crest to the Table. Climb on top of the Table (III) and follow the crenellated ridge above to the summit. c400m, 4–5hr from the Albert Premier Hut.

# Aiguille du Tour: North Summit

**277** **SOUTH-EAST FLANK**
F+   First ascent unrecorded

**99**

*The normal route to this summit from the Trient Plateau.*

From the Trient Plateau reach the deep gap between the 2 summits via a short couloir and some broken rock. Just below the level of the gap slant up R on a ledgeline to reach a poorly-defined rib. Scramble up this and the snow above to the summit. 2hr from the Trient Hut.

**278** **TRAVERSE OF MAIN RIDGE**
PD   First traverse not recorded

*A worthwhile introduction to the classic easy ridges in the range. It is equally as good in either direction and although more likely to be crossed from S to N, it is marginally easier the opposite way.*

From the S summit descend the NE ridge easily in c10mins to the gap before the N summit and follow Route 277 to its highest point. Descend the N ridge keeping to the R on snowy rocks to the Fenêtre du Pissoir (3410m). Either descend the steep glacier bay on the L (W) and return to the Albert Premier Hut, or walk easily onto the Trient Plateau and head back below the frontier ridge towards the Col du Tour. Allow 5–6hr for the round trip from the Albert Premier Hut.

# Fenêtre de Saleina 3261m

First reached by M Charlet, 1838

Frequently crossed by spring skiers on the initial stages of the Haute Route from Chamonix to Zermatt. This straightforward glacier pass provides the quickest route between the Trient and Saleina Huts.

**279** **NORTH-WEST SIDE**

F Follow Route 267 towards the Col du Tour and reach the pass by gentle slopes. 1¼hr from the Trient Hut, 2½hr from the Albert Premier Hut via the Col du Tour.

**280** **SOUTH-WEST SIDE**

F The middle section of the Saleina glacier is quite crevassed. When well snow-covered, such as would be expected in spring, it is possible to follow Route 238 towards the Col du Chardonnet and reach the Fenêtre directly via the glacier bay to its S. In the summer it is usually better to follow the path from the Saleina Hut down onto the glacier, cross it and continue up the R side to the S ridge of the Aig de la Varappe. Cross this ridge by means of a natural tunnel (the Fenêtre de Suzanne 3141m) and reach the glacier bay leading up to the pass. 2hr from the hut.

## Aiguilles Dorées 3519m

A granite chain 1300m long that rises abruptly out of the S end of the Trient Plateau. On the whole the rock is good, the routes are short and the mountain suitable for rock climbers with only moderate Alpine experience or wanting good quick routes when dubious weather dictates a short day.

**281** **TRAVERSE OF AIGUILLES DOREES**

AD+ First traversed in the direction described by Heiner and Crettez, 31 Aug 1898, but had been crossed in the reverse direction as early as

**103** 1892

*A classic ridge traverse, generally taken from E to W, which is one of the best and most enjoyable of its type in the range. The main difficulties come early and the route is still fairly popular, though climbed less often in recent years. There is a wide variety of climbing and the granite is quite solid where it matters, except for 1 section below the Aigs Penchées. In anything less than perfect conditions it will be at least D−. See also Photo 104*

From the Trient Hut cross the plateau and climb a small couloir immediately R of the Col Droit to a gap above Pt 3325m. Climb over large blocks to a second gap overlooking the Plines glacier.

Descend 4m in a couloir and traverse W along a large ledge system that rises across the SE face of the Tête Crettez to reach its summit (3419m, 1½hr).

From the Saleina Hut follow Route 282 to the summit of the Tête Crettez (3½hr).

Descend the summit block and reach the foot of the Aig Javelle easily. Climb a crack on the S side which widens into a deep chimney and leads to the ridge (IV, sustained). An easy crack leads to the twin summit blocks. Rappel back down to the base of the chimney and continue across ledges on the S side to reach a wide scree terrace on the ridge below the Trident. Climb easy chimneys to the summit blocks. The first block is easy but the second needs a delicate step from the gap between the two followed by a wall on the R. Return to the terrace (1½hr). Follow the ridge beyond the Trident, then use a ledge below a slab to reach Col Copt (3410m). Turn a step on the R and follow the snow ridge, turning the Aig Sans Nom on the R to a gully leading up to the ridge just S of Tête Biselx. Climb it and scramble easily to the top (1hr).

Descend slabs on the W face to a gap (III). Go down on the S side in a chimney (III) to a ledge which traverses across the face below PtFynn. Regain the ridge via a letterbox and follow the crest to a gap below the Aigs Penchées. Traverse across the N face (mixed climbing on rotten rock). Reach the ridge between the E and central summits. Turn the latter on the R and gain the W summit via an easy crack (2hr).

The continuation ridge is crenellated but easy. Turn a group of gendarmes on the R and go up broken rock to the summit of the Aig de la Varappe which is climbed via a steep chimney (IV, the highest point of the Dorées). Reach the slightly lower W summit that follows, by a ramp on the N side (1hr). Continue down the ridge for 50m then descend the NW ridge steeply to the R as far as a yellow buttress. Turn this on the L side and slant back R down the side of the ridge to reach the rimaye. Rappel over this to the Trient Plateau (2hr). In dry years when stonefall could be problematical, it is better to slant L below the yellow buttress on the ridge leading to the Fenêtre de Saleina and reach an easy chimney leading to a gully. Climb up the gully, turning a step on the Trient side, then continue on the Saleina side before descending alongside the rocks to the Trient Plateau. The rimaye here is enormous! A fast party will take 10hr for the round trip from the Trient Hut, 12hr is more usual. 14–15hr from the Saleina Hut.

# Tête Crettez 3419m

**282**
PD
104

**SOUTH FACE**
E Jeanneret-Perret and Wasserfallen with P Delez, 1 Aug 1893

*A nice little scramble and a pleasant start to the main ridge traverse when coming from the Saleina Hut.*

The SE spur of the Tête Crettez divides the Plines glacier into two. Go up the glacier on the E side, then slant R up the flank of the spur. Rocky couloirs and chimneys lead to the summit. 3½hr from the hut.

**283**
V
103

**NORTH FACE**
M and P Cretton, 11 July 1959

*Nice steep climbing on sound granite.*

Start almost directly below the summit at a double crack leading to a prominent chimney system. The climb follows this, overcoming short walls separated by narrow ledges. From the huge terrace walk up easier snowy ground and climb the summit block by a crack of IV on the L. 150m, 3hr

A similar but much harder and more strenuous climb takes the overhanging dièdre and chimney system (V+) leading directly to the snowfield in line with the Brèche Crettez-Javelle.

# Le Trident 3436m

**284**
VI
103

**NORTH FACE DIRECT**
J Corbaz and E Nuzzlé; F Jequier and Y Dunant, 8 Sept 1957.
Winter: T Gross, C Lemrich and B Nicoulin, 7 Jan 1973

*A fine free rock climb on excellent granite.*

Start on the L below a triangular wall split by a crooked crack. Climb a small flake (IV) then the crack above (V) to the foot of the wall. Climb the crooked crack (V+), move easily L and climb another wall to a large ledge (IV+). Climb a grey dièdre below a detached flake and work L to 2 parallel cracks. Climb these (V) to a ledge. Traverse L then climb up directly for 15m before trending up to the slanting dièdre on the R side of the spur. Climb a succession of 4 dièdres that increase in difficulty and lead to a huge platform on the R of the summit. The last dièdre is 25m long and VI. 200m, 5hr

## Col Copt

This lies between the Trident and the Aig Sans Nom. The N side provides an excellent little ice route.

**285**    **NORTH FACE DIRECT**

AD/AD+    First ascent unknown

**103**

The most elegant route takes the middle of the couloir directly to finish just R of the Aig Sans Nom. The average angle is 53° but it is steeper than this at the finish. The L bank of the couloir has a fixed rappel descent alongside the rocks of the Tête Biselx.c200m, 3hr from the hut.

## Aiguille Sans Nom 3444m

*A double tower to the SE of the Tête Biselx.*

**286**    **SOUTH RIDGE**

AD+    G Formaz and C Vouilloz, 18 Sept 1961

**104**

*This is a delightful little climb and thoroughly recommended. The granite is excellent throughout.*

From the Trient or Orny Huts cross the Col S des Plines (Col Droit) by Route 294 and reach the base of a scree couloir coming down from the shoulder on the S ridge at the point where the latter bends to the SE.

    From the Saleina Hut follow Route 295 towards the Col S des Plines then go up the Plines glacier on the R side of the lower ridge (terminating at 3005m) to reach the couloir mentioned above.

    Climb the couloir to the ridge which takes the form of 2 parallel and steep buttresses. Climb the crest of the Rhand buttress until it merges into the final wall. Go L along a terrace and climb a wall with a detached flake, then follow the sharp ridge to the S summit.4hr from the Trient Hut, a little longer from the Saleina Hut.

## Aiguille Sans Nom: South-East Face

On the R of the S ridge, in the middle of the wall, is a huge dièdre directly in line with the summit. There are at least 4 routes on this wall giving technical climbing in plenty of warm sunshine with an abundance of in-situ protection or aid.

**287    ORIGINAL ROUTE**

V+/A1/2    J Coquoz, B Gross, J Hauser and J Hiroz, 1974

104
40

This climbs the dièdre, or crack lines just to the L of the dièdre in 3 or 4 sustained pitches of V+ and A1/2. Traverse horizontally L on a prominent ledge that leads across to the S ridge but before reaching the latter climb a 15m dièdre (V+) and slab above to pendule R into another dièdre. Climb this (V+) after which 2 pitches of III+ lead to the S summit. c280m, 5hr

**288    1987 ROUTE**

VII    W Josi, V von Kaenel and A Leibundgut, 17 and 19 Aug 1987

104
40

This gives some very varied and sustained free climbing starting just R of the huge dièdre. It is well equipped with pegs and bolts. Each stance has a fixed rappel point and the route climbs almost directly to the N summit. c300m, 6hr

## Tête Biselx 3509m

Perhaps the most prominent summit of the chain, with an imposing barrel-shaped buttress of impeccable granite on the N side, seamed with crack lines. Most of the routes were originally climbed with considerable aid from wide-angle pegs and large wooden wedges. This aid could be substantially reduced by the expert crack climber!

**289    NORTH-NORTH-EAST FACE**

V+/A2    G Genoud, D and J Troillet, 1 July 1972

103

This climbs the most prominent crackline on the L side of the pillar which falls from the centre of the upper terrace. It is clearly visible from the Trient Hut. Finish up Route 290. Sustained climbing but with all the necessary pegs in place. c200m to the terrace, 6hr

**290    ORIGINAL ROUTE**

IV/A2    Y and M Vaucher, 2 July 1964. Winter: P Froidevaux, E Lettry and A Villinger, 9–10 March 1969

103

*30m to the R of Route 289 is a line of cracks descending from the R edge of the upper terrace. Reach this from the Trient Plateau via a short ice slope and broken rock in 1–1½hr.*

Climb the cracks to a line of overhangs and pass them on the L. Return R on a series of flakes and climb more cracks to the terrace. Ascend a chimney on the R (IV) and the crack above (IV) to the Rhand ridge. Follow this to the summit. c250m, 10hr

**291**  **DIANETIC**
VI+  C and Y Remy, 28 July 1983

103

*A modern free climb taking a parallel line of cracks and dièdres just to the R of the Original Route. There is no in situ gear.*

Climb the dièdre (VI−) then reach an area of ledges via a flake (V). Go up to the R of a huge block, climb an overhanging flake and the crack above (VI+) to a terrace. Struggle up a wide crack (VI) and continue more easily past the R end of the upper terrace. Climb thin cracks between 2 prominent wider ones in the upper section of the face (IV+). Reach the Rhand ridge shortly below the summit via a finger crack (V−). 250m, 8 pitches. 4−5hr

# Aiguille de la Varappe 3519m

The culminating point in the chain gives some nice climbing on the sunny S side.

**292**  **SOUTH RIDGE**
AD  First descended by F Sandoz with A Crettez, 6 Aug 1897

104

A delightful little climb taking the crest of the ridge directly above the Fenêtre de Suzanne, which is reached on the approach to the Fenêtre de Saleina via Route 280. c350m, 4½hr

**293**  **SOUTH-EAST FACE**
V+  M Barrard and G Moyer, 10 April 1969

104

*Sustained free climbing on good rock.*

Reach the foot of the SE wall, lying to the R of the Fenêtre de Suzanne, in 1hr from the Saleina Hut. In the middle of the lower wall is a huge chimney-couloir. Start up easy rock (III) on the R of this and climb to a terrace (V+). Continue straight up turning an overhang on the L (V+) to the top of a gendarme. Climb up for 2 pitches (III and IV) to a crack. Climb this and the dièdre above (IV and V) to a platform, then traverse L beneath an overhang (V) and climb the slabs above (IV+). Traverse R (V, with some aid moves) to reach a dièdre on the L of a flake. Climb it to an overhang (IV and IV+) then continue up the grooves above (V) to the fore-summit. Slant R for 3 pitches on easy ground to the main summit. 300m, 5–6hr from the hut.

## Cols des Plines

Not marked as such on IGN. The N col (c3246m) is situated between the Roc des Plines and the Pt des Ravines Rousses. The S col (c3260m) is marked as Col Droit. Both are easy to cross and form a popular and most useful passage between the Trient and Saleina glaciers.

**294**    **NORTH SIDE**
F
Reached by a gentle walk across the Trient Plateau in ½hr from the hut.

**295**    **SOUTH SIDE**
F
Follow Route 280 towards the Fenêtre de Saleina until at the end of the moraine on the R side of the Saleina glacier. Head N up scree slopes and snow patches. It is normal to cross the N col, so first reach the Ravines Rousses glacier. Go up it and finish on the col via a short steep snow slope cut by a rimaye. 2½hr from the Saleina Hut.

## Le Portalet 3344m

E Dufour, E Javelle and F Paschoud, Aug 1876. Winter: M Legrand and P Roux, Feb 1931

A magnificent viewpoint with a variety of straightforward routes that are quite suitable for alpinists of limited experience.

The E ridge carries the monolithic granite thumb of the Chandelle (3281m) c25m high and difficult of ascent (VI) without resorting to rope-throwing tactics.

**296**    **NORTH FLANK AND WEST RIDGE**
F+
T Chapuis and E Pellis, 16 Aug 1877

**102**

*The normal route of ascent and the best for descent. Fairly interesting scrambling.*

Walk across the Orny glacier and gain the rocks to the R of the ice slope on the N face of the mountain. Climb these easily to the W ridge above Pt 3167m and follow it pleasantly to the summit. 400m, 3hr from the Trient Hut.

**297**    **NORTH FACE DIRECT**

AD−

R and R Gréloz, 9 Sept 1937. Winter: M Jobin and B Pivot, 4 Jan 1971

102

This climbs the snow/ice slope directly below the summit finishing on the L side of the rocky spur. A short but worthwhile outing from the Trient or Orny Huts. Average angle 44°, c350m, 3½hr fro either hut.

**298**    **NORTH-EAST FLANK**

F+

First ascent party

102

*The usual route from the Orny Hut which can be used to begin a pleasant traverse of the mountain.*

Cross the Orny glacier to the foot of a big snow couloir coming down from the vicinity of the Chandelle on the E ridge. Scramble up the broken rocks on the L side until at ¾ height it is possible to cross the couloir. Follow the rocks on the R side to the ridge above the Chandelle. Follow this easily in ½hr to the highest point. c400m, 3hr from the Orny Hut.

**299**    **WEST FLANK**

F

First ascent not recorded

*The quickest means of ascent from the Saleina Hut but it is easily reached from the Trient Hut by crossing the Col N des Plines. A perfectly straightforward scramble.*

By using Routes 295 or 294, reach the Ravines Rousses glacier and work up easy stony slopes on the W flank of the mountain finishing up the top section of the S ridge. 3½hr from the Saleina Hut; 2hr from the Trient Hut.

# Grand Clocher du Portalet 2983m

This easy peak, opposite the Orny Hut, has no special attraction.

**300**    **NORTH-EAST RIDGE**

F

Climbed from the gap between the Petit and Grand Clochers, and can be followed with no particular difficulty. 1hr to the summit.

**301**    **WEST RIDGE**
F    Reached at a gap (2951m) at the head of the tiny Portalet glacier, this is also straightforward. 3hr from the Orny Hut.

## Petit Clocher du Portalet 2823m

M Crettez and E Revaz, 26 Aug 1897

An amazing monolith of red granite whose sheer smooth sides are taken by some of the finest rock climbs in the range. The N face routes, which have a more serious atmosphere than their length would indicate, and sunny S and E faces, which come into condition rapidly after bad weather, give tremendous free climbing with considerable exposure.

**302**    **WEST RIDGE**
IV–    First ascent party
**100**

*The normal route, and the only easy means of reaching the summit. The route follows the sharp crest that rises from the gap between the Petit and Grand Clochers. Although very worthwhile it is nowadays almost exclusively used as a means of descent after climbing one of the harder free routes and is described as such. Grade given is for the ascent.*

From the summit go down the W ridge until a huge iron piton allows a long rappel down the crest. Continue to the top of a buttress about midway between the summit and the col. Another iron piton allows a rappel onto the S side and a system of grassy ledges which can be used to make a descending traverse of 60m to the col. Go down the couloir on the N side following easy rotten rock to the moraine. 2½hr to the Orny Hut.

*Petit Clocher du Portalet continued on page 250*

## Petit Clocher du Portalet: North Face

The upper part of this sombre and impressive wall is sheer and smooth for almost 200m. It is crossed by a number of routes. The older lines are climbed with a considerable amount of aid while one or two modern routes offer some extremely demanding cracks.

Below the upper vertical section of the N face is a large sloping triangular terrace with a well-defined buttress descending to the scree below.

**303**
A1/A2
100

### DARBELLAY ROUTE
D and M Darbellay, 1 Sept 1962. Winter: J Siebenmann and L Weissbaum, 28 Feb–1 March 1965

*The best and most serious of the traditional routes on the N face climbs a series of cracks in the overhanging wall that lies directly above the middle of the terrace. Higher up a wide L-ward-slanting crack is followed to join Route 305 near the top. Most of the aid points were left in place and there have been numerous ascents.*

Reach the crest of the well-defined buttress where there is a cairn and climb it for 3–4 pitches (III and IV, finish V) to the terrace. From here it is 6 pitches to the top. c300m, 8hr from the Orny Hut.

**304**
VII+
100

### LA GUERRE DES NERFS
L Abbet and F Roduit, Aug 1983

A completely free route taking a parallel line to the L of the previous climb and passing to the R of a detached flake. The third pitch is a difficult off-width where large Friends are essential for protection. 150m of difficulties.

**305**
VIII
100

### ETAT DE CHOC
C and Y Remy, 25 and 26 July 1983

For the connoisseur of smooth off-width cracks, this is it! The compellingly obvious dièdre on the L side of the face is reached directly in 2 pitches of III/IV. The next 200m gives some of the most strenuous and technical crack climbing to be found in the range, with unavoidable moves of VII/VII+. No 4 Friends are essential. 300m from the base.

---

*Petit Clocher du Portalet continued*

**306**
VI
100

### EAST FACE
I Gamboni and M Vaucher, 23 July 1958. Winter: E Oberson and A Villiger, 22–23 Dec 1970

*A strenuous and character-building climb that follows the vertical chimney system in the centre of this narrow face. The technical climbing in the back of these chimneys is probably unique to the range.*

From the Orny Hut go down across the glacier to reach the spur that descends from the E wall. Turn it on the L and scramble up easy ground working back R to the foot of the vertical face (1½hr). In the centre, 2 obvious impending cracks rise up to the big chimney. 5m to the L of these climb a third thin crack for 20m (A1) then pendule R and enter the big crack via a flake (VI). Climb the big crack and continue in the depths of the chimney (V+) until it narrows. Move L (V+) into another crack, climb it (IV) and return to the widening chimney again. Strenuous climbing up the back (V+/VI, many pegs) leads to a good terrace just below the summit. c240m, 6–7hr from the hut.

**307**    **SOUTH-EAST PILLAR**

VII/VII+   M Rey and C Vouilloz, 15 June 1961. Winter: E Lettry and A

[42]    Villiger, 27–28 Jan 1969

*An elegant line on rather less than vertical rock and is thoroughly recommended. It is one of the most enjoyable climbs in the area and still considered the best on the peak. It has been climbed completely free but is still a marvellous outing at V+ and A1, when the free climbing is of a more delicate nature. All the necessary pegs and bolts are in place.*

Use the same approach as the E face then follow a gangway around to the L and start just L of the crest climbing some easy steps (III). An approach is also possible via the gap in the W ridge between the Grand and Petit Clochers. Descend a couloir on the S side with 1 short rappel and scramble round grassy rock until below the E face. 220m, 6–7hr from hut to summit.

# Pointe d'Orny 3269m

E Javelle and P Rouget, 30 March 1872

A famous viewpoint beside the Trient glacier reached easily in ½hr from the Trient hut by snow and scree slopes to the N.

**308**    **NORTH-EAST COULOIR**

PD+    F and J Mathey, 17 May 1964

The N side of the Pt and the Aig d'Orny is seamed with interesting snow couloirs. They are quite long but for the fit alpinist offer no particular difficulty and are climbed regularly. The altitude is low and an early start is wise so it is best to bivouac somewhere high up in the Val d'Arpette.

The best excursion takes the couloir designated the Glacier d'Arpette. Above mid-height a narrower couloir branches R and climbs more steeply (45°) to the ridge, 50m N of the summit. c700m, 3hr

# Aiguille d'Orny 3167m

G Stouvenel with M Crettez, 6 Sept 1900

This little peak lying just to the W of the Orny Hut offers numerous worthwhile rock climbs on its sunny S face. In fact the whole wall here is littered with short technical routes, full details of which can be seen in the hut. Only a few are indicated below.

**309**     **SOUTH-EAST FLANK**
F+     First ascent party

*Normally used as a descent to the Orny Hut.*

From the gap between the 2 summits descend a steep chimney on the S face. Follow a ledge horizontally L to reach the easy E flank of the mountain below the summit tower. Go down easily to the SE and reach the stony cwm below the Col d'Arpette. 1hr to the hut.

**310**     **SOUTH-WEST COULOIR**
First ascent unknown but climbed in winter by J Jouvy, M Jobin, B Pivot and C Pistom, 6 Jan 1971

*A shorter descent to the Trient Hut.*

Go down the W ridge from the summit to a small shoulder. Descend L towards the rocky couloir on the WSW face, rappeling down a slab with a small overhang (III+ in ascent). Go down the couloir on grassy ledges and broken rock to the base where there is a commemorative plaque and walk up the glacier to the Trient Hut. 1½hr.

**311**     **SOUTH PILLAR**
V+/A1     S Schaffter and party, 1 July 1973

*A difficult little climb on sound rock but disappointing due to the lack of continuity and the ease with which the hard pitches can be avoided by broken rock towards the couloir on the L.*

The climb begins 25m to the R of the commemorative plaque mentioned in the previous route. Climb the crest of a small pillar to a series of good terraces, then move R along these and continue directly up the crest of the spur above, in cracks and dièdres, to the summit. 200m, 4hr

**312**　**SOUTH-WEST SPUR**
IV+/V−　T Gross and S Schaffter, Sept 1973

To the R of the summit of the Aig d'Orny is a couloir and this climb takes the crest of the spur immediately to the R again avoiding a vertical step on the L side. The penultimate pitch sports 2 bolts. 200m, 3hr

**313**　**GROSS-SCHAFFTER ROUTE**
V　T Gross and S Schaffter, 8 Sept 1973

This particular line climbs the S face of the Pt that forms a secondary summit to the W of the Aig d'Orny. Begin in a dièdre-chimney just to the R of an enormous block at the foot of the face and follow a fairly direct line up a series of corners and chimneys to the top. Not sustained, 200m, 3hr

## Pointe des Ecandies 2873m

P Beaumont with F Fournier and D Crettez, 16 June 1887

This minor summit at the head of the Val d'Arpette lies at the end of a bristling ridge extending NE from the Col des Ecandies. The ridge is 1km in length and is split halfway by a deep gap. The highest point lies in the N section and can be reached easily from the Fenêtre d'Arpette in 1hr. The main ridge offers one of the most interesting and enjoyable traverses in the Swiss part of the range and both flanks contain short difficult rock climbs to the summits of the various gendarmes.

**314**　**TRAVERSE SOUTH TO NORTH**
V　The route as described was pieced together by various parties before 1942

*A highly recommended classic, normally done from S to N and more difficult in this direction. Both parts can be climbed separately but the N section of the ridge is broader, not quite so interesting and only worth doing as part of the complete traverse to the Fenêtre d'Arpette. Many parties complete the S section only which, if it were higher and surrounded by snow and ice, would be a serious undertaking. In fact it*

POINTE DES ECANDIES

*can be done at any time of the day, via a long return walk from the main valleys.*

Reach the Col des Ecandies from the Arpette Chalets using Route H18 in 2½hr or from the Trient Hut reversing Route H19 in 1hr.

Follow ledges on the R side of the ridge to a crack (15m, III) which leads into a couloir. Follow the latter to a gap between the first and second towers. Reach the gap between the second and third towers by a traverse on the Trient side and climb the second tower by the N ridge (IV−, exposed). Climb the third tower by a strenuous chimney up to the R (IV−) and rappel 15m to the gap beyond. The fourth tower lies just off the ridge and is climbed easily by its SE face. Return to the gap and follow the ridge to the 'Razor', a 6m blade of granite. Climb it by a flake on the R side (V or III+ with the bolt). Go down the ridge crossing a delicate slab, then follow a ledge on the Trient side and regain the ridge above a small step. Climb a wall L of a large block and the next gendarme by its L ridge (V, or avoid it on the Trient side). Continue along the crest, crossing an exposed notch by a sensational stride, the 'Angel's Step'. Turn the Great Tower easily on the L and from the following gap climb a 25m buttress on the Arpette side by a traverse across a short slab, then the crack (IV) and chimney above to a gap (which can be reached on the Trient side via a dièdre and flake; sustained V). Move R and climb the L-ward-slanting crack to the top of the step and follow the ridge easily to the S summit (2783m). Descend a deep chimney to the E and follow ledges back onto the ridge. Go down this to the central gap (3–4hr).

The ridge can be left at this point descending easily down either flank to the Trient or Arpette footpaths.

To continue up to the N summit, climb the big wall above over a detached gendarme. Now slant up cracks on the R to a ridge on the Arpette side coming down from the first gendarme (IV). Reach a prominent couloir between the first gendarme and a smaller tower (from where the top of the gendarme can be easily reached), then climb the steep wall alongside the couloir to a gap in front of the second gendarme. Climb up to the R then descend to the gap between the second and third gendarmes. Start the third gendarme by slabs on the R returning L to a huge block on the crest. Traverse L and take a crack to the top (IV). One can also climb directly above the huge block using combined tactics (IV+).

The ridge is now much easier and after a moderately angled 40m slab, the last buttress is climbed up a crack on the R side (III) followed by a little descent in a couloir and up a dièdre (III+).

Grassy ledges and an awkward chimney mark the end of the difficulties and the highest point is reached in another 10mins (2–3hr).

Either descend the L side of the NE ridge easily to the Fenêtre d'Arpette in ¾hr or go back down the route of ascent for 10 mins and scramble down grassy rock and a stony couloir, on either flank, to reach the Trient or Arpette valleys (1–1½hr).

# General Index

# Index of Climbs

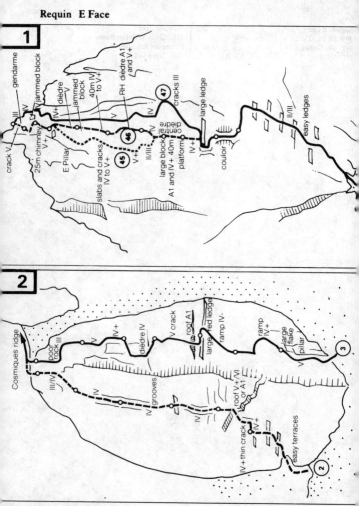

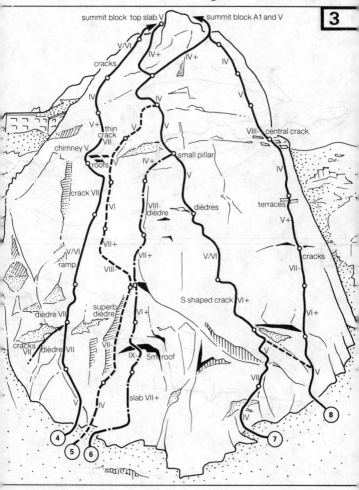

summit block top slab V
summit block A1 and V
V/VI
IV+
IV+
IV
cracks
IV
IV
V+
V
VIII central crack
thin crack VII
V
V
chimney V
roofs IV
IV+
small pillar
IV
crack VII
VI
V
VIII- dièdre
dièdres
terraces
V+
ramp
V/VI
VII+
VII+
V/VI
cracks
VII-
dièdre VII
superb dièdre
VI+
S shaped crack VI+
VI+
cracks VII
dièdre VII
VII
IX- 5m roof
VII
V
slab VII+
V
IV
IV

④
⑤
⑥
⑦
⑧

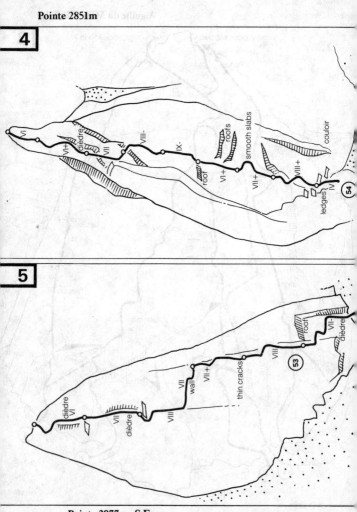

**Pointe 2977m  S Face**

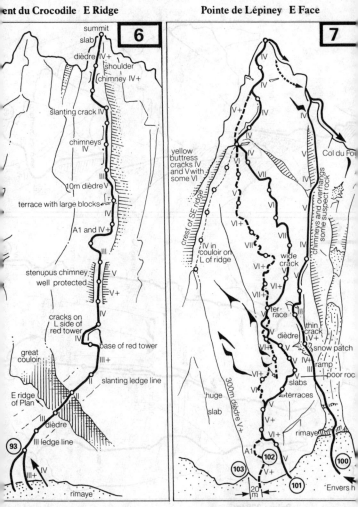

**ent du Crocodile E Ridge**

**6**

summit
slab
dièdre IV+
shoulder
chimney IV+
slanting crack IV
chimneys IV
10m dièdre V
terrace with large blocks
IV
A1 and IV+
III
strenuous chimney
well protected
V
V+
IV
cracks on
L side of
red tower
IV
great
couloir
base of red tower
III+
II
slanting ledge line
E ridge
of Plan
II
III
dièdre
III ledge line
93
IV
III+
rimaye

**Pointe de Lépiney E Face**

**7**

IV
V+
IV
IV
V
Col du Foi
yellow
buttress
cracks IV
and V with
some VI
IV
VI
VII
IV
V
VI
IV in
couloir on
L of ridge
VII
VI+
wide
crack
IV
VI+
VII+
V
ter-
race
III
thin
crack
IV+
V
dièdre
snow patch
VI+
IV+
III
ramp
poor roc
V+
slabs
terraces
huge
slab
300m dièdre V+
V
V+
VI+
rimaye
A1
102
V
103
V+
101
20
m
Envers h

271

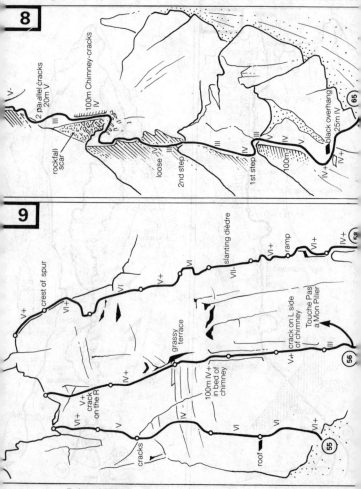

**Pointe 2784m**

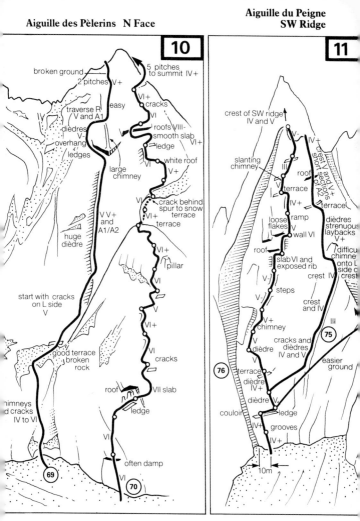

# Aiguille des Pèlerins  N Face

10

broken ground
2 pitches  V+
easy
traverse R
V and A1
dièdres
V-
overhang
ledges

5 pitches
to summit IV+

VI+
cracks

VI
roofs VIII-
smooth slab
VI+
ledge
white roof
VI  V+

large
chimney

V  VI
crack behind
spur to snow
VI+  terrace
terrace

huge
dièdre

V V+
and
A1/A2

VI+
pillar

VI

start with cracks
on L side
V

V
VI+

VI
cracks

good terrace
broken rock

roof
VII slab

himneys
d cracks
IV to VI

ledge
VI

often damp

VI

69
70

# Aiguille du Peigne
# SW Ridge

11

crest of SW ridge
IV and V

slanting
chimney

III
V-
IV
creasy and V-
short sections
of A2
roof

V  terrace

IV+  terrace

loose
flakes
ramp

wall VI

dièdres
strenuous
laybacks
V+

roof
slab VI and
exposed rib

V-  steps

difficu
chimne
onto L
side c
crest  IV  crest

crest
and IV

III

V-
V+
chimney

cracks and
dièdres
IV and V

dièdre

75

easier
ground

76

terrace
dièdre
IV+
dièdre  V

couloir

ledge
IV+  grooves
IV+

10m

summit

IV+

VI or A1

Lépiney
Crack
V

III

couloir

ledges
III

V+
chimney

wall III

IV

dièdre 10m V

platform

V

boulder platform

dièdre

parallel
cracks VII+

platform

VI flakes

crest
of pillar
V/VI

cracks and
grooves
IV and V

V+/VI- flake

platform

IV cracks

**80**

V and VI-

quartz crack

VI+

**81**

IV+

roof

VI+ slab

20m
right
of pillar

IV dièdre

easy
ledges

**82**

274

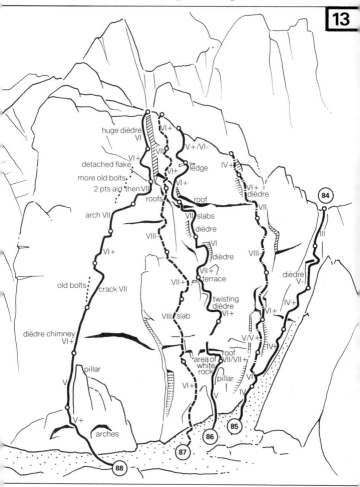

huge dièdre
VI

VI+

VII

V+/VI-

IV+

detached flake
VI+

ledge

more old bolts

VI+

VI+ dièdre

2 pts aid then VII

roofs

roof

VII

arch VII

VII slabs

dièdre

VIII-

VI

dièdre

VIII-

VII+ dièdre

terrace

old bolts

crack VII

VII+

dièdre
V-

IV+

twisting
dièdre
VI+

VI+

dièdre chimney
VI+

VIII slab

V/V+ IV+

roof
VII/VII+

pillar

area of
white
rock

pillar

VI

V

V

IV

V+

VI+

arches

84

III

85

86

87

88

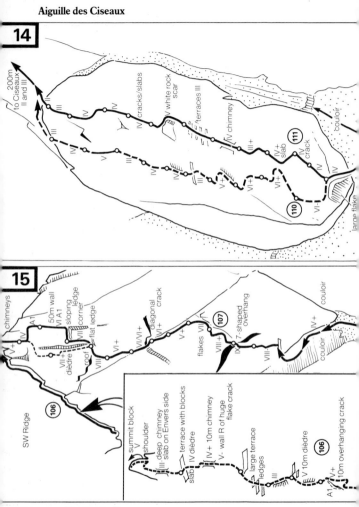

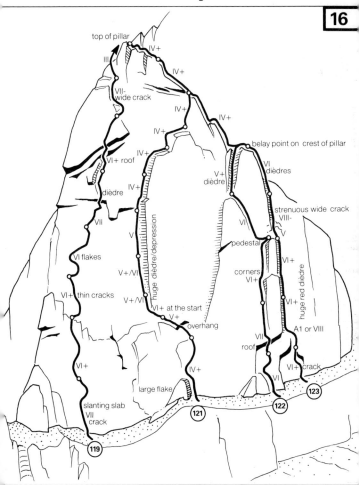

top of pillar

III

IV+

IV+

VII-
wide crack

IV+

IV+

IV+

IV+

belay point on crest of pillar

VI+ roof

VI
dièdres

dièdre

IV+

V+
dièdre

VII

strenuous wide crack
VIII-

V

V

huge dièdre/depression

VI

pedestal

VI flakes

VI+ thin cracks

V+/VI

corners
VI+

VI+

V+/VI

VI+ at the start

VI+

V+

huge red dièdre

VI+

overhang

VII
roof

A1 or VIII

VI+

VI+ crack

large flake

IV+

VI

slanting slab
VII
crack

119

121

122

123

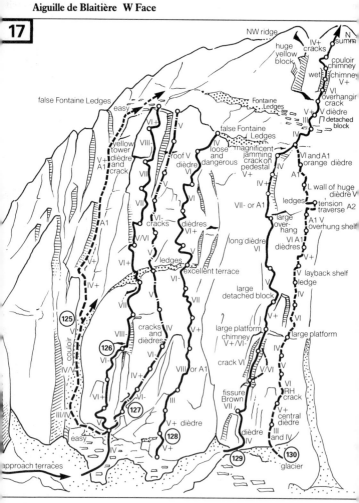

NW ridge

N
summ

huge
yellow
block

IV+
cracks

couloir
chimney

wet chimney

overhangir
crack
V+

false Fontaine Ledges

Fontaine
Ledges

V+ V dièdre

easy

VI+

V

detached
block

III

false Fontaine
Ledges

IV

IV
loose
and
dangerous

magnificent
jamming
crack on
pedestal
V+

VI and A1
orange dièdre

yellow
tower
dièdre
and
crack

VIII-

A1
V+
A1

roof V
dièdre

VII
V

VI

IV

IV V
A1

L wall of huge
dièdre V

VII- or A1

ledges

VII

VI
A1

tension
traverse  A2

VI-
cracks

dièdres
VI+

V/VI

V+

VI+

V

ledges

V

V

VI+

V
VIII

excellent terrace

large
overhang

overhung shelf
VI A1
dièdres

long dièdre
VI

V+

layback shelf
ledge

large
detached
block

IV

IV+

cracks
and
dièdres

V+

VIII

VI-

VI+

IV

III

large platform
chimney
V+/VI-

crack VI

V+

large platform

IV

V/VI

125

126

127

128

129

VIII or A1

IV+

couloir

IV/V

III/IV

easy

IV+

V+ dièdre

V+

fissure
Brown
VII

dièdre
IV

VI
RH
crack

V+
central
dièdre

III
and IV

130

glacier

approach terraces

278

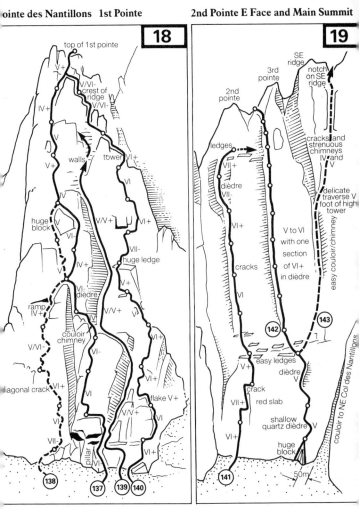

**18**

top of 1st pointe

V+

V/VI—
crest of
ridge
V/VI—

IV+

V

walls

tower  VI+

V+

VI

IV

V

huge
block

V
VI—

V/V+  VI+

VII—
huge ledge

IV+

V

V+

VI—
dièdre

ramp
IV+

V

couloir
chimney

V/V+

V/VI—

VI+

diagonal crack  VI+

VI

V/V+  VI

flake V+

VI

VI+

VII—

pillar  VI

VI+

(138)      (137)   (139)(140)

**19**

SE
ridge

notch
on SE
ridge

3rd
pointe

2nd
pointe

cracks and
strenuous
chimneys
IV and
V

ledges

VII+

dièdre
VII—

delicate
traverse V
foot of high
tower

VI+

V to VI
with one
section
of VI+
in dièdre

cracks

VI

(142)        (143)

easy ledges

V+

dièdre

crack

VII+

red slab

shallow
quartz dièdre  V

VI+

huge
block

(141)              50m

easy couloir/chimney

couloir to NE Col des Nantillons

279

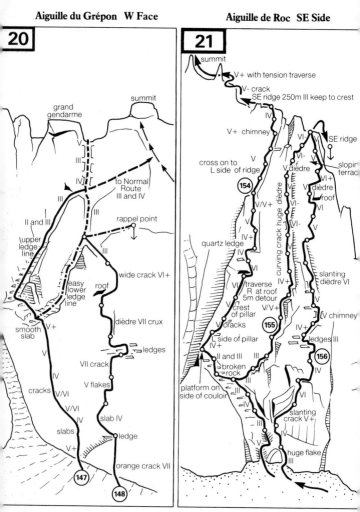

# Aiguille du Grépon  W Face

**20**

grand gendarme

summit

V

III

IV

III

to Normal Route III and IV

III

III

rappel point

upper ledge line

easy lower ledge line

roof

wide crack VI+

II and III

smooth slab

V+

V

dièdre VII crux

IV

ledges

cracks

VII crack

V/VI

V flakes

V/VI

IV

slab IV

slabs

ledge

V+

orange crack VII

**147**

**148**

# Aiguille de Roc  SE Side

**21**

summit

V+ with tension traverse

V- crack
SE ridge 250m III keep to crest

IV

V+ chimney

VI-

V    SE ridge

cross on to
L side of ridge

V    V dièdre

V-    sloping terrace

**154**

V/V+

VI+

dièdre
roof

VI

V

IV+

IV    curving crack huge dièdre

quartz ledge

IV

IV+

VI

slanting dièdre VI

VI    traverse
R at roof
5m detour

IV+

V/V+

V    crest
of pillar

V chimney

V cracks

IV+

L side of pillar

IV+    ledges III

**155**

II and III

III

**156**

II and III

broken rock

IV

platform on
side of couloir

III

IV

VI

IV

slanting crack V+

IV

huge flake

III

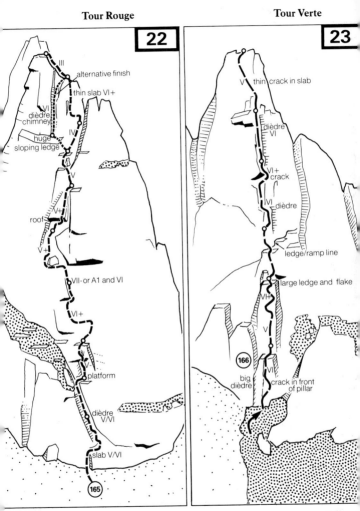

**Tour Rouge**

22

III

alternative finish

thin slab VI+

VI
dièdre
chimney

IV

huge
sloping ledge

V

V+

roof

V+

VII- or A1 and VI

VI+

platform

dièdre
V/VI

slab V/VI

165

**Tour Verte**

23

V thin crack in slab

dièdre
VI

VI+
crack

VI dièdre

ledge/ramp line

large ledge and flake

VI+

V

166

big
dièdre

VI

crack in front
of pillar

281

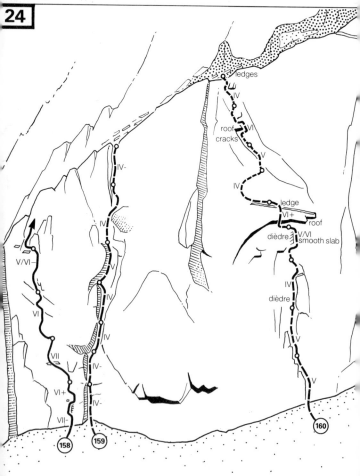

ledges

IV

roof
cracks

VI

V

IV

ledge
VI+
roof
V/VI
smooth slab

dièdre

IV

dièdre

V

V

V/VI

VI

VII

IV

IV

IV-

VI+

IV-

VII-

(158)

(159)

(160)

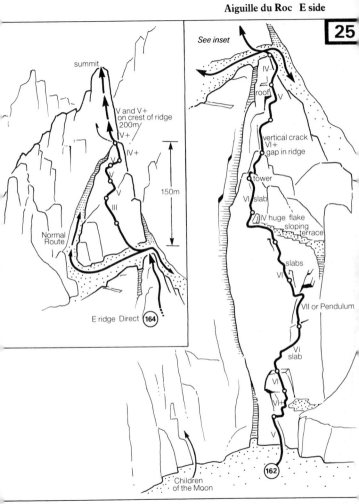

*See inset*

summit

V and V+
on crest of ridge
200m

IV+

IV+

V

V

III

150m

Normal
Route

I

E ridge Direct **164**

IV-

roof

V

vertical crack
VI+
gap in ridge

tower

VI slab

IV huge flake

sloping
terrace

slabs

VI

VII or Pendulum

Vi
slab

VI

VI+

V

**162**

Children
of the Moon

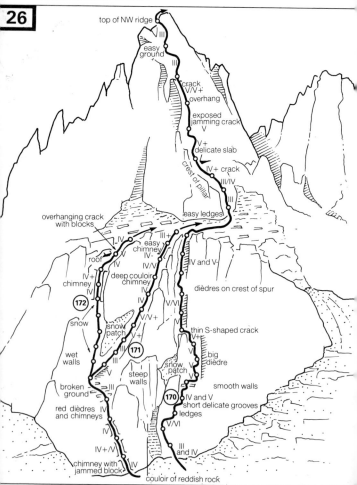

top of NW ridge

III

easy ground

III

crack V/V+

overhang

exposed jamming crack

V

V+ delicate slab

IV+ crack

III/IV

III

easy ledges

overhanging crack with blocks

I-IV

easy chimney

III+

roof V

IV-

IV and V-

IV+ chimney

IV/V

deep couloir chimney

IV

IV

V/VI

dièdres on crest of spur

(172)

snow

snow patch

V/V+

thin S-shaped crack

V+

III

(171)

V+

wet walls

V

big dièdre

snow patch

V

smooth walls

broken ground

V III

steep walls

II

(170)

IV and V

short delicate grooves

red dièdres and chimneys

IV

ledges

V/VI

IV+/V

III and IV

chimney with jammed block

IV

couloir of reddish rock

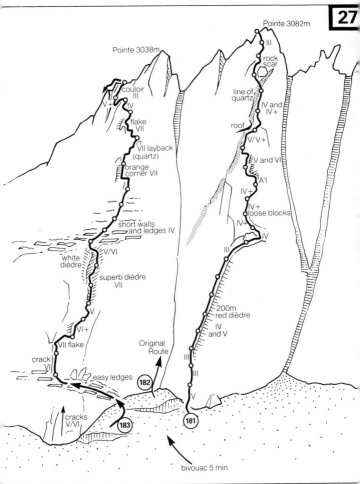

Pointe 3082m

III

rock
scar

line of
quartz

IV and
IV+

roof

V/V+

V and VI

A1

IV+

IV+
loose blocks

IV+

IV

III

200m
red dièdre

IV
and V

III

III

V

Pointe 3038m

couloir
III

V+      IV

flake
VII

VII layback
(quartz)

orange
corner VII

short walls
and ledges IV

V/VI

white
dièdre

superb dièdre
VII

V

VI+

VII flake

crack
VI

easy ledges

cracks
V/VI

Original
Route

182

181

183

bivouac 5 min

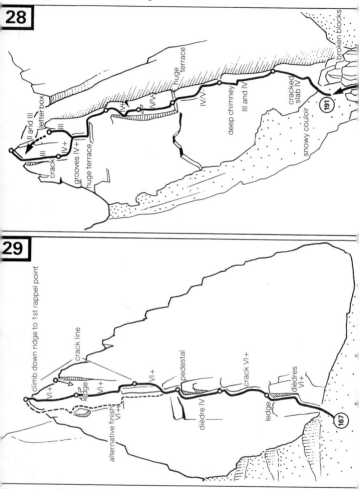

**28**

broken blocks

huge terrace

letter box

III and III

III

crack

III

IV+

grooves IV+

huge terrace

VI+

V+

IV/V-

deep chimney

III and IV

cracked slab IV

snowy couloir

**191**

**29**

climb down ridge to 1st rappel point

crack line

VI+

ledge

VI+

VI+

alternative finish VI+

diédre IV

pedestal

crack VI+

ledge

diédres VI+

**167**

**Pointe Elisabeth   SE Face**

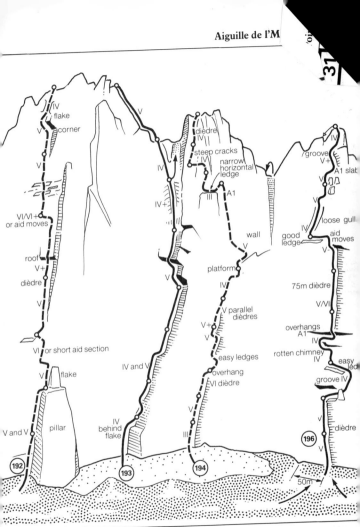

IV flake
V corner

V

V

VI/VI+
or aid moves

roof
V+

dièdre

V

VI or short aid section

V flake

V and V        pillar

(192)

V

diédre
IV

steep cracks
IV                narrow
              horizontal
              ledge
III            A1

IV+

IV and V

IV
behind
flake

(193)

A1

wall

V

platform

IV

V parallel
    dièdres
V+
V

easy ledges
overhang
VI dièdre

V

III

(194)

IV

/groove
V+

A1 slab

V

IV           loose gull
good        aid
ledge       moves
V

75m dièdre

V/VI

overhangs
A1
IV
rotten chimney
IV         easy
          led
groove IV

V

V      dièdre

(196)

50m

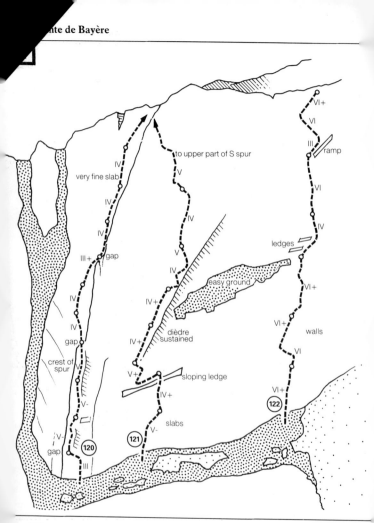

very fine slab

to upper part of S spur

ramp

ledges

easy ground

dièdre
sustained

walls

sloping ledge

crest of
spur

slabs

gap

gap

gap

(120)

(121)

(122)

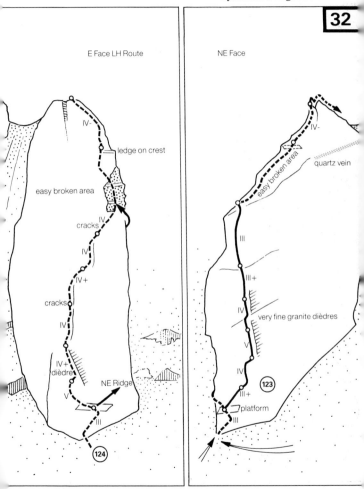

E Face LH Route

IV-

ledge on crest

easy broken area

cracks

IV

IV

IV+

cracks

IV

IV+
dièdre

V

NE Ridge

III

124

NE Face

IV-

easy broken area

quartz vein

III

III+

IV

very fine granite dièdres

V

IV

III+

123

platform

III

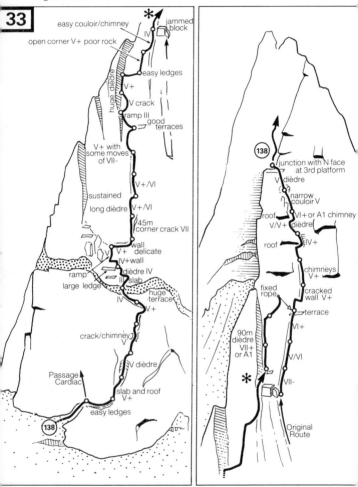

**33**

easy couloir/chimney

open corner V+ poor rock

IV — jammed block

easy ledges

V+

V crack

ramp III

good terraces

V+ with some moves of VII−

V+/VI

sustained

long dièdre V+/VI

45m corner crack VII

wall

V+ delicate

IV+ wall

dièdre IV

III slab

ramp

large ledge

IV — huge terrace

V+

crack/chimney V

V dièdre

Passage Cardiac

slab and roof V+

easy ledges

**138**

**138** — junction with N face at 3rd platform

V dièdre

narrow couloir V

roof — VI+ or A1 chimney

V/V+ dièdre

roof — IV+

chimneys V+

cracked wall V+

fixed rope — terrace

90m dièdre VII+ or A1

VI+

V/VI

VII−

Original Route

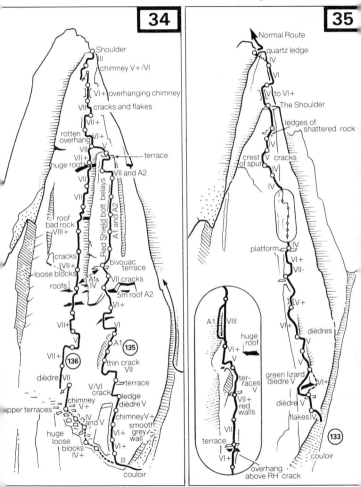

**34**

Shoulder III
chimney V+/VI
VI+ overhanging chimney
VII cracks and flakes
VII+
rotten VI+
overhang V
VII
VII+
huge roof
VII and A2
terrace
VII
VII
A1 and A2
roof
bad rock
VIII+
cracks
(VII+)
loose blocks
IV
roofs
A1 &
bivouac
terrace
VII cracks
5m roof A2
VI+
VII+
V
VI
A1
VII (136) (135)
thin crack
VII
dièdre VII
terrace
V/VI
crack
ledge
dièdre V
chimney
V+
chimney V+
IV
and V
smooth
grey
wall
VI+
huge
loose
blocks IV+
VI+
III
couloir

**35**

Normal Route
quartz ledge IV
VI
V to VI+
The Shoulder
ledges of
shattered rock
IV
crest cracks
of spur IV
IV
platform IV
VI+
VII-
IV+
VI+ dièdres
green lizard
dièdre V VI+
dièdre V
flakes IV
(133)
couloir

A1 VIII
huge
roof
VI+
terraces
V
VII+
red walls
VII
terrace
VI+
overhang
above RH crack

291

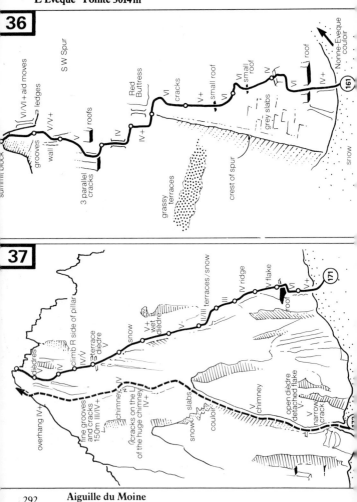

**36**

SW Spur

VI/VI+ aid moves

ledges

VI/V+

grooves

wall

V/V+

V

IV

3 parallel cracks

IV

IV+

V

roofs

Red Buttress

VI

cracks

V+

small roof

VI

VI small roof

IV

grey slabs

VI

roof

IV+

Nonne-Eveque couloir

161

snow

crest of spur

grassy terraces

summit block

**37**

diedres

V

overhang IV+

fine grooves and cracks 150 m III/IV+

chimney IV

cracks on the L of the huge chimney IV+

climb R side of pillar IV/V

terrace diedre

snow

V+ wet diedre

V/III terraces / snow

III

snow slabs

couloir

chimney

IV ridge

flake

IV roof

V+

171

open diedre detached flake

narrow crack

V+

VI/VI+    V

IV+      III

IV+      IV    V+  gap

III    V      A1

V      IV

gap

V+/A1        III to

V           VI-

IV+              shoulder

IV+          IV+

IV            V

V/V+         IV+        V

V/A1         IV+

S Face 1967      IV+     IV

III/IV        roof

large terrace

VI/          IV+

VI+          IV+

IV and V

VI-

228          229          227

**39**

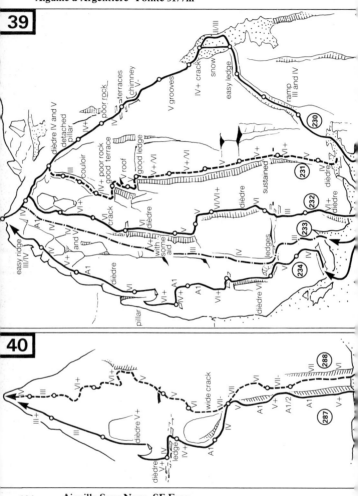

II/III

V groove

IV+ crack

snow

easy ledge

ramp
III and IV

230

terraces

chimney
V-

IV

V+

poor rock

detached
pillar

dièdre IV and V

couloir

VI+

poor rock
good terrace

V roof

good ledge

V+/VI

V+/VI

V+

IV+

231

crack

VI
dièdre

VI

VI/VI+

dièdre

VI

sustained

dièdre
IV

232

V+
with
some
aid

IV

III

ledges

V+/VI+
dièdre

233

easy ridge
III/IV

IV

IV
and V

V

III

IV

234

IV

diedre

A1

V+

A1

VI

pillar

A1

VI+

dièdre VI

**40**

III

VI+

V+/I+

VI+

V

288

VI

VI

VII

III

diedre V+

III

ledge
IV+

diedre
V+

IV+

A1

IV

wide crack

VII-

VII-

A1

A1/2

A1

V+

VI

VII-

287

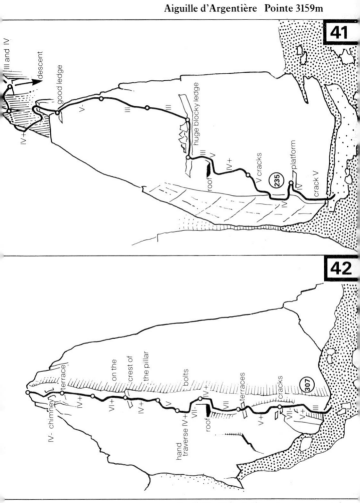

41

III and IV

descent

good ledge

III

IV+

V-

III

III

huge blocky ledge

III

V+

V cracks

platform

IV+

roof

V

235

IV

crack V

IV

V

42

IV- chimney

terrace

IV+

VI+

on the
crest of

IV+
the pillar

bolts

terraces

cracks

307

IV+

VII

VII

III

hand
traverse IV+

roof

IV+

V+

VII
V+

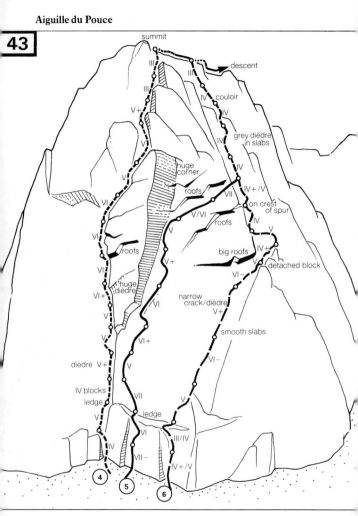

## Aiguille du Pouce

**43**

- summit
- III
- descent
- III
- III
- IV  couloir
- V+
- IV
- V
- IV  grey dièdre in slabs
- huge corner
- IV
- roofs
- VII
- IV+/V
- VI
- V/VI
- on crest of spur
- roofs
- IV
- VI
- roofs
- V
- big roofs
- IV+
- VI
- V
- detached block
- huge dièdre
- VI−
- VI+
- V
- narrow crack/dièdre
- V+
- VI
- V
- smooth slabs
- VI+
- VI−
- dièdre  V+
- V
- IV blocks
- ledge
- VII
- V
- ledge
- V
- IV
- VI
- III/IV
- VII−
- IV+/V
- (4)
- (5)
- (6)

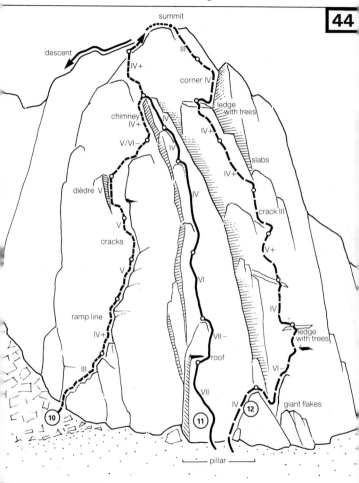

summit

descent

III

IV+

corner IV

chimney
IV+   IV

ledge
with trees

V/VI−   IV

IV+

dièdre V   IV

slabs

IV+

cracks

crack III

V

IV

V+

V

VI

ramp line

IV+

IV

VII−

ledge
with trees

III

roof

VI−

VII

IV   12

giant flakes

10

11

pillar

298

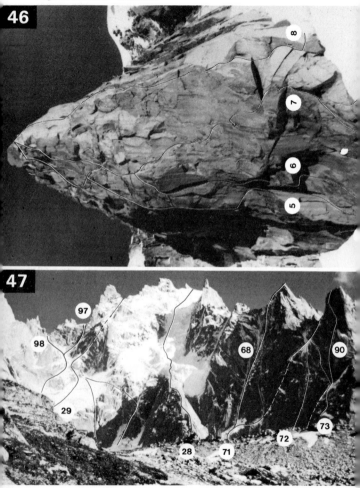

**50**

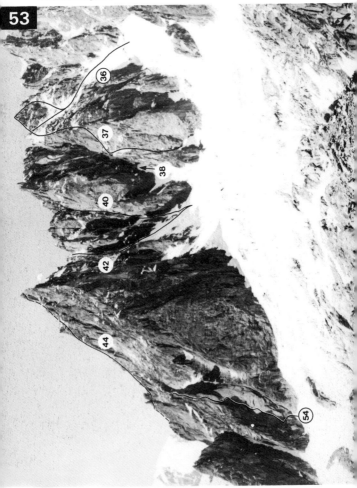

**54**

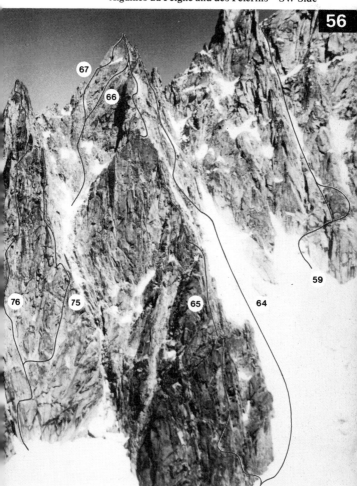

**61**

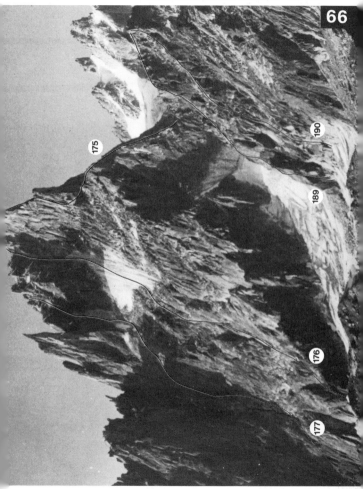

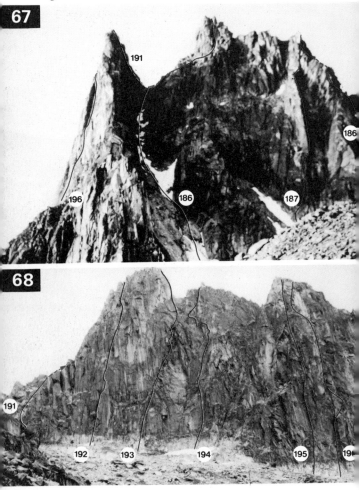

**Aiguille de l'M   NW Face**

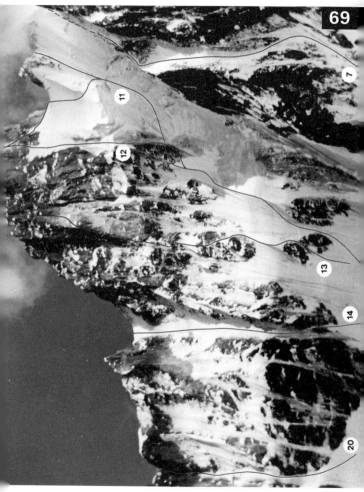

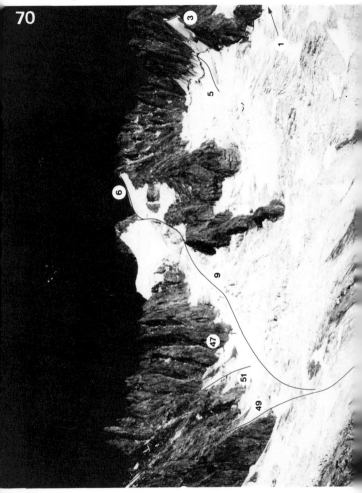

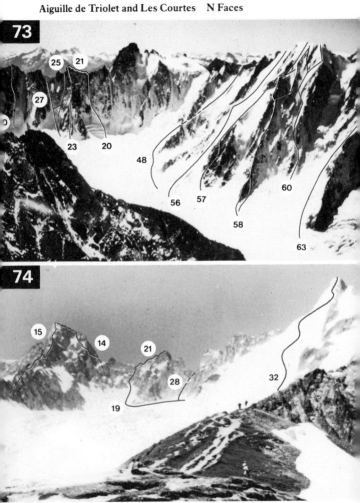

Aiguille du Triolet and Mont Dolent   S Side

Les Droites and Les Courtes   S Side

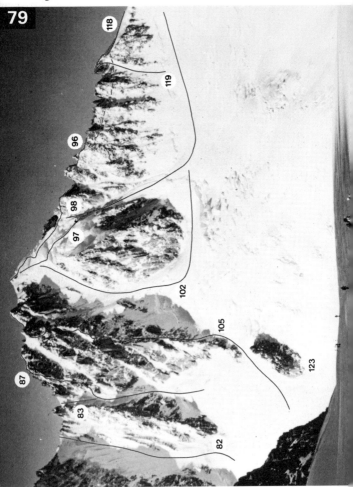

**81**

113

1

95   114   112

131 129 128 127 126

185 190 191 192 184 188 213

**Grande Lui and Aiguil**

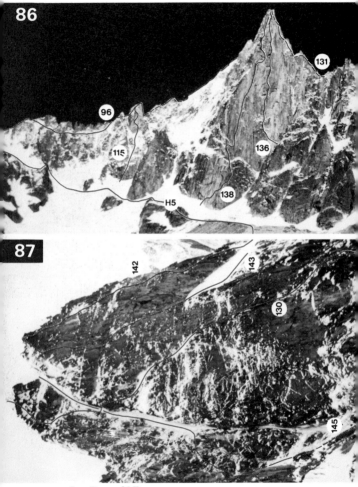

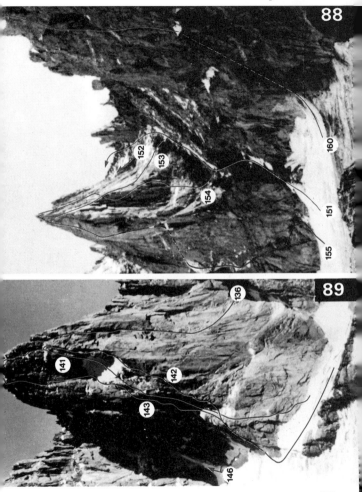

172  171                    164

**92**

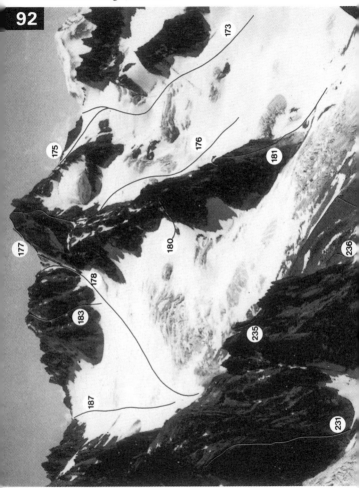

**93**

**94**

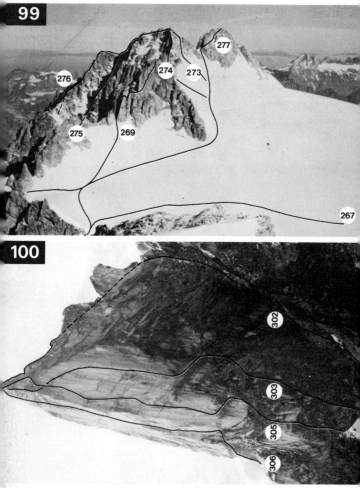

**99**

276
275
269
274
273
277
267

**100**

302
303
305
306

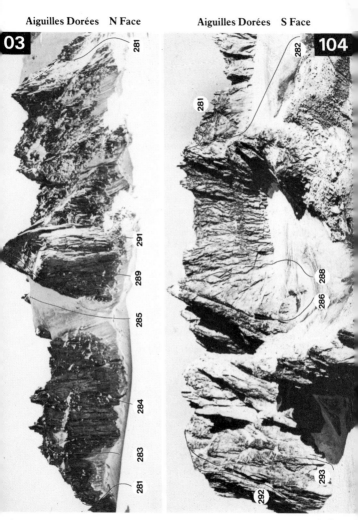

281

282

281

291

289

285

288

286

284

283

281

293

292

# Addendum

Various changes to the existing routes in Volume II have been noted in this reprint, pending a complete rewrite in the next edition. Alterations in route description have been kept to a minimum and generally concentrate on the more popular classics. Due to recent climatic changes it is now, more than ever, essential to note that approaches involving travel over snow slopes and glaciers are changing dramatically from one year to the next. Climbers are urged to assess the current conditions and employ common sense.

Since the guide was written there have been numerous and generally well-equipped rock climbs of high quality established in various sectors of the Chamonix Aiguilles, in the Aiguilles Rouges, on the various Pointes of the Flammes de Pierre Ridge and the long southerly arêtes of the Aiguille d'Argentière, around the Orny Hut and notably on the excellent granite of the South Faces of the Aiguille Dorées. More modern ice routes and goulottes have been climbed in the Chamonix Aiguilles and the Argentière Glacier Basin. A recent trend has been the equipping of many of the more popular ice couloirs with fixed belay and rappel anchors, greatly reducing the commitment for the now almost mandatory winter/spring ascent.

Additional First Winter Ascents (FWA) have been noted in the list below where deemed appropriate. Arabic numerals refer to French rock grades, which will be standard in the next edition. Adjectival grades are maintained for snow/ice routes, though it is anticipated that the numerical dual grading system, currently applied to Continental icefall climbing, will be added in the next edition.

## General Information

Page 1      Add Michel Piola to acknowledgements.

Page16/    Digitally displayed weather forecast etc. at Tourist Office in
17        Place de l'Eglise. Full five-day weather forecast and comprehensive snow/avalanche bulletin on the board in the Office de la Haute Montagne (OHM).
          New guides of relevance to this volume include Francois Damilano and Godefroy Perroux's, 'Neige, Glace et Mixte', Nigel Shepherd's 'Chamonix Cragging' and Romain Vogler's topo guide. There is now a new English edition to 'The 100 Finest Routes'.
          Information on all new routes can generally be obtained from the OHM.

Page 20     More accurate grading table in later AC Guides eg. Bernina and Bregaglia.

## Huts

H1     Cosmiques Hut new in 1991. Private. Room for 120. Reservations obligatory, Tel: 50 54 46 16. Very Expensive! Currently an overnight camp still appears to be tolerated (just!) in this region.

H8     An alternative approach uses the recently created first stage of the Balcon de la Mer de Glace, a high-level route for experienced walkers that circumnavigates the glacier in several days. From Montenvers, descend the ladders to the Mer de Glace and cross it directly to the far side, where a conspicuous painted triangle at the base of the Echelets marks the start of a set of ladders which lead up onto a previously disused track. Follow this track under the base of the Flammes de Pierre Ridge and beneath the Chapoua Glacier to the hut.

H9     Rarely crowded. Note that the Pierre à Béranger is a good bivouac site.

H10    Grands Montets Téléphérique: first cable car at 6am in season and 8am out of season.

H17    Tel: 26 83 14 38. Plenty of short, popular and well-equipped rock routes now exist close to the hut.

H20    Reservations essential. Tel: 26 83 18 87.

H22    Currently being enlarged.

H22a   Envers des Dorées bivouac hut (2,980m). Property of the CAS. Situated midway between the Pointes des Plines and Trident. 23 places, 12 by reservations. Tel: 021 921 85 50. Bring sleeping bags and gaz stove. 1½hr from the Saleina Hut or 1hr from the Trient Hut.

H23    Tel: 26 83 24 24.

H26    Comfortable room for c20. Tel: 0165 895 44.

## Routes

### Chamonix Aiguilles

10     A popular combination is now to climb the lower 350m section of Route 12 and then traverse R across a rib to finish up the narrow icy/mixed section of Route 10 (D+).

12     The upper section is rarely in good condition. See above.

14     Now very popular in the 'winter/spring' season is the Mallory/ Porter Route (AD+) to the R.

15     Most parties now avoid the top buttress on ice slopes to the R.

19     The couloir left of the spur normally has a 10m section at 80°– 85°. Above this the left hand exit is TD– /TD.

21     Branches out left from the couloir variant to Route 19 after c100m. Three ice pitches (crux 85°) in the lower section leading to short steps above. Popular but can be thinly iced.

48/    Hardly ever climbed these days.

| 49 | Rarely climbed. The thin gully just left of the main couloir was climbed in the winter of 1993 at D. |
|----|----|
| 70 | There is now a five pitch, independent finish at 6a+. |
| 103 | The Anker/Piola/Strappazzon route, Je t'ai Conquis, Je t'Adore, is considered to be one of the finest rock climbs in the range despite the lack of line. This route has superseded the other existing climbs and having a bolted rappel descent has reduced the commitment needed to climb on the Lépiney. |
| 107 | The Colas/Grenier route, Les Ailes du Désir, was retrobolted and subsequently climbed free at 7c. FWA 1994. There are six routes on this face to date, most involving sections of hard aid. |
| 131 | The previously unclimbed lower section is now Magie d'Orient (5+: excellent rock: natural protection). |
| 144 | Can be climbed completely free at 6a. |
| 165 | One of the finest and most popular short rock routes in the range and now completely re-equipped. There are nearly a dozen routes on this face to date. |
| 173 | The huge diêdre was climbed in October 1993 as Birthright (Backes/Twight: ED3), a 10 pitch, thinly iced, ephemeral runnel with minimal protection. |
| 183 | Lower down the ridge the E Face of Pt 2,784m now has many fine, short and easily accessible rock routes (Ratheaux *et al*). |
| 192 | 6b all free. |
| 193 | 5+ all free. |
| 194 | Climbed free in 1991 by Ball and Ettle at 6b. |

## Aiguilles Rouges

| 2 | More like III+ at the crux. |
|----|----|
| 8 | Avoid the first step on the R. The elegant S Diêdre was climbed in 1994 at D (300m: nine pitches: 5: delightful climbing). |

## Col de Talèfre to Swiss Val Ferret

| 11 | Rarely climbed at present due to the very dangerous state of the seracs. |
|----|----|
| 12 | As Route 11. |
| 15 | Increasingly popular are the many excellent rock routes now on the various summits of Monts Rouges de Triolet. They lie at a relatively low altitude, face the sun and can be approached easily from the Triolet Hut. |
| 22 | A winter classic taking the first main pencil of ice to the R of the Domino's summit (80°– 85°). Very popular and now has an equipped rappel descent. |
| 23 | The crest of the monolithic N Spur to the left of this route is now the Voie Kevin (500m: TD – : 5). |

| | |
|---|---|
| 30 | Sustained and generally thinly iced with a hard mixed crux to gain the upper runnel. 85° maximum with a well-equipped rappel descent. |
| 31 | A number of repeat ascents have confirmed that in good conditions (rare) this route is probably overgraded at ED2. However it is narrow (c1m), thinly iced and sustained (85° maximum) but has a well-equipped rappel descent. |
| 32 | In the last couple of summers the summit crest has been a broken rocky ridge. |
| 33 | Also equipped for a rappel descent and now an increasingly popular winter objective. |
| 34 | Wrongly marked on photo 71. It takes the obvious couloir immediately to the R. |
| 35 | Certain parties consider the approach couloir hard for grade IV. |
| 58 | The Red Tower variation is rarely climbed. |
| 63 | Also here is the modern ice climb of Ainsi Soit'il (ED1). |
| 69 | The true crest of the pillar was climbed throughout in 1991 by Dale and Kerr at ED2 (6b). |
| 72 | Recent hot and dry summers have seen routes such as this climbed in rock boots throughout. |
| 79 | This route was first climbed, as described, by Brooks and Colton in 1977. |
| 81 | Rappel anchors in place. |
| 83 | True FWA: P Biedermann in 1992. 75° maximum. |
| 88 | Rarely climbed and AD+. |
| 99 | More like TD+/ED1. |
| 128 | Sustained jamming in wide cracks and thought to warrant TD+. Near the top, instead of crossing the wide couloir on the L to reach the upper section of the South Pillar, it is possible to continue up the crest and then take an unlikely looking diagonal line out R across a steep wall (5+) to join the seldom repeated Voie Pierre below the second crux. 12hr to summit. |
| 133 | The accepted descent from the Flammes de Pierre now goes straight down from the foot of gendarme 3,361m. Five rappels on steep rock are well-sheltered from stonefall until the couloir is reached. This descent is generally feasible in rock boots and most parties now leave equipment on the Flammes and aim to complete the round trip in a day. |
| 135 | FWA in 1984. |
| 136 | With two or three rest points on the slimy second roof (the best effort so far) this route is ED4 (7b). 18 pitches to the Shoulder. To reach this and other neighbouring routes, the best approach is to climb the American Direct to the first terraces, follow these around to the |

R until below a series of dièdres and then use one of these to reach the upper terraces at the base of the climb.

142 With a succession of huge rock falls in recent years it is no longer possible to say that this face has little objective danger.

148/ Many good routes on these sunny walls up to 350m in height and
149 7a in standard.

161 Many more excellent routes here of a similar character.

168 The pitches of IV+ noted in lines 8, 15 and 21 of the description are thought to be nearer V. The 'easy couloir' runs parallel to the ridge and therefore it is not possible to 'climb it to the ridge': the chimney and chockstone exit pitch occurs after 60m and is a good deal harder than IV.

171 The crux on pitch 2 is probably 6a if the pegs in the main dièdre are followed and 6b if the thin crack out R is taken. Vogler's 1992 route, Mystique, (400m: 6c+, 6b obl) was pronounced to be one of the finest rock routes in the range.

206 After recent dry summers this has become more tricky: probably PD/PD+.

214/ Nowadays probably undergraded at AD.
216

217 Reduced snow cover has exposed extensive areas of very shattered rock. AD+.

227 All free at 6a.

278 The snow/ice couloir on the NW Face of the Aiguille du Tour, leading to the gap between the two summits, is a recommended alternative to the crowded classics on the other flanks. It is 250m and PD+.

286 Maximum difficulties of 5 − /5.

288 Christened Don Quichotte and thought to be a potential modern classic at 6b.

293 Totally neglected in favour of such modern classics as Eole Danza per Noi (380m: TD+: 5+/6a: 5+ obl and undoubtedly one of the finest rock routes in the range: Very popular), Et je suis le Vent (ED1: 6b+, 6a+ obl) and C'est Mozart qu'on Assassin (6a+). Magnificent granite.

303 Climbed free in 1989 at 8a.

305 6c and now a modern classic.

309/ Considerable development of all the rock around the Orny Hut. Also
etc the Dalles du Plan de l'Arche down the approach path towards Champex. Full details at the Hut.